Public Microeconomics

Public Microeconomics

NEIL M. SINGER

University of Maryland

Little, Brown and Company

Boston

Library of Congress Catalog Card Number: 74-182406

First Printing

Published simultaneously in Canada
by Little, Brown & Company (Canada) Limited

PRINTED IN THE UNITED STATES OF AMERICA

ACKNOWLEDGMENTS

The author wishes to thank the following copyright holders for permission to use material reprinted in this book:

Prentice-Hall, Inc. For Table 15.1, on page 273, from William A. Niskanen, "The Defense Resource Allocation Process," in Stephen Enke (ed.), *Defense Management* (Englewood Cliffs, N.J., 1967), p. 8

Rand Corporation. For Table 15.2, on page 274, from David Novick, "The Department of Defense," in Novick (ed.), *Program Budgeting* (Santa Monica, Calif., 1965), p. 61.

John Wiley & Sons, Inc. For Table 14.1, on page 260, from Roland N. McKean, *Efficiency in Government Through Systems Analysis with Emphasis on Water Resource* (New York, 1958).

For Elizabeth and Danny, whose world it will be

Preface

The subject of public finance has undergone an extensive metamorphosis in the last fifteen years. Prior to the mid-1950's, the principal topic for study was the finances of the public sector: revenues from taxes and the issuance of debt, and the management of the economy through fiscal and monetary measures. The chief microeconomic subjects were the incidence of taxation and implementation problems such as timing and administrative feasibility. The major themes of macroeconomics were the choice among alternative fiscal instruments and the extent to which monetary policy offered a useful supplement to fiscal measures. We were all Keynesians then.

Since that time has come an awareness of the complexity of stabilization policy and considerable uncertainty about the relative effectiveness of monetary and fiscal measures. The macroeconomic aspects of public finance have merged with monetary economics and macroeconomic theory under the banner of aggregative economics. Students of taxation have reached general agreement on the theory of tax incidence, and questions of tax administration have become the domain of professional administrators rather than of economists. In place of these traditional macroeconomic and microeconomic topics, the study of public finance has focused on resource allocation in the public sector.

In recent years the two major themes in the professional literature on public finance have been a growing sophistication about the theory of public expenditures and a better understanding of governmental resource allocation decisions in the real world. The application of welfare economics to the public sector, with an intellectual history dating at least from Wicksell and Pigou, was codified by Samuelson's well known papers in the mid-1950's and has since been extended by many scholars. Their work has clarified the questions of the government's ability to compensate for departures from the competitive model (for example, decreasing-cost production and externalities) and of the relationship between public resource allocation and income redistribution. The use of economic analysis in governmental expenditure decisions has an equally long history, but entered a new era of sophistication and influence with the development of systems analysis studies and program budgeting techniques during the late 1950's. Some of the public sector programs that have been the subject of systems analysis include manpower retraining, education, urban renewal, urban mass transit, pure research and development activities, pollution control, and military weapons systems. In addition, the analysis of water resources systems has become much more sophisticated during this period.

I have tried to incorporate the new direction in public finance into this text. As a result, this is a rather unconventional book. The reader will find no discussion of traditional topics such as debt management and compensatory fiscal policy. Instead, he will discover a treatment of the theory of public expenditures that is more rigorous and intensive than that in any other undergraduate textbook. Much of the material on budgeting techniques, the methodology of systems analysis, and discounting public investments cannot be found elsewhere outside the professional literature. I feel that the emphasis on these topics, reflecting recent developments in public finance, facilitates the discussion of current policy issues and indicates both the role and the limitations of economic analysis as a factor in governmental resource allocation decisions. I have tried throughout to illustrate principles of analysis with examples from the real world, and the chapters in Part Five demonstrate how the many topics discussed earlier in the text arise in various program areas.

The level of presentation throughout is appropriate for a second-level course in economics. No mathematics is used beyond that of an introductory course. The emphasis, however, is on economic analysis, especially on the integration of microeconomic theory with governmental resource allocation. This stress carries over into the section on taxation, where I have concentrated on the economic aspects of taxes rather than on either administrative or descriptive material. Overall, I hope the result is a textbook that challenges the student intellectually while focusing his attention on timely issues.

I would like to express my thanks to several classes of students at the University of Maryland for reading, using, and commenting on preliminary versions of the manuscript, and to my colleagues Eugene McLoone and Henry Einhorn for their willingness to use the text in draft form and to suggest improvements. I am especially grateful to Richard Caves of Harvard University and to Ronald Grieson of M.I.T., who read the entire manuscript in detail, offered many valuable suggestions, and saved me from more errors than I care to remember. Among my colleagues at Maryland, I owe a special debt to Henry Aaron for his detailed critique of Part Three. John Cumberland, Thomas King, Martin McGuire, Mancur Olson, and J. J. Shipley aided me considerably with their comments on individual chapters. Greatest of all, however, are the thanks due my wife, who edited the entire manuscript with skill, care, and remarkably good humor. All remaining aberrations, whether analytical or stylistic, are mine alone.

N.M.S.

Contents

Figures and Tables

TABLES

Public Microeconomics

PART ONE The Role
of Government
in a Market Economy

Our concern in this book is with the economic activities of governments; more precisely, we will study some of the ways that governments in developed, free-market economies influence the market's determination of economic activity. Chapter 1 is a description of different kinds of government activity and their interrelationships. In Chapter 2 the growth of public expenditures at different levels of government is examined. Some trends can be discerned in the types of economic activity that have become the responsibilities of federal, state, and local governments. In Chapter 3 the question of how well markets function is discussed. Several reasons for expecting public sector decisions about economic policy to be less rational and consistent than private decisions are set forth, and two models of allocation that try to incorporate these features of policy-making in the public sector are presented.

BIBLIOGRAPHY

The division of government activity into allocation, distribution, and stabilization was first presented by Richard A. Musgrave in *The Theory of Public Finance* (New York: McGraw-Hill, 1959), chapters 1 and 2. A good discussion of the objectives of government policy and the instruments used by governments can be found in the second chapter of Leif Johansen's *Public Economics* (Chicago: Rand McNally, 1965).

1

The categorization of public expenditures in Chapter 2 was first made by Francis Bator in *The Question of Government Spending* (New York: Harper and Row, 1969), especially in chapters 2, 3, and 8 and in the appended tables. Chapter 7 of Bator's book contains some comments on how efficiently private and public sectors respond to demand, a subject discussed here in Chapter 3.

A heretical view of the responsiveness of the private sector to consumers' demand is given by John Kenneth Galbraith in *The New Industrial State* (Boston: Houghton Mifflin, 1967). For a more orthodox presentation, see Robert H. Haveman and Kenyon A. Knopf's *The Market System,* 2nd edition (New York: Wiley, 1970).

1 Allocation, Distribution, and Stabilization Activities

Public finance is the study of the conduct of the public sector in an economy predominantly organized around markets. Historically, the study of public finance has encompassed descriptions of the institutional processes leading to governmental economic policies, analyses of how effectively governmental policies attain their objectives, and normative discussions of what the scope of governmental policies should be in a market-oriented economy. In economies like that of the United States, where market behavior is often influenced by either the fact or the prospect of government intervention, the scope of public finance is very broad. Only in the purely competitive model of economic theory and in its antithesis, the purely collectivist economy, is there no role for the study of public sector economics.

Economists and political philosophers have never been able to agree on the scope of legitimate government economic activity. Instead, particular economic policies and programs of the public sector are developed haphazardly, when the public perceives an economic problem and the private sector fails to solve it. Public responsibility for some programs is universally recognized, but in other cases the question of whether an economic activity is in the public or private sphere is still unresolved.

Some of the programs that are usually located in the public domain include national defense, the provision of law enforcement (although police protection and security are frequently provided privately), and

3

education up to some minimum level. Public responsibility for other programs has developed more recently: the provision of retirement and disability insurance; the maintenance of full employment and price stability, coupled with sustained economic growth; and the regulation of monopoly in industry and transportation. Some other areas of public concern are only now emerging as the responsibility of the public sector: problems of poverty, including hunger, lack of opportunity, and inability to sustain minimal levels of consumption; and environmental protection from many types of pollution, including the effects of chemical and bacteriological accumulation, heat transfer, noise, and nuclear radiation.

In its attempts to implement these programs, the government in a market-oriented economy can work only through a limited set of policy instruments. Its chief instrument, of course, is the power to tax. Modern governments levy a wide variety of taxes, all of which differ in their incidence, revenue yield, and incentive or disincentive effects. Moreover, there are usually "subinstruments" within taxes; for example, exemption and deduction allowances are instruments within the tax rate schedule of the personal income tax. Another instrument frequently available to a government is the creation and regulation of the money supply. All modern central governments have primary authority over the money supply,[1] but lower-level (state and municipal) governments can often exert some influence over the supply of money and credit through regulation of local financial institutions (banks and savings and loan associations).

Once revenues are obtained, through either taxation or borrowing, a government can try to achieve its policy goals through its disbursements. Expenditures are one type of disbursement, in which the government buys goods and services related to its policy objective. Transfers, direct grants of either money or goods, are a second type. In the case of a transfer (such as social security retirement benefits), the grant itself is the policy objective, for the government does not usually require that the recipient of the grant supply either goods or services in exchange.

Regulatory activities offer governments another instrument for achieving their policy objectives. One of the principal forms of regulation is ensuring that private firms comply with legislation, such as the Sherman and Clayton antitrust acts, which is usually intended to improve the functioning of the market. The other main type of reg-

---

[1] The U.S. Federal Reserve Board is autonomous, but it is nonetheless a government agency.

ulatory activity is the administration of public and semipublic enterprises, frequently in transportation, utilities, and communications.

Both economic and non-economic factors can limit the government's choice of instruments to achieve its objectives. For example,
the goal of price stability can place limitations on the revenue available for expenditure programs. Pressures to achieve a balance-of-
payments surplus can constrain both general monetary policy and
particular expenditures such as for foreign aid and national defense.
Non-economic factors can affect both the revenue and the expenditure sides of government budgets. Taxpayers are generally reluctant
to accept increases in tax rates (for reasons to be explored in Chapter
3), and special-interest groups are frequently very effective in maintaining their favored positions in the tax law. Once a policy objective
attains the status of a legislated, funded program, however, the favorable views of the beneficiaries of the program may well carry more
legislative weight than the general aversion of taxpayers at large. As
a result, a government may find a large fraction of its revenues committed to the continuation of obsolete programs, leaving only small
amounts of funds that can be reallocated to attain new objectives.
Among the obsolete federal programs that owe their continuation to
special-interest groups are some major ones (agricultural price supports) and many minor ones (regulation of interstate trucking rates).

A second problem that a government must face in selecting the instruments to be used in reaching its objectives is that many instruments can have secondary effects on other policies. A program of
highway construction will affect both the level of employment and
price stability. Subsidies for education will result, in the long run, in
increased rates of economic growth due to greater labor productivity.
A tax increase to choke off an investment boom may necessitate
higher levels of transfers to sustain poor families whose disposable
personal income has been reduced. The presence of these interrelationships of programs and instruments makes it useful to classify
public programs according to the economic objective toward which
they are directed.

ALLOCATION, DISTRIBUTION, AND STABILIZATION

Allocation. The public sector's allocation function is to use resources
to satisfy wants not met by the private sector. In a market-oriented
economy, most goods are produced by private sector firms that allocate resources according to the preferences expressed by consumers

through market demand. The criterion that is usually satisfied (at least to an approximation) is that the goods private firms produce with the resources they buy are the goods consumers most prefer. There are many reasons why this criterion may not be met, but the most prevalent reason is that consumers are unable to express all their preferences through the market. For example, it is difficult to imagine national defense being supplied by the private sector in response to market demand.

In a market-oriented economy, producers must receive information about the intensity of consumers' preferences in order to allocate resources. This process works well for private sector goods like clothing and food. But in many cases (defense, environmental purity, the control of crime) individual consumers cannot indicate their preferences through market behavior. In these cases, it becomes the government's job to determine the strength of society's demand for the good and to express it to producers. Although the strength of demand for public sector goods is usually determined through the political process, the economic guideline for public sector allocation is that the value of goods produced in response to the government's demand must be at least as great as the value of the alternative goods that the private sector could have produced in response to private sector demand. In other words, the market criterion underlying private resource allocation is the appropriate criterion for the public sector to use in deciding whether resources should be taken from the private sector and devoted to satisfying wants not expressed through the market. A concise statement of this criterion is: "The *opportunity cost* of public sector resource allocation must not exceed the value of the goods produced to satisfy the public sector's demand."

Even if the criterion for public sector resource allocation is met, it does not follow that the good must be produced by the public sector. In many cases private firms will be able to satisfy the demand the government expresses. Although the demand for national defense is certainly expressed through the political decision and financed by taxes, most public expenditures for national defense are purchases of military equipment from the private sector. The demand for highways and freeways is expressed in government appropriations (at the federal, state, and local levels), but the construction of most highways is performed by private construction contractors. There are many instances (to be explored in Chapter 5) in which the private sector is not able to satisfy the demand the government expresses, and other cases in which a demand expressed in the market by individual consumers must be satisfied by the public sector instead of by private firms. But it is important here to distinguish between public expression of demand and public production. The allocation function of the public sector encompasses both activities, but not necessarily for the same goods.

Many, perhaps most, public expenditures are made in response to an allocation failure of the private market. Public demand is expressed for national defense, education, the administration of justice, space exploration, and (to an increasing extent) environmental protection. The demand for transportation facilities is usually expressed through the public sector, and research programs in many areas including health, technology, and pure science satisfy a public demand. Most of these goods are provided privately, although education (especially primary and secondary) and some components of national defense (notably manpower) are publicly supplied. Regulatory activities are a publicly supplied service that satisfies a publicly expressed demand. In many cases, public supply of utilities (water, electricity, gas) is engendered by the inability of unregulated private firms to supply the service without creating monopolies.

Distribution. The public sector's distribution function is to see that goods and services are distributed according to some "fair" criterion. Economists have never been very successful in describing the fair distribution of income, wealth, or consumption, and the process of determining the criterion of equity is political. Usually underlying the distributional criterion is the notion that all individuals or families should be able to provide themselves with the necessities of life; that is, that every person should be able to sustain at least some minimum level of well-being. No single economic criterion corresponds to this notion of equity. Economic well-being or welfare depends on income (measured in both money and nonmoney terms), consumption, wealth, and personal preferences. Several economists have suggested that income (measured in goods and services) and intangibles such as freedom and opportunity may be mutually inconsistent and that society may have to choose between high levels of income and a greater degree of personal freedom. Whether or not their claim is correct, it emphasizes the different concepts of fairness that are a part of the distributional decision.

Distributional policy in the United States is focused on current income, wealth, and a wide variety of specific types of consumption, of which education, health, food, and housing are some of the most important. The distributional judgments about these components of welfare are made through many different instruments. The distributions of total personal income and wealth are altered primarily through taxation (especially income and estate taxes, but also some excises and the corporation income tax) in ways that will be discussed in Part Three. In addition, some programs such as social security transfer income, general purchasing power, to particular segments of the population. The provision for minimum levels of consumption of specific goods is made through a variety of expenditure programs at different levels of government. Local governments are primarily responsible for funding minimum levels of education, although they frequently receive some state aid and a smaller amount of federal assistance. Health care (usually limited to hospitalization) is provided by all levels of government. Food subsidies are primarily a federal program, although the participation of state and county governments usually is required. Public housing programs are operated by all levels of government.

Two concepts that economists like to apply to discussions of the distribution of welfare are "horizontal equity" and "vertical equity." Horizontal equity means that families or individuals in similar economic circumstances should be treated similarly with respect to taxation and the availability of public subsidies for particular kinds of consumption. Vertical equity is said to exist if families in different economic circumstances are treated differently, paying different taxes and receiving different consumption subsidies in systematic accord with the prevailing distributional ethic. For example, vertical equity might entail that a bachelor with an income of $8000 pay higher taxes than a family of five living on the same income. Horizontal equity would require that two families of five, with equal incomes and similar age distributions, pay equal taxes. It is difficult to judge whether either concept of equity is met by current practice in the United States, since decisions about distributional equity are made by so many different levels of government and agencies within each level. But most economists agree that abuses of both concepts of equity are widespread.

The ethic of fairness in the distribution of welfare does not specify any particular distribution. One concept of fairness is related to individual liberty, holding that any person should be able to amass and allocate his personal fortune as he sees fit, with no governmental interference. A distributional policy consistent with this equity concept would levy no tax and offer no consumption subsidy that interfered with the distribution of well-being determined in the market by the productivity and remuneration of factors of production. On the other hand, the progressive personal income tax might be taken as evidence that the distributional policy of the federal government is egalitarian; that is, that the federal government disagrees with the statement that the fair distribution of income is the one determined by market forces. When combined with other taxes (at both the federal and lower levels of government) and subsidy programs, however, the distributional impact of the personal income tax is much weaker than it initially appears to be. There is no clear-cut equity decision underlying the distributional judgments of American governments, but it is clear that the distribution of welfare determined in the market on the basis of productivity is altered in many ways by public policies.

The distribution function of the public sector, as distinguished from the allocation function, would be met if governments altered individuals' abilities to satisfy their wants without affecting their resource allocation decisions at the margin. Thus purely distributional programs would consist only of taxing the income (or wealth) of some people and transferring income to others in order to alter the distribution of welfare determined in the private sector. Public distributional activities would produce no goods and satisfy no wants directly and would consist only of pure tax and transfer programs, a Robin Hood kind of activity. The distributional public programs described earlier bear little relation to these normative distributional tax and transfer activities, and consequently it is impossible to determine what society's explicit distributional goals are and whether they are being reached.

Stabilization. Stabilization policy is usually administered through fiscal and monetary means—tax rates, interest rates, the money supply. and public expenditures. In a simple Keynesian world where the equilibrium level of national income is determined by aggregate demand, the government could attain its stabilization goal of full employment (or any other level of employment consistent with the desired rate of price inflation) by altering its surplus or deficit to compensate for the deficiency or excess in private aggregate demand. This point can be illustrated by a simple algebraic model.

Let the economy have a linear aggregate consumption function,

$$C = a + bY,$$

and a level of investment $\bar{I}$ determined by the expectations of investors (independent of the level of income or consumption). If $\bar{I}$ equals 15, with a equaling 10 and b equaling 0.8, then every student of elementary economics can calculate that the equilibrium level of income (Y) is 125. Suppose, however, that the level of income consistent with full employment is 150. The introduction of a government sector levying a lump-sum tax (T), which may be negative, enables the economy to reach full employment. Now,

$$C = a + b(Y - T).$$

If $\bar{I}$ is still 15, and the values of a and b are unchanged, then it is easy to calculate that T must be -6.25 if the economy is to reach an income level of 150.[2] In other words, the government must increase aggregate demand by transferring 6.25 to consumers, producing a government deficit of 6.25. (Note that the government does not use any goods and services, so G — government demand — is zero.) Conversely, if aggregate demand were to exceed the full-employment level of income, the government could stabilize the economy at its full-employment level by levying a tax and thus operating at a surplus.

If the government's stabilization activities are to be distinguished analytically from its allocation and distribution functions, its surplus or deficit should not alter either the socially preferred allocation of resources or the distribution of welfare. An approximation to such a stabilization policy might be a tax or transfer that left the relative income distribution unchanged; that is, T equals tY with t positive in the case of taxes and negative in the case of transfers. In the model above, this policy would change the consumption function to

$$C = a + b(1 - t)Y.$$

If the equilibrium income level is still 150 and all other parameters are unchanged, the equilibrium value of t is $-5/120$, or -0.0417. In this case, the government could achieve its desired full-employment equilibrium by offering proportional transfers at the rate of 0.0417.

When we leave the simple Keynesian world of the model, we also leave behind the easy determination of the stabilization policy consistent with full-employment equilibrium. In more complex models and in the real world, consumption and investment behavior respond to many different policy instruments in ways that still are not fully understood. Economists have not adequately explained the mechanism through which monetary policy influences the level of income and employment. The effectiveness of fiscal policy in the absence of reinforcing monetary measures is also in dispute. The stabilization policies used by modern governments involve manipulating dozens of tax variables, hundreds of expenditure and transfer decisions, and a wide variety of monetary variables and interest rates. These activities are sometimes supplemented by non-economic persuasion (for example, the wage-price guideposts of the mid-1960's or the "freeze" of 1971).

---

[2] Notice that a transfer of 5.0 would increase equilibrium aggregate demand by only 20, instead of the 25 needed to reach full employment. In the example, the marginal propensity to consume, whether out of transfer income or earned income, is only 0.8.

The objectives of stabilization policy, too, are different in fact from those used in the simple model above. There is no single point of "full-employment equilibrium with stable prices." The Phillips curve analysis has convinced economists that there are different combinations of unemployment and price inflation but that low unemployment is almost always accompanied by high rates of inflation. One of the problems of formulating stabilization policy is to choose among the alternative points on the Phillips curve, in effect trading the lost output caused by underemployment for the distributional costs of inflation. Other objectives, such as rapid economic growth and balance-of-payments equilibrium, may place further constraints upon stabilization policy. If the economy is operating near full employment, for example, a policy of encouraging rapid growth will generate inflationary pressures in the industrial sectors that are growing most rapidly; these pressures, in turn, will lead to a balance-of-payments deficit as domestic prices rise relative to foreign prices and increases in domestic disposable income lead to increased imports.

This discussion has only hinted at the problems inherent in the choice of stabilization policies. There are too many policy instruments and conflicting objectives and too little knowledge about the mechanisms through which these policies work and the time lags present in their operation to permit anything like a comprehensive treatment of stabilization. The instruments through which stabilization policy operates, however, can never be completely independent of the allocation and distribution functions of the public sector, even though such a separation of functions might be implied by the simple aggregate-demand model.

INTERRELATEDNESS OF PUBLIC SECTOR FUNCTIONS

One way to illustrate the three aspects of governmental economic behavior is through the production possibility curve (Figure 1.1). The horizontal axis shows the value of goods that society may produce and consume if all resources are allocated to private sector goods; the maximum of such production is P, in the event that all resources are allocated to the private sector. The vertical axis shows the value of goods that may be produced if resources are allocated to the public sector. For simplicity, let us assume that all government resource allocation is through demand, so that all goods and services are produced by private sector firms even if all resources are initially allocated to the public sector. The maximum value of public sector goods that the economy can produce is G.

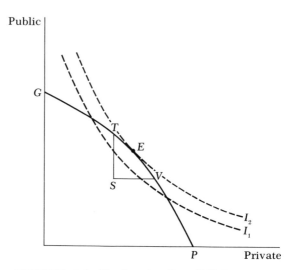

FIGURE 1.1   Production Possibilities

The curve GP traces the production (and consumption) possibilities available to society. The points on GP are determined by the allocation alternatives, which in turn reflect the resources required to produce public and private sector goods. Under the normal assumption of diminishing rates of transformation, the production possibility curve will be convex to the origin, as in Figure 1.1. The function of the allocation activities of the government, then, is to determine the location of the curve GP and to express effectively the demand for the public sector goods that society chooses once a point on GP is selected.

The stabilization responsibilities of the public sector consist, first, of making sure that the economy produces somewhere on GP. If the economy is located at an interior point such as S, it is clear that any number of preferable locations are available (on the arc TV, for example) if stabilization policy can just move the economy to a position of maximum resource use. Second, stabilization policies must regulate the growth of the economy (depicted by an outward shift of the production possibility curve), assuming that other problems of the real world such as inflation and the balance of payments do not intrude into this model.

The public sector's distributional activities are related to the choice of one point on GP as the preferred production point. This choice may be made on the basis of a social welfare function (shown in Figure 1.1 by the dashed social indifference curves I_1 and I_2), or there may be some give-and-take in the political process leading to the selection of a point such as E as the social optimum. Once point E is chosen from the production possibilities defined by allocation considerations, stabilization policies must be directed toward reaching the curve *GP* at point *E*, and the government must obtain enough resources from the private sector to demand the appropriate level of public sector goods.[3]

This model of the allocation, distribution, and stabilization functions of the public sector is useful for the clarity with which it defines these responsibilities, but it bears little relation to the real-world activities of governments. No government stabilization program can be perfectly neutral with respect to allocation and distribution, so the movement from *S* to the production possibility curve will itself shift the curve and change the socially preferred point on it. Distributional policies alter patterns of factor ownership and income and thus affect resource allocation (since preferences about factor employment and consumption will differ among individuals) and stabilization (by altering the responsiveness of the economy to fiscal and monetary measures). A reallocation of resources from the private to the public sector will increase the incomes of owners of those factors of production needed to produce public sector goods and will therefore alter the distribution of income and welfare.

These points can be clarified with some examples. Suppose that the public sector expands its programs of educational support in response to public demand for higher levels of education. (We leave aside for the moment the question of the "publicness" of education, but we shall turn to it in Chapter 16.) Public expenditures for education are primarily an allocation function, reflecting demand for this public sector good over alternative private sector consumption. But not all students are capable of profiting equally from education (even if all receive equal amounts, which is not usually the case), and public expenditures for education will therefore confer a distributional benefit on people who place a high value on the education they receive and on students whose future incomes rise the most as a result of the additional education. Stabilization policy will be affected also, for the taxes or borrowing necessary to finance the additional education expenditures will cause further adjustments in aggregate demand, asset holdings, and the full spectrum of stabilization instrument variables.

As a second example, let the government increase the benefits paid to widows and orphans under the social security program. This primarily distributional policy will immediately generate a secondary effect on stabilization, since aggregate demand will rise because the

---

[3] Recall the assumption made earlier that even public sector goods are produced by private sector producers.

consumption propensities of widows and orphans are greater than those of the average taxpayer who finances the increase in benefits. There will also be two allocational effects: (1) some widows and orphans may retire from the labor force, since at their new, higher income levels they will prefer more leisure; and (2) the consumption patterns of the widows and orphans probably will differ from that of the average taxpayer, leading to a reallocation of resources within the private sector and between the private and public sectors.

A third example is provided by anti-inflationary tax increases, clearly a stabilization measure. Since the tax system (especially the personal and corporate income taxes that are manipulated as part of stabilization policies) is not neutral with respect to the distribution of income and wealth, there will be an immediate redistribution toward those taxpayers whose tax liabilities have risen the least. The relative increase in income these taxpayers enjoy will lead to a change in overall resource allocation, as indicated in the preceding example.

Although any government policy affects all three functions simultaneously, it is useful to separate them conceptually in order to evaluate public programs at the margin. The impact of allocation expenditures on stabilization policy, for example, may be negligible if the expenditure is small relative to the overall size of the public sector. The emphasis in the following chapters will be on the allocative activities of the public sector, with a discussion of the distributional consequences of these activities when distributional judgments are likely to be a part of the allocation decision. We will ignore stabilization policy, assuming that if public sector activities are evaluated on the basis of their allocational validity and distributional impacts, then stabilization measures consistent with these allocational decisions will be available.

2 Patterns of Public Expenditures

CATEGORIZATION OF PUBLIC EXPENDITURES

A casual look at trends in public spending in the United States leaves the impression that growth of the public sector has proceeded unchecked during the twentieth century. The single most remarkable phenomenon has been the rapid increase in federal spending above its pre–World War I level, but state and local expenditures have increased nearly fifty-fold in the same period. Since 1929 (the first year for which reliable National Income Accounts data are available), total government spending has increased from about 10 percent of gross national product to over 30 percent.

Although these figures are startling, they do not begin to give an accurate picture of how well the different levels of government have met the demands of taxpayers. Governments are not monolithic but are instead composed of many, frequently hundreds of, separate departments, bureaus, and operating agencies. The budget for each of these agencies typically is determined by many people in different sectors of the economy and the government: employees of each agency (program managers and budget officers) who estimate the benefits and costs of providing different levels of services; officials of the government's central budgeting agency who must reconcile the requests of agency personnel with the availability of funds; taxpayers, either individually or organized into lobbying groups, who influence the priorities of executive and legislative funding; and legislators who respond to the expressed demands of the electorate (as they perceive them)

15

and to political realities. The result of these fragmented decisions is a fragmented budget, one in which allocations for each program are made primarily on the program's own political and economic merits and only secondarily in response either to a total revenue constraint or to the merits of alternative expenditures.

This view of government budgets agrees with the contention in Chapter 1 that the public sector allocates and redistributes resources because the allocation and distribution resulting from private sector activities are unsatisfactory to the electorate. According to this viewpoint, the level of government budgets is significant, if at all, only for stabilization policy. Growth in government budgets over time is much less important than the behavior of the individual allocations of government revenues, for only by examining the funding of individual programs can we tell how the public sector has responded to taxpayers' preferences.

Our emphasis on individual government programs neglects the contention of many eminent economists and political philosophers that large government budgets are bad no matter what programs are funded. The alternative to public spending is consumption and investment within the private sector, allocations always made in response to the preferences expressed by individual consumers and producers. In the view of many conservative economists, government spending reduces individuals' freedom by substituting collective decisions for the individual decisions made in the market.[1] In the interests of preserving freedom, therefore, government budgets should always be kept at minimum levels, and only unavoidable expenses (such as war and justice) should be funded publicly. This position attaches significance to the overall size of the public sector budget, for it asserts that large budgets reduce individual freedom regardless of the merits of particular programs.

Such instinctive disapproval of large government budgets oversimplifies the issue of public expenditures and individuals' freedom. Small budgets do not necessarily mean that markets can operate freely, and large ones do not have to prevent individual consumers from expressing their preferences in the marketplace. At one extreme, imagine that all prices and wages were controlled by an agency of the federal government. (A situation similar to this existed during World War II, when the federal controlling agency was the Office of Price Administration.) The federal budget could be very small, since price

---

[1] Two lucid presentations of this view are made by Milton Friedman, *Capitalism and Freedom* (Chicago: University of Chicago Press, 1962); and Henry Wallich, *The Cost of Freedom* (New York: Collier Books, 1962).

control is not a resource-intensive activity, but individuals would have little freedom to express their wants because relative prices would not be free to vary in response to consumer demand. The allocation of re-sources would not be that which consumers and producers wanted except in the special case that the controlled prices were exactly the ones that would have prevailed in a perfectly competitive economy. Moreover, firms would not be able to adjust to changing patterns of demand because relative prices would remain constant. In this case, markets would not function at all freely, but the degree of federal control could not be inferred from the size of the federal budget.

At the other extreme, suppose that the government taxed away three-quarters of everyone's income and then redistributed the rev-enues through a set of cash transfer payments. Public expenditures would be large relative to GNP, but the freedom of markets would be virtually unhampered since the government would not be buying any goods or services. There would be some effects on the supply of factors of production (as we shall discuss in Part Three), but the effects could be minimized by a careful selection of tax policies. Any one taxpayer's freedom to allocate his earned income would be severely limited by the public tax transfer policy, but the overall impact of the federal government on the economy's allocation of resources would be much less than commensurate with the size of the federal budget.

Thus, even if we are concerned about the impact of public spending on individual freedom, incentives, and the functioning of markets, we must look beyond the sum total of government budgets to the pro-grams included in the budgets. We may discover that the growth of public expenditures has caused a reduction in the freedom of individ-ual consumers, or we may find that public programs differ widely in their effects on private markets. To investigate these issues, we must first distinguish between public programs that remove resources from the control of the private market and those that leave private allocation mechanisms unaffected.

Exhaustive. In Chapter 1 several public programs were described as responses to an allocation failure of the private market. Some of the programs in this category are national defense, education, the admin-istration of justice, space exploration, and environmental protection. The common characteristic of these programs is that they all provide a good or service that benefits consumers directly and that consumers cannot obtain in private markets. The production of these goods and services, whether performed publicly or privately, removes resources from the production of private consumption and investment goods. These programs are called "exhaustive" because they require resources to be allocated away from private sector goods to the public sector.

In terms of Figure 1.1, increases in exhaustive expenditures move the economy along the production possibility curve, away from P and toward G. If we are initially at a point such as V, we may want to increase our public sector allocation of resources in order to approach point E. Thus, exhaustive expenditures are a measure of the resources devoted to producing goods and services that are not subject to the "test of the market," consumers' willingness to buy the goods at the prices at which they are supplied. For the reasons already discussed, exhaustive expenditures are not a perfect indicator of the extent to which the public sector interferes with the freedom of the market, but they do tell roughly how much of its resources the economy is spending on the production of public sector goods.

Non-exhaustive. Many public programs consist simply of transfers of resources from one consumer or producer to another. These programs do not directly reallocate resources, although they will usually cause some changes in allocation because different consumers and producers have differing preferences. The primary purpose of these programs, however, is to change the distribution of income or wealth by taxing income away from some people and transferring it to others. The best examples of these programs are pure income transfers such as unemployment compensation, public relief assistance, and social security (disability, survivors', and retirement benefits). But governments also operate many programs that transfer income in the form of specific goods and services. Food, health care, housing, and education are some of the most important.

Transfers in kind necessarily involve the public sector in reallocating resources, as well as in redistributing them. The government's decision to transfer specific goods entails the allocation of resources to produce them and thus reduces the amount of resources available to produce the goods and services demanded in private sector markets. Accordingly, transfers in kind must be considered an exhaustive expenditure. Pure income transfers, however, do not affect the total amount of resources available to the private sector. Instead, they cause changes only in the patterns of demand and supply within private markets. Expenditures on these programs are called "non-exhaustive" because they do not reduce the amount of goods that can be produced in response to private sector demand.

To interpret non-exhaustive expenditures in terms of Figure 1.1, recall that consumers' preferences depend on their incomes (among other factors). Transfers of income among consumer groups, therefore, will affect society's preferences for various public and private sector goods. In effect, more weight will be given to the preferences of the recipients of transfers, and less weight will be attached to the preferences of those who are taxed. If we assume that exhaustive expenditures are unaffected by the level of non-exhaustive expenditures, then only the composition of private sector goods will vary as a result of changes in the level of non-exhaustive spending. More generally, we may expect a shift in society's preferences (denoted by the social indifference curves, I_1 and I_2, in Figure 1.1), leading to the selection of some point other than E as the new optimum. We shall return to the interdependence of non-exhaustive spending and resource allocation in Chapter 6.

Although all public expenditures can be classed as exhaustive or non-exhaustive, it is worth repeating that neither category alone nor the total of all public spending is an accurate measure of governmental intervention in private sector allocation. Even if the government does not impose wage and price controls, it influences private markets in many ways that do not appear in the public budget. For example, federal and state regulation of transportation, communication, and banking creates prices that differ greatly from the free-market prices. Public utilities boards control the price and supply of electricity, water, and natural gas. Federal antitrust activities affect the market behavior of many private firms. Quotas on imports for goods including oil, sugar, and textiles both distort the allocation procedures of domestic producers and affect the equilibrium prices and quantities supplied in domestic markets. Policies like these may either increase individuals' freedom or reduce it, but we cannot judge their effects merely by looking at the size of public budgets.

PATTERNS OF EXHAUSTIVE EXPENDITURES

Trends in exhaustive spending by different levels of government are shown in Table 2.1. The outstanding feature of Table 2.1 is the difference between the growth of federal exhaustive expenditures and state and local purchases. During the period since the Korean War, federal purchases of goods and services have increased by a little less than 100 percent, from \$53.9 billion to \$101.6 billion. In the same period, however, state and local exhaustive spending has increased nearly fivefold, from \$22.9 billion in 1952 to \$100.7 billion in 1968. In 1952 the ratio of state and local exhaustive expenditures to federal purchases was only about 40 percent, but rapid increases in state and local spending brought the ratio to 100 percent by 1965. Despite the increases in federal purchases caused by the Vietnam War in the

1966–1968 period, state and local expenditures have remained virtually equal to federal spending.

TABLE 2.1   Exhaustive Expenditures, 1952–1968

YEAR	FEDERAL EXHAUSTIVE EXPENDITURES		STATE AND LOCAL EXHAUSTIVE EXPENDITURES		TOTAL EXHAUSTIVE EXPENDITURES	
	$ (millions)	% of GNP	$ (millions)	% of GNP	$ (millions)	% of GNP
1952	53,867	15.6	22.882	6.6	76,749	22.2
1953	59,012	16.2	24,611	6.8	83,623	22.9
1954	49,153	13.5	27,418	7.5	76,571	21.0
1955	46,132	11.6	30,106	7.6	76,238	19.2
1956	47,454	11.3	32,994	7.9	80,448	19.2
1957	51,313	11.6	36,585	8.3	87,898	19.9
1958	55,392	12.4	40,564	9.1	95,956	21.5
1959	55,508	11.5	43,346	9.0	98,854	20.4
1960	55,413	11.0	46,090	9.1	101,503	20.2
1961	59,500	11.4	50,217	9.7	109,717	21.1
1962	65,555	11.7	53,731	9.6	119,286	21.3
1963	66,423	11.2	58,240	9.9	124,663	21.1
1964	67,347	10.7	63,725	10.1	131,072	20.7
1965	68,996	10.1	69,399	10.2	138,395	20.3
1966	80,057	10.7	79,040	10.5	159,097	21.2
1967	92,987	11.7	89,336	11.3	182,323	23.0
1968	101,627	11.7	100,745	11.6	202,372	23.4

SOURCE: *Survey of Current Business* (July 1969) and *U.S. Income and Output, 1929–1965* (U.S. Department of Commerce, Office of Business Economics).

A second noteworthy feature of Table 2.1 is that the ratio of federal
exhaustive expenditures to GNP has been nearly constant since the
end of the Korean War buildup in 1954. In fact, during the mid-1960's
(before the Vietnam buildup), the federal government used a smaller
percentage of the economy's resources than at any time during the
preceding fifteen years. The data in Table 2.1 do not support the contention that the American economy is becoming increasingly dominated by the federal government.

While the federal government's exhaustive expenditures were increasing more slowly than GNP, however, state and local exhaustive
spending rose more rapidly. The share of state and local purchases in
GNP rose steadily (with two temporary setbacks in 1959 and 1962)

during the entire post-Korean period. But despite this increase in state and local spending, the public sector as a whole kept its exhaustive expenditures at a remarkably constant proportion of GNP. No trend in public exhaustive expenditures can be found for the period 1954–1966, when total exhaustive expenditures stayed between 19.2 and 21.5 percent of GNP. The increase in exhaustive expenditures in 1967 and 1968 was primarily attributable to the Vietnam War.

Federal. A more detailed picture of federal exhaustive spending is available in Table 2.2, which shows the breakdown of expenditures by function for 1952–1968. The data in Table 2.2 make clear the preponderant role of national defense in federal exhaustive expenditures. Since the cold war erupted in Korea in 1952, federal purchases for defense have been less than three-quarters of total federal exhaustive spending only twice, and during 1952–1961 defense took more than 80 percent of all federal purchases. The impact of Vietnam can clearly be seen in Table 2.2: federal purchases increased by $32.6 billion from 1965 to 1968, and defense expenditures rose by $27.9 billion (over 85 percent of the total increase).

Another interesting aspect of Table 2.2 is the role of the space program, which has claimed the second largest portion of federal purchases since 1963. Although expenditures on space research and technology began to fall in 1967, the total of spending on defense and space has comprised at least 80 percent of federal exhaustive expenditures in every year since 1952. The other "nondomestic" federal program, international affairs and foreign aid, has been a decreasing percentage of total federal exhaustive expenditures since 1961.

Trends are harder to identify among the "domestic" programs because of frequent changes in the administration of many of them. Agricultural research and support, for example, has fluctuated greatly as a fraction of total federal purchases because of frequent changes in the statutory nature of federal programs. Federal purchases of farm commodities appear as exhaustive expenditures, but federal payments in return for acreage limitation are non-exhaustive cash transfers. Federal exhaustive expenditures have not risen rapidly for any domestic program, however, and only education and health, labor, and welfare show a rising trend over the entire 1952–1968 period.

The remarkable aspect of federal domestic programs is their small size. The decade of the 1960's was marked by the passage of path-breaking federal legislation in the areas of education, health, and welfare, and (at least until 1966) by reductions in defense spending as a percentage of GNP. But even during 1964 and 1965, the years in which many Great Society programs were begun, expenditures on federal domestic programs (excluding defense, space, international

TABLE 2.2   Federal Exhaustive Expenditures by Function, 1952–1968

	1952		1956		1960		1961		1962	
	$ (millions)	%	$ (millions)	%	$ (millions)	%	$ (millions)	%	$ (millions)	%
DEFENSE	45,928	85.3	40,330	85.0	44,946	81.1	47,825	80.4	51,582	78.7
SPACE	—	—	—	—	572	1.0	890	1.5	1,785	2.7
GENERAL GOVERNMENT	1,260	2.3	1,361	2.9	1,465	2.7	1,421	2.4	1,583	2.4
INTERNATIONAL AFFAIRS[a]	2,380	4.4	2,147	4.5	2,233	4.0	2,530	4.3	2,585	3.9
EDUCATION	92	0.2	129	0.3	231	0.4	261	0.4	319	0.5
HEALTH, LABOR, AND WELFARE	352	0.7	761	1.6	899	1.6	1,258	2.1	1,545	2.4
VETERANS	1,203	2.2	979	2.1	1,183	2.1	1,290	2.2	1,343	2.0
COMMERCE, HOUSING, AND TRANSPORTATION	756	1.4	713	1.5	1,550	2.8	1,734	2.9	1,887	2.9
AGRICULTURE	702	1.3	64	0.1	944	1.7	630	1.1	1,141	1.7
NATURAL RESOURCES	1,194	2.2	1,007	2.1	1,393	2.5	1,667	2.8	1,794	2.7
TOTAL	53,867	100.0	47,454	100.0	55,413	100.0	59,500	100.0	65,555	100.0

[a] Includes foreign economic assistance and other transfers.

TABLE 2.2 (Continued)

	1963		1964		1965		1966		1967		1968	
	$ (millions)	%	$ (millions)	%	$ (millions)	%	$ (millions)	%	$ (millions)	%	$ (millions)	%
DEFENSE	50,760	76.4	49,985	74.2	50,143	72.7	60,688	75.8	72,353	77.8	78,031	76.8
SPACE	3,351	5.0	4,606	6.8	5,562	8.1	5,907	7.4	4,815	5.2	4,494	4.4
GENERAL GOVERNMENT	1,758	2.6	1,959	2.9	2,069	3.0	2,156	2.7	2,408	2.6	2,562	2.5
INTERNATIONAL AFFAIRS	2,611	3.9	2,660	3.9	2,668	3.9	2,858	3.6	2,871	3.1	2,731	2.7
EDUCATION	374	0.6	428	0.6	430	0.6	516	0.6	695	0.7	778	0.8
HEALTH, LABOR, AND WELFARE	1,629	2.5	1,683	2.5	2,143	3.1	2,756	3.4	3,301	3.5	3,662	3.6
VETERANS	1,370	2.1	1,450	2.2	1,445	2.1	1,536	1.9	1,588	1.7	1,727	1.7
COMMERCE, HOUSING, AND TRANSPORTATION	2,080	3.1	2,192	3.3	2,109	3.1	2,429	3.0	2,544	2.7	2,881	2.8
AGRICULTURE	606	0.9	435	0.6	373	0.5	-1,152	-1.4	-73	-0.1	2,458	2.4
NATURAL RESOURCES	1,891	2.9	1,955	2.9	2,058	3.0	2,371	3.0	2,503	2.7	2,303	2.3
TOTAL	66,423	100.0	67,347	100.0	68,996	100.0	80,057	100.0	92,987	100.0	101,627	100.0

SOURCE: Same as for Table 2.1.

affairs, and general administration) comprised less than 12.5 percent of all federal purchases of goods and services.

State and Local. With the bulk of federal exhaustive expenditures going to defense and space, the burden of financing and operating domestic programs has fallen largely on state and local governments. The resulting pattern of state and local exhaustive expenditures is shown in Table 2.3.

Education is both the largest and the fastest-growing state and local program, as measured by exhaustive spending. From 1952 to 1968, exhaustive spending on education increased over 500 percent, and the share of education in total state and local purchases rose accordingly. About two-thirds of most state and local educational expenditures in 1968 were on primary and secondary schooling; about one-quarter was spent on higher education, with the balance going to miscellaneous compensatory and remedial programs.

Expenditures on health, labor, and welfare increased over fourfold between 1952 and 1968 and remained a stable fraction (almost one-quarter) of all state and local purchases. Much of this increase was due to the rapid increases in the costs of health care and hospitalization rather than to the provision of expanded facilities and coverage. Civilian safety (mostly police) was the other large category of expenditures under this function.

Under the heading "Commerce, transportation, and housing" were two large programs. Transportation was second only to education during 1952–1958. Highway maintenance and construction consumed the bulk of state and local purchases for transportation (95.5 percent in 1968), but a large fraction of state and local highway expenditures was financed through federal grants. The operation of public utilities was also a major category of state and local purchases during this period.

These functional categories (education; health, labor, and welfare; and commerce, housing, and transportation) took the bulk of all state and local exhaustive expenditures throughout the 1952–1968 period: 88.4 percent in 1952, 87.8 percent in 1960, and 87.2 percent in 1968. All the reduction in the share of these three program categories can be attributed to the rising costs of general government administration, which climbed more than 500 percent in the seventeen years.

PATTERNS OF NON-EXHAUSTIVE EXPENDITURES

Table 2.4 shows the trends in non-exhaustive expenditures by federal, state, and local governments from 1952–1968. The data for federal

TABLE 2.3 State and Local Exhaustive Expenditures by Function, 1952–1968

	1952		1956		1960		1961		1962	
	$ (mil-lions)	%	$ (mil-lions)	%	$ (mil-lions)	%	$ (mil-lions)	%	$ (mil-lions)	%
DEFENSE	124	0.5	177	1.5	278	0.6	309	0.6	337	0.6
GENERAL GOVERNMENT	1,607	7.0	2,275	6.9	3,375	7.3	3,603	7.2	3,903	7.3
EDUCATION	8,233	36.0	12,900	29.1	18,465	40.1	20,408	40.7	21,795	40.6
HEALTH, LABOR, AND WELFARE	5,612	24.5	7,473	22.6	10,395	22.6	11,257	22.4	12,249	22.8
VETERANS	14	0.1	13	0.0	16	0.0	17	0.0	18	0.0
COMMERCE, HOUSING, AND TRANSPORTATION	6,374	27.9	8,829	26.8	11,550	25.1	12,422	24.7	13,247	24.7
AGRICULTURE	301	1.3	383	1.2	531	1.2	620	1.2	656	1.2
NATURAL RESOURCES	617	2.7	944	2.9	1,480	3.2	1,581	3.1	1,521	2.8
TOTAL	22,882	100.0	32,994	100.0	46,090	100.0	50,217	100.0	53,731	100.0

TABLE 2.3 (Continued)

	1963		1964		1965		1966		1967		1968	
	$ (mil-lions)	%	$ (mil-lions)	%	$ (mil-lions)	%	$ (mil-lions)	%	$ (mil-lions)	%	$ (mil-lions)	%
DEFENSE	359	0.6	373	0.5	376	0.5	421	0.5	447	0.5	501	0.5
GENERAL GOVERNMENT	4,289	7.4	4,944	7.8	5,860	8.4	5,976	7.6	6,946	7.8	8,506	8.4
EDUCATION	23,773	40.8	26,256	41.2	28,634	41.3	34,656	43.8	39,099	43.8	42,861	42.5
HEALTH, LABOR, AND WELFARE	13,146	22.6	14,332	22.5	15,558	22.4	17,353	22.0	20,094	22.5	24,007	23.8
VETERANS	18	0.0	18	0.0	18	0.0	18	0.0	19	0.0	24	0.0
COMMERCE, HOUSING, AND TRANSPORTATION	14,142	24.3	15,070	23.6	16,258	23.4	17,676	22.4	19,314	21.6	21,029	20.9
AGRICULTURE	748	1.3	801	1.3	744	1.1	864	1.1	1,007	1.1	1,102	1.1
NATURAL RESOURCES	1,765	3.0	1,931	3.0	1,951	2.8	2,075	2.6	2,410	2.7	2,715	2.7
TOTAL	58,240	100.0	63,725	100.0	69,399	100.0	79,040	100.0	89,336	100.0	100,745	100.0

SOURCE: Same as for Table 2.1.

expenditures in Table 2.4 are the totals of direct transfers and interest paid to persons, grants-in-aid to state and local governments, and subsidies (net of the surplus of government enterprises) paid to private firms. The state and local data represent the sums of direct transfers and interest paid less the current surpluses of government enterprises.

TABLE 2.4   Non-exhaustive Expenditures, 1952–1968

YEAR	FEDERAL NON-EXHAUSTIVE EXPENDITURES		STATE AND LOCAL NON-EXHAUSTIVE EXPENDITURES		TOTAL NON-EXHAUSTIVE EXPENDITURES	
	$ (millions)	% of GNP	$ (millions)	% of GNP	$ (millions)	% of GNP
1952	17,178	5.0	2,371	0.7	19,549	5.7
1953	17,977	4.9	2,417	0.7	20,394	5.6
1954	20,575	5.6	2,478	0.7	23,053	6.3
1955	21,962	5.5	2,557	0.6	24,519	6.2
1956	24,407	5.8	2,573	0.6	26,980	6.4
1957	28,255	6.4	2,923	0.7	31,178	7.1
1958	33,478	7.5	3,413	0.8	36,891	8.2
1959	35,480	7.3	3,482	0.7	38,962	8.1
1960	37,603	7.5	3,546	0.7	41,149	8.2
1961	42,584	8.2	3,906	0.8	46,490	8.9
1962	44,688	8.0	3,914	0.7	48,602	8.7
1963	47,434	8.0	3,964	0.7	51,398	8.7
1964	50,764	8.0	4,161	0.7	54,925	8.7
1965	54,360	8.0	4,257	0.6	58,617	8.6
1966	62,689	8.4	4,866	0.6	67,555	9.0
1967	70,769	8.9	5,654	0.7	76,423	9.6
1968	79,884	9.2	6,887	0.8	86,771	10.0

SOURCE: Same as for Table 2.1.

The surpluses and deficits of public enterprises are included as non-exhaustive expenditures because they are more closely comparable to governmental transfers than to exhaustive expenditures. The post office, for example, sells services to the private sector. If its revenues exactly equal its costs, the net surplus is zero. If it operates at a deficit, the post office is, in effect, providing a transfer payment to the users of postal services and financing the transfer out of general revenues. Conversely, a highway toll bridge that operates at a surplus is taxing users an amount in addition to the cost of providing the bridge. (We will discuss pricing policies and costs with more precision in Chapter 5.) In either case, the net surplus of the public enterprise is equivalent to a negative transfer payment and is treated accordingly as a (negative) non-exhaustive expenditure.

A glance at Table 2.4 indicates that state and local non-exhaustive expenditures roughly tripled from 1952–1968, just keeping up with the growth in GNP. The share of state and local non-exhaustive spending in GNP was virtually constant over the entire period. Federal non-exhaustive expenditures, however, grew steadily as a percentage of GNP from 1952 to 1962. After a brief period of proportional growth, federal spending rose sharply in 1966–1968 as some of the Great Society programs enacted in the mid-1960's made an impact on the federal budget. Over the entire period, federal non-exhaustive spending increased over 400 percent, or at about the same rate as state and local exhaustive expenditures. The rise in federal spending was responsible for the increase in total non-exhaustive spending as a percentage of GNP.

Federal. A more detailed breakdown of federal non-exhaustive spending by function during 1952–1968 is presented in Table 2.5. One of the major components of non-exhaustive spending is general government, which includes both the administrative activities of the central executive agencies and the legislative and judicial branches of the federal government. General government also includes the activity of paying interest on the public debt. Interest payments are treated as transfer payments under the reasoning that the majority of the public debt was acquired during the First and Second World Wars and that current productive capacity cannot legitimately be related to these federal obligations. Interest payments rose from $4.7 billion in 1952 to $11.6 billion in 1968, accounting for about 80 percent of the increase in non-exhaustive spending for general government.

By far the largest dollar increase in federal non-exhaustive expenditures occurred in the health, labor, and welfare category. The major program in this category, of course, is social security, and the largest program within social security is old age and retirement benefits. These pension payments totaled $2.7 billion in 1952, but by 1968 they had grown to $31.8 billion. Most of the rest of the increase in this category was due to larger federal grants-in-aid to states for public assistance and relief, better known as "welfare." These grants climbed from $1.3 billion in 1952 to $5.5 billion in 1968.

Expenditures on veterans' programs were the third largest category of federal non-exhaustive spending in 1952, but they declined steadily

TABLE 2.5 Federal Non-exhaustive Expenditures by Function, 1952–1968

	1952		1956		1960		1961		1962	
	$ (millions)	%	$ (millions)	%	$ (millions)	%	$ (millions)	%	$ (millions)	%
DEFENSE	817	4.8	783	3.2	939	2.5	1,071	2.5	1,205	2.7
SPACE	—	—	—	—	2	0.0	3	0.0	11	0.0
GENERAL GOVERNMENT	5,066	29.5	5,863	24.0	8,024	21.4	7,652	18.0	8,330	18.6
EDUCATION	231	1.3	250	1.0	458	1.2	507	1.2	573	1.3
HEALTH, LABOR, AND WELFARE	5,496	32.0	9,840	40.3	18,180	48.3	21,472	50.4	22,428	50.2
VETERANS	3,794	22.1	4,174	17.1	4,485	11.9	4,853	11.4	4,611	10.3
COMMERCE, HOUSING, AND TRANSPORTATION	1,198	7.0	1,433	5.9	3,294	8.8	3,726	8.7	4,024	9.0
AGRICULTURE	565	3.3	2,105	8.6	2,245	6.0	3,350	7.9	3,553	8.0
NATURAL RESOURCES	11	0.1	-41	-0.2	-29	-0.1	-50	-0.1	-37	-0.1
TOTAL	17,178	100.0	24,407	100.0	37,603	100.0	42,584	100.0	44,688	100.0

TABLE 2.5 (Continued)

	1963		1964		1965		1966		1967		1968	
	$ (millions)	%	$ (millions)	%	$ (millions)	%	$ (millions)	%	$ (millions)	%	$ (millions)	%
DEFENSE	1,370	2.9	1,567	3.1	1,712	3.1	1,940	3.1	2,162	3.1	2,408	3.0
SPACE	19	0.0	23	0.1	30	0.1	40	0.1	41	0.1	55	0.1
GENERAL GOVERNMENT	9,028	19.0	9,754	19.2	10,294	18.9	11,371	18.1	12,394	17.5	13,919	17.4
EDUCATION	640	1.4	723	1.4	841	1.5	3,033	4.8	3,200	4.5	3,677	4.6
HEALTH, LABOR, AND WELFARE	23,682	49.9	24,638	48.5	27,451	50.5	30,678	48.9	37,341	52.8	43,337	54.2
VETERANS	4,840	10.2	4,722	9.3	4,920	9.1	4,861	7.8	5,554	7.8	5,892	7.4
COMMERCE, HOUSING, AND TRANSPORTATION	4,464	9.4	5,303	10.4	5,078	9.3	5,572	8.9	5,712	8.1	6,120	7.7
AGRICULTURE	3,431	7.2	4,080	8.0	4,037	7.4	5,128	8.2	4,242	6.0	4,249	5.3
NATURAL RESOURCES	-40	-0.1	-55	-0.1	-3	10.0	66	0.1	123	0.1	227	0.3
TOTAL	47,434	100.0	50,764	100.0	54,360	100.0	62,689	100.0	70,769	100.0	79,884	100.0

SOURCE: Same as for Table 2.1.

in relative importance throughout the period. The dollar cost of veterans' benefits less than doubled between 1952 and 1968, due primarily to low levels of military manpower during much of this period.

The other category in which expenditure was large was commerce, housing, and transportation. A substantial increase in dollar expenditures in this category occurred between 1956 and 1960, when the interstate highway network was first funded. Federal grants-in-aid for highway construction rose from $773 million in 1956 to $2.5 billion in 1960 and then continued to grow at a somewhat slower rate to $4.4 billion by 1968. Highways accounted for two-thirds to three-quarters of federal non-exhaustive expenditures in this category throughout the 1952–1968 period. Most of the rest of the expenditure total was due to the deficit in the provision of postal services.

An interesting feature of Table 2.5 is the unimportance of federal transfers and grants-in-aid for education. In 1952, only 1.3 percent of all federal non-exhaustive spending was on education, and the percentage did not increase significantly until 1966. Even though federal grants-in-aid more than tripled between 1965 and 1966, the share of education in total non-exhaustive spending actually fell in the following year. The dollar amount of funds involved in the peak year 1966, about $3 billion, was less than 10 percent of state and local expenditures in the same year.

State and Local. The description of patterns of government expenditures by function is completed in Table 2.6. The column totals, state and local non-exhaustive expenditures in each year, conceal information about the size of individual expenditures due to the large negative entries in the category of commerce, transportation, and housing. State and local governments operate a variety of public enterprises in transportation, housing, and (most important) utilities. In 1968, for example, public utilities earned nearly $2.0 billion for state and local governments. Most of the rest of the total (of $3.4 billion in 1968) came from transportation facilities such as toll highways and airports. Although receipts from public enterprises rose steadily from 1952 to 1968 (except in 1966), they failed to increase as rapidly as non-exhaustive outlays, and their threefold increase was much less than the 500 percent growth in state and local exhaustive expenditures.

General government expenses were an important category of state and local, as well as of federal, non-exhaustive expenditures. Unlike the federal government, however, state and local governments had only minor interest expenses, since most state and local bond issues are included in specific exhaustive expenditures. Most transfers for general government were pension costs.

TABLE 2.6   State and Local Non-exhaustive Expenditures by Function, 1952–1968

	1952		1956		1960		1961		1962	
	$ (mil-lions)	%	$ (mil-lions)	%	$ (mil-lions)	%	$ (mil-lions)	%	$ (mil-lions)	%
GENERAL GOVERNMENT	870	36.7	1,436	55.8	2,172	61.3	2,416	61.9	2,637	67.4
EDUCATION	30	1.3	53	2.1	96	2.7	114	2.9	134	3.4
HEALTH, LABOR, AND WELFARE	2,454	103.5	2,746	106.7	3,424	96.6	3,610	92.4	3,656	93.4
VETERANS	148	6.2	29	1.1	71	2.0	106	2.7	27	0.7
COMMERCE, HOUSING, AND TRANSPORTATION	− 1,134	− 47.8	− 1,696	− 65.9	− 2,195	− 61.9	− 2,308	− 59.1	− 2,497	− 63.8
AGRICULTURE	2	0.1	7	0.3	7	0.2	7	0.2	8	0.2
NATURAL RESOURCES	1	0.0	− 2	− 0.1	− 29	− 0.8	− 39	− 1.0	− 51	− 1.0
TOTAL	2,371	100.0	2,573	100.0	3,546	100.0	3,906	100.0	3,914	100.0

TABLE 2.6 (Continued)

	1963		1964		1965		1966		1967		1968	
	$ (mil-lions)	%	$ (mil-lions)	%	$ (mil-lions)	%	$ (mil-lions)	%	$ (mil-lions)	%	$ (mil-lions)	%
GENERAL GOVERNMENT	2,714	68.5	2,841	68.3	2,906	68.3	2,971	61.1	3,113	55.1	3,570	51.8
EDUCATION	168	4.2	203	4.9	229	5.4	323	6.6	431	7.6	537	7.8
HEALTH, LABOR, AND WELFARE	3,792	95.7	3,991	95.9	4,177	98.1	4,624	95.0	5,383	95.2	6,250	90.8
VETERANS	13	0.3	12	0.3	12	0.3	2	0.0	6	0.1	10	0.1
COMMERCE, HOUSING, AND TRANSPORTATION	-2,664	-67.2	-2,825	-67.9	-3,007	-70.6	-2,981	-61.3	-3,200	-56.6	-3,397	-49.3
AGRICULTURE	8	0.2	9	0.2	10	0.2	11	0.2	13	0.2	14	0.2
NATURAL RESOURCES	-67	-1.7	-70	-1.7	-70	-1.6	-84	-1.7	-92	-1.6	-97	-1.4
TOTAL	3,964	100.0	4,161	100.0	4,257	100.0	4,866	100.0	5,654	100.0	6,887	100.0

SOURCE: Same as for Table 2.1.

The largest category of state and local non-exhaustive expenditures was health, labor, and welfare. The increase of $3.8 billion between 1952 and 1968 is all attributable to greater outlays for public assistance and relief. Most state and local transfers for "welfare," however, were financed by federal grants-in-aid. In 1968, federal grants accounted for $5.5 billion of the total outlay of $6.1 billion.

Other categories of state and local non-exhaustive spending were minor, although transfers for education increased sixfold as a percentage of all non-exhaustive expenditures. States and localities generally earned surpluses from their conservation and natural resource development activities. Agricultural transfer payments were subsidies for farmers' conservation activities.

SUMMARY

A comparison of Tables 2.1 and 2.4 indicates that federal expenditures during the 1952–1968 period remained at a nearly constant percentage of GNP (a low of 17.1 percent in 1955 and a high of 21.1 percent in the war year of 1953). Federal non-exhaustive expenditures rose during this period while federal exhaustive expenditures fell slightly as a percentage of GNP. The most dramatic rise was shown by state and local exhaustive expenditures, which nearly doubled as a share of GNP. State and local non-exhaustive expenditures remained at a constant percentage of GNP throughout the entire period.

About 80 percent of federal exhaustive spending was on the non-domestic categories of national defense and space research and technology. Expenditures on domestic programs ranged from 8.0 percent of total exhaustive expenditures in 1952 to only 12.4 percent in 1965. Federal non-exhaustive spending, however, financed social security payments directly and public relief and transportation programs indirectly. The main thrust of federal expenditures during this period was to increase federal distributional activities while actually reducing the proportion of GNP spent on federal resource allocation.

Virtually the opposite picture appears when we study state and local expenditures during 1952–1968. Exhaustive spending on education, transportation, and health rose rapidly as the resources devoted to state and local allocation activities increased from less than $23 billion to over $100 billion. Some of these state and local programs were funded by the federal government through grants-in-aid, an indication that the electorate seemed to prefer allocating public sector resources at low levels of government. The redistributive activities financed by state and local non-exhaustive expenditures barely kept pace with GNP growth during this period.

3 Allocation Criteria: Theory and Practice

In discussing the allocation, distribution, and stabilization functions of the public sector in Chapter 1, we assumed that governmental programs and policies are rational responses to rational demands expressed by the private sector. The opportunity-cost criteria for allocation and tax-and-transfer distributional programs are examples of such governmental responses. Our summary of public expenditure patterns in Chapter 2 implicitly assumed that the structure of government expenditures is not capricious but instead reflects some basic social consensus about what functions governments should perform and what levels of government should perform them. In this chapter, we will examine these premises to see whether the assumptions of rational behavior by consumers, producers, and governments conform closely enough to reality to provide the basis for constructing a theory of public sector resource allocation and an analysis of observed governmental taxes and expenditures.

PRIVATE RESOURCE ALLOCATION

The economists' model of competitive behavior assumes that producers and consumers behave as pure maximizers of profits or utility. The pure theory of public sector resource allocation is also derived from these postulates. If actual consumer or producer behavior does not conform (even approximately) to the maximization of utility or profits, however, both public and private resource allocation will deviate from the norms of the model.

In the competitive model all goods and services are supplied in response to what consumers demand in the market. Consumers, in turn, decide what goods and services to demand by examining the relative prices of all goods and then selecting the combination that yields the greatest total satisfaction or utility (subject to the usual budget constraint that total spending does not exceed total income). Each consumer's definition of utility usually is assumed to depend only on his own levels of consumption, although "consumption" may be defined broadly to include savings of different kinds of assets. In this form, the theory of consumer behavior is a general theory of utility maximization over both current and future consumption.

One problem with this theory is the generality of utility maximization. Each year, consumers must make thousands of separate decisions about allocating their incomes. The implicit maximization problem would challenge a sophisticated computer even if consumers had full knowledge of their utility functions. To compound the difficulty, some consumption goods (consumer durables and savings) yield utility over a period of years, and in each year their utility depends on the consumption alternatives available at that time. Thus, each consumer's problem of utility maximization has a time dimension that multiplies the complexity of the allocation process.

A more difficult conceptual problem is that in order to maximize utility, the consumer must know the amounts of utility that he will derive from each of the consumption possibilities available to him. This information may be difficult and costly to obtain. The primary source of information is the consumer's own experience, which naturally excludes consumption of most of the alternatives available to him. In particular, a consumer may find it difficult to evaluate durable goods (such as automobiles and major appliances) because of the infrequency of purchase and the variability of maintenance and repair costs. As an alternative to relying on his own experience, the consumer may try to obtain information from other sources, such as commercial testing services. In either case, information will be costly, and the consumer will not try to behave as a pure maximizer since at some point the cost of additional information will exceed its value.

Utility maximization is difficult to achieve even in these simple cases, where the consumer's satisfaction depends only on his own consumption choices. If we allow utilities to depend on others' consumption, the maximization process is much more complex. A full discussion of interdependences will be left until Chapter 5. For now, it is enough to note that the postulate of consumers' utility maximization cannot be satisfied perfectly due to the difficulties of obtaining information about preferences, processing the information to yield an optimal allocation, and adapting this allocation to the complexities and interdependences of individuals' preferences.

Similar problems arise on the production side of the market. The competitive model assumes that the goal of all producers is to maximize their profits by producing at minimum cost the goods and services that consumers demand. In their single-minded pursuit of profits, producers are driven by competition to introduce new technologies as they become available and to adjust quickly to variations in consumer preferences.

Even if we defer a discussion of interdependences among producers, we cannot accept this model of competitive behavior as an adequate description of real-world production decisions. One difficulty is that the criterion of profit maximization is rather naive. Most economists agree that profits are not the only objective in producers' utility functions. Some of the others, even in essentially competitive markets, include the long-run stability of the company, the company's share of the total market, total sales (subject to the constraint that profits be above some minimum level), and doing well enough not to disturb the company's stockholders ("satisficing").[1] Pure profit maximization may conflict with any or all of these other goals.

Another shortcoming of the profit maximization rule is that it does not specify the time period over which profits are to be maximized. In the long run, producers must evaluate the advantages of investing in new capital equipment and of altering their old production techniques to adapt to new technologies or changes in the relative prices of factors of production. When a change is made in a company's capital equipment, the new equipment customarily will contribute to the total cost of production over the lifetime of the capital good. These capital costs incurred by the firm are just as real as the costs of labor and raw materials, but unlike the latter costs the capital costs cannot be varied in response to short-run fluctuations in production. Thus, the firm's profit-maximizing output and price in the long run may differ from its short-run equilibrium.

A third reason why producers may not behave as pure profit maximizers is that they may not have all the information they need. Just as utility maximization by consumers requires each consumer to know the utility derivable from all consumption alternatives, profit maximization can only be achieved if each producer knows the costs and productivities of every alternative technology. But this information can be obtained only by trying different techniques of production,

---

[1] A word that combines "satisfying" and "sufficing," it suggests why business managers may not try to maximize their profits.

and real-world producers rarely can afford such experiments. As in the consumer example, the cost of obtaining the information is high. Profit maximization consequently can only be carried to the point at which the cost of additional information about productivity equals the expected increment in profits. Since information is not free, this point clearly is not the one at which incremental profit is zero.

In spite of these deficiencies in the objectives that we postulate for consumers and producers, economists continue to rely on the competitive model as the norm for the behavior of free markets. One reason is that the underlying premises of the competitive model are very appealing. Even if he does not push utility maximization to the margin, the consumer usually *should* prefer to allocate his income in ways that yield the largest increments in satisfaction. Similarly, other things being equal, we should expect producers to choose the allocations that offer the largest increments in profits. Utility and profit maximization are not hard and fast rules but are instead descriptions of the motivations that underlie market behavior.

Since most choices about allocation are expressed through markets, utility and profit maximization are the criteria governing most resource allocation decisions. The normative equilibrium of the purely competitive model, accordingly, is broadly descriptive of the real-world equilibrium that results from the allocation decisions made by producers and consumers under their imperfect applications of the maximization criteria. Even though real markets are, at best, only approximations to purely competitive ones, we may use the competitive model to predict the effects of policies that disturb market equilibria.

PUBLIC RESOURCE ALLOCATION

Allocation between the public and private sectors and within the public sector is subject to the same imperfections that characterize allocation within the private sector. Government managers must decide how to allocate factors of production to produce public goods and services, and in doing so they are confronted with the same uncertainties about factor productivity as producers in the private sector. The simple profit motive does not explain the response of government producers to public demand, but the actual maximands of public managers—budgetary appropriations, personnel ceilings, legislative approval, and the long-run stability of the government agency—are not very different from private producers' goals (sales maximization, long-run stability, and satisficing). Profit maximization in the private sector simply denotes the willingness of the private producer to supply the goods demanded in the market by consumers. The willingness of public managers to respond to expressed demand and the difficulties they encounter may make them behave very much like private producers. Real-world market imperfections may not make the supply of public sector goods deviate from the competitive model by much more than the supply of private sector goods.

The greatest departure from the competitive model occurs in consumers' demand for the output of the public sector. The theoretical allocation criterion stated in Chapter 1 was that the opportunity cost of public sector production should be no greater than the value of the public sector goods produced. This allocation criterion is consistent with consumers' utility maximization, for if the value consumers place upon public production is greater than the value of the private sector goods that could have been produced with the same resources (the opportunity cost), consumers will rationally demand public sector goods at the expense of private sector ones. The difficulty with this criterion is that consumers cannot easily evaluate public sector goods, nor can they always express their demand once they have determined the amount of public sector goods that they prefer.

The value of private sector goods is set, in the market, by the price that consumers are willing to pay. No market is available to determine the equilibrium price of public sector goods, except in those few cases of publicly produced goods such as postal services, some government documents, or the outputs of public utilities. Even in these cases, the public sector rarely uses price as a mechanism to equate demand and supply. Instead, the prices of government outputs are usually set by administrative or political procedures, and supply is left to adjust to demand at the predetermined price.

This situation is shown in Figure 3.1. Suppose that the demand and supply curves are those for third-class postage. (There is every reason to expect the curves to have the normal shapes.) The equilibrium price for this good is obviously p_0, and q_0 is the equilibrium quantity demanded. But if the government decides that the market price should be p_1, users of third-class mail will demand q_1, and the cost of supplying the good will rise to c_1 (at the margin). The important point is *not* that the post office will have a built-in deficit but that consumers will use too much of the third-class mail service (q_1 instead of q_0). The marginal valuation of the good provided through the "market" (p_1) is less than *both* the marginal resource cost (c_1) of supplying q_1 of the good *and* the marginal opportunity cost of the good in equilibrium (p_0). As long as the government maintains the price of third-class mail at p_1, the allocation criterion based on opportunity cost cannot be met

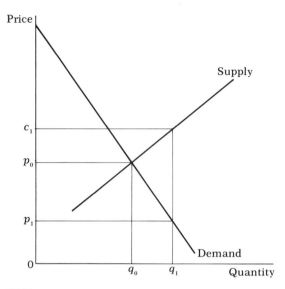

FIGURE 3.1   Postal Services

even if consumers are able to express their preferences by buying the government's output.

Even this approximation to private sector resource allocation does not apply to most exhaustive public sector expenditures, for most government goods and services either are not marketed to specific individuals at all or are made available at a zero price. Examples of nonspecific goods are defense, foreign aid (which confers general benefits on all domestic consumers but specific benefits on foreign ones), space exploration, and police protection. Examples of goods usually supplied to specific consumers at a zero price are education, social insurance, highways (except for some state toll roads, bridges, and tunnels), and many forms of public assistance. In all these cases and in many more, it is impossible to determine the strength of consumers' demand for the public sector good since there is no market in which consumers must make the trade-off between the government goods and private sector alternatives.

The valuation of public sector goods, however, is not quite a hopeless problem. In some instances (such as social security) we may be able to estimate the value of the public sector goods by observing how consumers evaluate close substitutes supplied by the private sector. Other government goods may be viewed as investments, and their value may be inferred from their effects on private sector goods. For example, many studies estimate the value of education on the basis of the increased lifetime income attributable to education. Estimates of the value of antipollution programs can be made on the basis of the increase in the market value of private property or the reduction in private expenditures (such as cleaning bills) to counteract the effects of pollution. In Part Five we shall explore in greater depth the possibility of evaluating public programs like these.

If we try to use the market prices of private sector goods and services to evaluate public sector output, then we must be careful that the prices we use really reflect consumers' preferences. At the beginning of this chapter we discussed several factors that may cause private sector resource allocation to deviate from the competitive norms. But if market prices are not accurate reflections of the value that consumers place upon private sector goods, these prices will not indicate the true value of public sector substitutes. Thus, market imperfections that affect private sector resource allocation also influence public expenditures. In Chapter 12 we will return to the problem of using private sector prices to estimate the value of public sector goods and services.

In using market behavior to make inferences about the value of public programs, we must also be careful not to violate two of the basic postulates of market analysis. The first is the interrelationship of allocation, distribution, and stabilization mentioned in Chapter 1. If the government were not supplying social insurance, for example, some people who now buy no private insurance would purchase life, disability, or hospitalization coverage, probably causing the market price to rise. If we value the government's program at the *current* market price for private insurance, therefore, we are actually underestimating the true value of the good to consumers. The problem is that the government's activity violates the requirements of partial analysis, that other demands not be affected by changes in the price of the good in question. In this case, an increase in the price of social security would cause a large reduction in most consumers' real incomes and subsequent changes in allocation, distribution, and stabilization. The same analysis would apply to public education and to many other public programs that are large relative to the total market for the good.

The second problem is that many public sector goods are received by all consumers in equal amounts (for example, defense and space exploration). The goods do not, however, have the same value for all consumers. It would simplify the analysis of public programs if we could assume that all individuals were willing to pay their proportional share of the total cost (as we infer from market demand that the value of private goods is at least equal to market price). But this assumption about the public sector involves some unsatisfactory judgments about the political process, as we shall see in Chapter 6.

This discussion of the problems of valuing public sector programs rests on the assumption that consumers consider rationally the trade-offs between public and private goods. But there are several reasons to expect that individuals will behave non-economically in choosing between private goods and government programs.

The Myth of Government Nonproductivity. There is a long tradition of treating the public sector as a final demander of the goods and services produced by the private sector rather than as a supplier of goods and services in competition with the private sector. In the National Income and Product Accounts, all government purchases of goods and services from the private sector are considered to be final consumption. Thus, the Accounts compare the services of a statistical analyst in the Treasury Department to those of a household domestic worker rather than to the services rendered by an accountant employed in private industry. Public schools and hospitals (but not private ones) are conceptually compared to washing machines and other consumer durables instead of to business investment in structures and equipment.

The basis for this treatment of government output lies in the concept of "value added," the difference between the value of a firm's output and the cost of the goods it purchases from other firms (excluding labor and the return to invested capital). Government output cannot generally be evaluated, so national income accountants have been unable to measure its value added. Due to our inability to compare government outputs to private ones, the convention has been to define government "value added" as the cost of labor inputs. But this convention certainly understates the value of the government's production, for it ignores government capital inputs (assuming, in effect, a zero return to public investment). While we may be confident that the value of government investment is greater than zero, the problem of estimating the correct rate of return has proved to be difficult, as we shall discover in Chapter 13.

Even if the government does not produce the goods that the public wants but only expresses public demand to private firms, it may still be performing a productive function. When private sector firms provide information to consumers or help them express their demands, the private firms are called advertisers or brokers. Their activities are included in the nation's business sector, and they are treated as productive users of resources in the same manner as any other private firm. The same brokerage function is performed by many public agencies; for example, most of the budget for national defense is used for the purchase of defense systems from private contractors, not for public production. The services of a Defense Department contract officer are a cost of expressing the demand for public sector goods, for without his activities the private sector could not be informed of consumers' demand. But the tradition of nonproductivity is expressed in the politician's statement that "a dollar that goes to Washington comes back as 85 cents."

Nonspecific Benefits. If consumers were aware of the goods and services either produced by the government or made available through public expression of demand, the traditional view of the nonproductive nature of public programs could be replaced by an economically rational determination of the proper allocation of resources between sectors. Many public programs, however, confer benefits in a general way. In some cases, the benefits are stated negatively; the benefits of police protection are that people are *not* robbed or maimed; the benefits of pollution control are that the environment is *not* polluted. Other public programs offer only uncertain linkages between the expenditure and the eventual benefit. Education is an excellent example, since the benefits that any student receives (in the form of higher income) are highly uncertain and are difficult to attribute to the educational process. Still other programs may offer certain benefits linked directly to the public expenditure, but the length of time between the expenditure and the receipt of benefits may bias consumers against the program. Examples of this kind of expenditure are many public works projects (dams, highways) and other programs with deferred benefits such as social security.

Grouping of Projects. Even if consumers are aware of the benefits they derive from public programs, their decisions between public and private sector goods may be distorted by institutional factors. Consumers allocate resources among private goods by trading off one good against another. But the choice among public goods projects is usually made by proxy, by electing a representative who is committed to particular positions on a large group of issues, many of which (perhaps including the most important) may not be at all concerned with economics. The consumer in such instances obviously has little opportunity to express the strength of his demand for individual public programs.

Accept-or-Reject Decisions. Consumers may be able to indicate their demands for particular public programs when one issue is predominant in an election or when a special bond issue is proposed. But the choice is usually between accepting the project as proposed (endorsing a candidate's position) and rejecting it completely (electing his opponent). Only rarely is the consumer able to express his preference for a third alternative. The choice of projects to present to the electorate frequently is determined by a political process that includes the participation of interested citizens, as we shall discuss in Chapter 6. But the possibility of evaluating public programs at the margin generally does not exist.

For all these reasons, allocating resources between public and private sectors and within the public sector is different in the real world from the description in the normative economic model of competition and individual rationality. Nonetheless, the competitive model can provide insights into the problems of determining the proper role of the government and assessing the effects of governmental economic policies. The application of economic analysis to the public sector is the subject of Part Two. The real-world budgetary process is described and analyzed more fully in Chapter 11.

TWO MODELS OF ALLOCATION
IN IMPERFECT MARKETS

Downs's Model of the Size of the Government Budget. Many of the imperfections in the allocation process have been incorporated by Anthony Downs into a model of government budget-making in a democracy.[2] Downs reasons that the primary objective of real-world democratic governments is to win elections and thereby remain in office. One way to attain this objective is to undertake those economic programs for which the votes gained by the programs' benefits are more numerous than the votes lost by the additional tax cost. Vote gains and vote losses depend on the size and distribution of the benefits of each program and the taxes needed to finance it, and upon voters' perceptions of costs and benefits.

Downs distinguishes three states of voter perception: zero ignorance, or perfect knowledge of costs and benefits for all programs; partial ignorance, in which voters are not aware of all costs and benefits but do know the nature of all government programs; and preponderant ignorance, when voters do not know what programs the government is undertaking or what the costs and benefits are. He defines the "correct" government budget as the one the government

---

[2] Anthony Downs, *An Economic Theory of Democracy* (New York: Harper and Row, 1957).

would choose if all voters had zero ignorance. This is the budget that corresponds to the allocation criterion set forth in Chapter 1, for if the opportunity cost of some public programs is less than the value of the public sector goods *and* if all voters know this to be the case, then (abstracting from redistributional effects) these programs will attract the support of the electorate. Programs that do not satisfy this criterion will not be accepted by voters. Thus, a government seeking to maintain itself in office will limit its budget proposals to those that offer a net vote gain, which is equivalent to an economic gain above their opportunity cost.

The state of zero ignorance never exists in the real world, however, because information about the costs and benefits of public sector goods is hard to acquire. Some of the problems have been mentioned: the difficulty of measuring government output and value added and the related problem of public investment, remoteness or uncertainty of benefits, and the rarity of evaluating public programs individually. For these reasons, even if voters are aware of most of the programs undertaken by the government, they will tend to underestimate the value of the benefits they receive from public sector goods.

There will not be as strong a tendency to understate the opportunity cost of public programs since taxes are not uncertain, distant in time, or difficult to measure. Each voter, therefore, will identify programs in the budget that he would like the government to eliminate—those for which his tax cost exceeds the benefits that he perceives. Different programs will be enacted only if the government can establish what Downs calls "revolving majorities" of voters who receive net benefits from the programs in the budget and who will vote for each of the programs in turn. But voters' tendency to undervalue benefits means that the government will not be able to find majorities for many programs that produce "hidden" (unrecognized) benefits. Particularly affected will be programs with nonspecific, uncertain, or remote benefits that would be included in the budget preferences of "zero ignorance" voters. Relative to this ideal budget, therefore, the government's budget will be too small in a world of partial ignorance.

Even this description may exaggerate the extent of voters' information. Surely many economic activities of the federal government are not known to most taxpayers. The same condition is undoubtedly true at the state level and even for moderately large local governments. If voters are preponderantly ignorant of public programs, there will be strong incentives for each minority group to insert its own pet program into the budget at the cost of a small general tax increase. Since no one minority can achieve this goal by itself, revolving majorities will be established through "log-rolling," and the ensuing budget will have many programs whose benefits are smaller than their opportunity cost.

This tendency to overinflate the size of the budget, however, will be partially offset by the need to finance the programs with higher taxes. Even though taxpayers are preponderantly ignorant of the items in the budget, their taxes will still be highly visible. The strength of their opposition to budget increases may depend on the kind of taxes used to finance the additional programs. (Income taxes are usually thought to be more visible than sales taxation.) Nonetheless, the net effect of "preponderant ignorance" is to make the government's budget somewhat larger than in the case of "zero ignorance." But even in this case, the undervaluation caused by "partial ignorance" will reduce minority groups' demands for special public programs. Downs suggests that the likely result is for the government budget to be somewhat smaller than the "zero ignorance" budget. It also seems likely that some of the programs that do find their way into the budget will not provide benefits in excess of their opportunity cost.

Downs's model is attractive because its theory of government budgeting postulates a government objective (continued tenure) that is more reasonable than that of the competitive model. Whether the budget is "too small," however, is not the main issue. We will profit very little if we vote uncritically for larger (or smaller) public sector budgets. The central point of Downs's model is to illustrate how the problems of expressing public sector demand lead to departures from the "correct" set of public programs. One major problem confronting the public sector is to improve its responsiveness to the true preferences of consumers and thereby reach the "correct" budget. The methodology of microeconomics can help to attain this goal.

Galbraith's Model of "Social Balance." In *The Affluent Society,* John Kenneth Galbraith set forth his view of how the departure of modern economics from the competitive model has led to the relative starvation of the public sector.[3] One of Galbraith's central tenets was the assertion that scarcity is no longer a major problem in economies approaching the standard of living of the United States. Poverty is no longer an "all-pervasive fact" of life; instead, the modern economy is more concerned with maintaining demand for the products of industry at a level high enough to promote full employment.

In Galbraith's model, consumer demand may be satisfied either through additional private sector output or by allocating resources to

[3] John Kenneth Galbraith, *The Affluent Society* (Boston: Houghton Mifflin, 1958).

public sector goods. There are several sources of bias, however, against public sector allocation. One important bias can be found in the political tradition of liberalism, which places a value on the freedom of individuals to choose their own allocation. Public programs, says Galbraith, are always linked to socialism in the minds of the electorate. A related factor is the opposition of the wealthy to increases in public expenditures financed largely by progressive taxation. The effect of these factors, as in Downs's model, is to cause consumers to undervalue public sector goods relative to those of the private sector.

But this undervaluation is not sufficient to explain the persistent unwillingness of consumers to approve public programs. The basis of the theory of consumer demand is the concept of diminishing marginal utility, according to which consumers should demand relatively more public sector goods as the incremental utility of private sector consumption falls. Especially in affluent societies should we find public sector allocation rising rapidly, since the immediate private needs (food, clothing, and shelter) are all well provided. To Galbraith, the value of many public programs (education, hospitalization, transportation) is so great that the failure of the electorate to express its demand for these programs is a remarkable, almost incomprehensible, phenomenon.

Galbraith finds the explanation in the activity of "want creation," or the "dependence effect." He postulates that the general level of affluence has satisfied all "natural" private wants but that the private sector has ingeniously created new wants through advertising. Producers have successfully prevented the marginal utility of private consumption from falling by producing new goods that consumers do not "naturally" desire and then convincing consumers through advertising that they have wants that can only be satisfied by the purchase of new goods. The dependence effect is this relationship between consumers' utilities and the advertising activities of producers.

The utility generated by advertising is, to Galbraith, less "real" than that arising in "spontaneous consumer need." In fact, the net result of the dependence effect is to cause resources to be wasted in the production of private sector goods. Since the goods would not be demanded in the absence of advertising (which is part of the production process), "the marginal utility of present aggregate output, ex advertising and salesmanship, is zero." The dependence effect thus works to take resources from the public sector (where their output is undervalued) and allocates them instead to the private sector (where their true productivity, in utility terms, is zero).

The implications of this theory for the intersectoral allocation of resources are obvious. Far too few resources are used to produce public sector goods; instead, our economy is unbalanced in favor of the private sector. The consumer is unable to express his true preferences because the dependence effect blinds him to their nature. There is no tendency to redress the imbalance because the private sector is always able to stimulate new wants in order to market its output. An improvement in resource allocation, Galbraith concludes, can come only if social balance is seen as the overriding problem of the modern economy, and other thorny issues (such as distributional equity) are put aside until the balance of allocation is improved.

It is easy to criticize the analytical steps that lead Galbraith to his conclusion. His assertion that scarcity is now a secondary problem is naive, not only overlooking all but a handful of countries but also neglecting serious problems of poverty within developed countries like the United States. To claim that the average American family of four, living on $6000 or $7000 a year, has no unsatisfied material wants is to reduce the human condition to mere biological necessities. Most economists go to one extreme in refusing to differentiate between "valid" and "invalid" wants. Galbraith goes to the other in lumping all private wants (in excess of pure subsistence) as needless frivolities.

But it is hard to deny that the imbalances cited by Galbraith do exist in the American economy (and to some extent in other developed economies). The social imbalance he describes is, in another guise, a failure of the public sector to undertake the programs that satisfy the "correct" allocation criterion of Chapter 1. The question that will concern us is whether, in a market-oriented economy, the performance of the public sector in meeting the allocation criterion (subject to constraints of distributional equity) can be improved.

PART TWO Economic Efficiency and Public Sector Allocation

The theory of efficient resource allocation is recapitulated in Chapter 4, where we discuss the aspects of the competitive model pertinent to the analysis of government allocation and redistribution. Since the conditions of pure competition are never met in the real world, we also try to assess the efficiency cost of small deviations. Chapter 5 discusses the role of the government in three of the most important deviations from pure competition: monopolistic behavior of producers, production conditions not conducive to pure competition, and interdependencies in either the supply or demand decisions of individual producers and consumers. In all these cases, the good produced is consumed by individual consumers at the expense of others. This condition is dropped in Chapter 6, and we examine the demand and supply of goods that are consumed simultaneously by many people.

BIBLIOGRAPHY

Several works that cover the material of Chapter 4 are footnoted at the beginning of that chapter. A less sophisticated treatment can be found in any elementary textbook or in chapter 2 of Robert H. Haveman's *The Economics of the Public Sector* (New York: Wiley, 1970).

Much of the material in Chapters 5 and 6 can be found in a simplified form in chapter 3 of Haveman's book. Although more technical, an excellent discussion of efficiency in production and exchange and of the different policies a government may pursue is given by I. M. D. Little in *A Critique of Welfare Economics* (New York: Oxford University Press, 1960); see chapters 8 and 9 and especially chapters 10 and 11. A thorough treatment of the theory of external effects (interdependence) is available in R. H. Coase's article "The Problem of Social Cost" in *Journal of Law and Economics* 3 (October 1960): 1–44.

One of the original analyses of publicly consumed goods is by Paul A. Samuelson, "The Pure Theory of Public Expenditure," in *Review of Economics and Statistics* 36 (November 1964): 387–89, and "Diagrammatic Exposition of a Theory of Public Expenditure," in *Review of Economics and Statistics* 37 (November 1955): 350–56. A summary can be found in chapter 4 of Richard A. Musgrave's *The Theory of Public Finance* (New York: McGraw-Hill, 1959). Musgrave's chapter 6 discusses mechanisms for public sector decisions. Another treatment of the same material is available in James Buchanan's *The Demand and Supply of Public Goods* (Chicago: Rand McNally, 1968), chapters 7 through 9. Collective decisions are explored at length by Buchanan and Gordon Tullock in *The Calculus of Consent* (Ann Arbor: University of Michigan Press, 1962), and by Mancur Olson in *The Logic of Collective Action* (Cambridge, Mass: Harvard University Press, 1965).

4 Microeconomic Analysis
for the Public Sector

In Chapter 1 we discussed some of the aspects of the government's role in a market-oriented economy and concluded that public sector resource allocation was justified when the value of the public sector goods exceeded their opportunity cost, the value of private sector production. But much of the simplicity of this allocation criterion was lost in Chapter 3, when we discussed the many reasons why there may be a bias against public sector allocation. The departure from the competitive model of resource allocation is greatest when we consider the expression of demand for public sector goods, but the supply and demand for private goods and the supply of public ones may not conform closely to the norms of the purely competitive model. The task of this chapter is to restate the competitive norms and their implications for allocation and distribution and then to examine how efficient allocation and equitable distribution are affected by small deviations from pure competition.

EQUILIBRIUM UNDER PURE COMPETITION[1]

In the model of pure competition, the product market is the arena of exchange between consumers and producers of final goods. We postu-

---

[1] The material in this section is intended to review basic microeconomic theory at a level slightly beyond that of the elementary course but in less detail than in an intermediate course. Students who feel that their backgrounds are inadequate might review the appropriate chapters in any elementary textbook. Intermediate textbooks that cover the material in this section include

late that each consumer allocates his resources (both income and assets) with the objective of maximizing his well-being, or utility. Although economists have never developed a satisfactory definition of what utility is, the behavioral rule of utility maximization states that consumers will choose those allocations of their resources that they prefer to all other allocations. This is the only rule that can describe consumers' behavior in free markets, where they are able to allocate resources in whatever way they choose. Thus the postulate of utility maximization is both plausible intuitively and compatible with the behavior we can observe in the market.

As a concession to economists' inability to define utility, the model of pure competition admits that there is no basis for comparing the utilities that different consumers derive from their allocations. Stated formally, this is the axiom that interpersonal comparisons of utility are inadmissible (that is, impossible to make). Early utility theorists believed that interpersonal comparisons were possible and that governmental redistributive policy should tax people with low utilities for income and transfer to those with high utilities for income. We will take a closer look at some of these approaches to taxation in Chapter 7.

Although economists have discarded the notion of interpersonal comparisons, they have retained a second assumption although it is equally unrealistic. In our discussion of resource allocation in Chapter 3, we assumed that each consumer's utility was independent of every other consumer's allocation patterns and instead depended only on his own consumption (defining "consumption" broadly, to include the purchase of assets as well as current consumption). The model of pure competition generally assumes that individual decisions (of producers as well as of consumers) are independent of the actions of all other economic units (producers and consumers). In Chapter 5 we will examine the allocation of resources when this assumption of independent utility functions is discarded.

Consumer equilibrium in pure competition exists when each consumer has maximized the utility he derives from his own allocation of resources. Although we cannot compare the utilities of different consumers, the axioms of consumer behavior ensure that each consumer will choose the allocation in which the utility derived from the last dollar's worth of consumption of each good is equal to that derived from the last dollar's worth of consumption of every other good chosen.

James E. Hibdon, *Price and Welfare Theory* (New York: McGraw-Hill, 1969); Edwin Mansfield, *Microeconomics* (New York: Norton, 1970); and Kelvin Lancaster, *Introduction to Modern Microeconomics* (Chicago: Rand McNally, 1969).

In addition, the marginal utility (MU) of every good chosen must be at least as great as the marginal utility the consumer would derive from switching his choices to include some good that he is not now consuming; that is, the marginal utility of each good chosen must be at least as great as the opportunity cost to the consumer. If these conditions did not hold, the consumer would be able to increase his utility by transferring some of his resources to the goods that offered greater marginal utility per dollar. These goods might be more of the ones already chosen or some not then being bought by the consumer. In either case, the original allocation would be changed, so the consumer could not initially have been in equilibrium. Letting p_i be the market price of good i, the equilibrium condition for each consumer is

$$\frac{MU_i}{p_i} = \frac{MU_j}{p_j};$$

the marginal utility per dollar from consuming good i must equal that from consuming good j for every pair of goods.

An alternative way of deriving the same maximization criterion is to consider the consumer's willingness to exchange units of one good (B, for beer) for another (A, for ale). Suppose that total spending on B and A is held constant and that the consumer considers switching some of his consumption from beer to ale. Whether he actually does exchange beer for ale depends on the market price ratio, p_A/p_B, and the satisfaction he gets from both goods. Economists call the willingness to trade goods the marginal rate of substitution (MRS)—in this case, of ale for beer, MRS_{AB}.

If the consumer's total level of satisfaction is held constant, his MRS_{AB} is equal to $\Delta B/\Delta A$, the ratio of the (negative) number of glasses of beer that he is willing to give up in order to get a (positive) additional glass of ale. A reasonable postulate about the magnitude of MRS_{AB} is that it declines as more ale is substituted for beer, since the consumer probably places lower and lower valuations on additional ale and higher and higher ones on the beer he must give up. Thus, the consumer is willing to give up fewer glasses of beer for an additional one of ale, and $\Delta B/\Delta A$ falls.

While the MRS states the consumer's willingness to trade beer for ale, his opportunities to do so are determined by market prices. Since his total consumption is being held constant (as stated earlier),

$$(\Delta B)p_B + (\Delta A)p_A = 0$$

and
$$-(\Delta B)p_B = (\Delta A)p_A,$$

the change in spending on beer must equal the additional expenditures on ale. By simple division, we get the market condition for exchanging beer and ale:

$$\Delta B/\Delta A = -(p_A/p_B).$$

The consumer will be in equilibrium when his opportunities to exchange match his willingness to do so, but since

$$MRS_{AB} = \Delta B/\Delta A,$$

he will be in equilibrium when the $\Delta B/\Delta A$ that he prefers equals the $\Delta B/\Delta A$ in the market, and thus

$$MRS_{AB} = -(p_A/p_B).$$

In utility terms, the MRS must be equal to the ratio of the marginal utilities of the goods in question. To see this, simply recognize that, in the case of beer and ale, utility maximization requires that

$$MU_A/MU_B = p_A/p_B.$$

But this condition is equivalent to the maximization criterion in terms of the MRS if

$$-(MU_A/MU_B) = MRS_{AB},$$

the marginal rate of substitution of ale for beer is equal to the negative of the ratio of the marginal utility of ale and the marginal utility of beer. (The negative sign reflects the fact that the MRS expresses the willingness to *reduce* consumption of beer in order to consume more ale.) The consumer will choose ale over beer, at the margin, when the marginal utility of a dollar's worth of ale exceeds the marginal utility of a dollar's worth of beer.

The theory of consumer equilibrium developed around the marginal rate of substitution is somewhat more general (and mathematically more elegant) than the theory of utility. But both approaches make the same assumptions about the motivation behind consumer behavior, the inadmissibility of interpersonal comparisons, and the independence of the behavior of individual consumers. The familiar postulate that the marginal utility of consumption for any good diminishes as more of the good is consumed is equivalent to the postulate that the marginal rate of substitution between any two goods falls as consumption of the second good falls relative to that of the first. (To show that the MRS condition is equivalent to the MU condition, examine the behavior of MU_A/MU_B as the consumption of ale rises and that of beer falls.)

Either utility theory or indifference-curve analysis (using the MRS) makes the consumer's well-being depend on his consumption of all goods and his income level. Since his consumption depends on the prices of the different goods, the consumer's level of well-being is a function of the (relative) prices of all consumption goods and assets, his income level, his total assets, and his personal preferences or tastes. Of all these factors, the price of each good is usually singled out as the most important determinant of the level of consumption of the good; for example, the price of beer is treated as the most important determinant of the amount of beer consumed. This relationship is formalized in the demand curve, which describes the quantities of a good that a consumer will demand as the price of that good varies, *other things being held constant* (including all other prices, income, wealth, and preferences).

A typical consumer's demand curve for ale is illustrated in Figure 4.1. Each point on the demand curve (D_A) indicates the marginal value (MV) of an additional glass of ale (that is, the dollar value of the utility derived from the additional ale). Our assumption that all other variables are held constant means that the price of beer, p_B, is constant over the entire range of the demand curve. As p_A falls, therefore, the consumer's MRS_{AB} must fall, which means that he must consume more ale and less beer. (Total expenditures are held constant in deriving the demand curve.) Thus, a reduction in p_A must be accompanied by an increase in q_A, the quantity (q) of ale demanded, so that the demand curve must be downward sloping. The negative slope of the demand curve can also be derived from the postulate of diminishing marginal utility, for we saw earlier that this postulate is equivalent to that of the diminishing marginal rate of substitution.

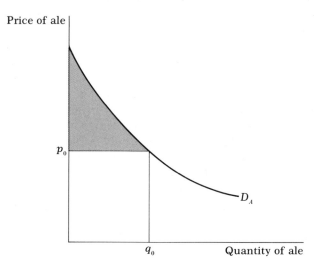

FIGURE 4.1   The Demand for Ale

Since all glasses of ale are physically identical (or very nearly so), the consumer will buy ale until the marginal utility of the last glass equals the market price (p_0 in Figure 4.1). The dollar equivalent of the marginal utility of ale in excess of q_0 obviously is less than p_0, but the dollar equivalent of the utility derived from drinking the first few glasses will always be greater than p_0 unless the demand curve is perfectly horizontal at p_0. The area between the demand curve and the market price (shaded in Figure 4.1) indicates the amount that the consumer would have been willing to pay for the ale he consumed, in addition to the market price that he actually paid. Because this shaded area represents the value of the utility the consumer received without paying for it, it is called "consumer's surplus." Clearly, the consumer's surplus on the q_0th glass of ale is zero.

The model of pure competition makes even more stringent assumptions about the behavior of producers than about that of consumers. One central requirement for pure competition is that there must be a large number of producers (of basically the same product) selling to a large number of consumers, so that no one producer or consumer (or group of a few producers or consumers) can control the functioning of the market. The other principal requirement for pure competition is that firms must be free to enter or leave the industry as demand and supply conditions vary.

Both of these requirements are troublesome in the real world. The many-producers condition may be satisfied in some industries (agricultural produce, many retail stores, gas stations, and barber shops), but it obviously does not describe many others (automobiles, steel, aluminum, chemicals, and pharmaceutical products). Perhaps the typical condition is an industry with a moderately large number of producers (enough to satisfy the spirit of the many-producers requirement) but a substantial degree of concentration, so that two or three firms are the acknowledged leaders in setting price, introducing new products, and trying new techniques of production. In such an industry, producers will not behave as pure profit maximizers, but the long-run responsiveness of firms to changes in demand or production costs should be similar to what the competitive model predicts.

The free-entry condition can be met only if the capital required to enter an industry and compete with existing firms is small and if there are enough potential entrepreneurs willing to take the risks of entering. In some industries entry is virtually impossible because consumer buying habits are ingrained; an example is provided by the attempted introduction of Kaiser and Frazer automobiles in the early 1950's. (A counter-example, indicating that buying habits may have changed, can be found in the capture of a substantial fraction of the

American automobile market by European and Japanese manufacturers in the 1960's.) In most industries, however, the barriers to the entry of new firms probably are not high enough to allow producers already in the industry to earn large monopoly profits over an extended time. Although it is easy to think of industries that do not fit this description, in most industries either the fact or the threat of entry by new firms keeps profits near their competitive level.

Under these assumptions, producers in the private sector are "price takers" who see themselves as unable to affect the market prices for their products. Their ability to sell any amount at the prevailing price appears in Figure 4.2 as a horizontal (perfectly elastic) demand curve for each producer's output, leading to the familiar condition that marginal revenue (MR), the revenue from selling an extra unit of output, is equal to the market price (p_0). In pure competition and approximately in real markets (as discussed in Chapter 3), producers strive to maximize profits. They can do this when the profit on the last unit sold is zero and the profit on any additional unit would be negative. Economists usually assume that the law of diminishing returns causes the marginal cost (MC) of production to be rising in the short run, as shown by the MC curve in Figure 4.2. Profit maximization leads the producer to sell q_0 of his product, since at that output the profit maximization condition (usually abbreviated $MC = MR$) is met.

A qualification to the foregoing description of the competitor's determination of output is that at q_0 the producer must not fail to meet his short-run costs of production. If he did not cover these costs, of course, he would prefer not to produce at all and would simply absorb his fixed costs as a short-run loss. In Figure 4.2, the producer is not only covering his average variable costs (denoted by the AVC curve) but also his average total costs of production (shown by the ATC curve). In the long run, we may expect firms to enter this industry, increasing total supply and reducing the market price to p_1 and each firm's output to q_1. As price falls from p_0 to p_1, each competitor will reduce his output so as to produce the amount for which the marginal cost is equal to the market price. For any given scale of production (ATC), therefore, the marginal-cost curve is the competitor's supply curve, and MC is equal to p at all times in the purely competitive model.

At this point we must take a closer look at the determinants of each firm's (or industry's) MC curve. Producers attempting to increase their outputs will have to buy additional factors of production on the open market, where factor payments reflect the value of the marginal products of the factors in other industries. A firm making, say, women's lingerie will be able to afford to hire labor away from, say,

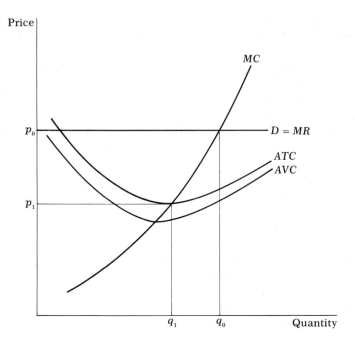

FIGURE 4.2   Equilibrium for the Pure Competitor

manufacturers of children's clothing only if the value of the output produced by the additional labor in the lingerie firm (and industry) is greater than its productivity in making children's clothes. We define the marginal rate of transformation (MRT) between lingerie and çhildren's clothing, MRT_{LC}, as the amount of children's clothing that must be given up to produce an additional unit of lingerie. (The MRT is always negative in sign, since the increase in lingerie requires a reduction in children's clothing.)

Suppose that a dollar's worth of labor is bid away from children's clothing by lingerie manufacturers. Output of children's clothing falls by the marginal productivity of a dollar's worth of labor in that industry, since marginal productivity is defined as $\Delta TP/\Delta q_f$, the ratio of the change in total output to the change in factor input. But the marginal cost of children's clothing can be written as $p_f(\Delta q_f)/\Delta TP$, since the numerator is the change in the cost of the labor associated with the change in output (the denominator). Since we have taken p_f equal to 1 by limiting our discussion to the shift of one dollar's worth of labor, we can see that

$$MC_C = \Delta q_f/\Delta TP = 1/MP_f.$$

Thus, the fall in output of children's clothing, $-MP_f$, is equal to $-1/MC_C$. Similarly, the increase in the output of lingerie resulting from the additional dollar's worth of labor input is $1/MC_L$.

In this example, the value of the MRT, which is the ratio of the change in children's clothing to the change in lingerie, is $-(MC_L/MC_C)$. But if both industries are competitive,

$$MC_L = p_L$$

and

$$MC_C = p_C,$$

so that

$$MRT_{LC} = -(p_L/p_C).$$

We have shown that for any two competitive industries in equilibrium (in either the short run or the long run), the marginal rate of transformation is equal to the ratio of the product prices.

The MRT tells us what the technological opportunities are for substituting one product for another. Consumers' willingness to substitute, on the other hand, is indicated by the value of the marginal rate of substitution (MRS). We saw earlier that each consumer will be in equilibrium when he has maximized his utility; that is, when

$$MRS_{ij} = -(p_i/p_j).$$

But if the industries producing goods i and j are competitive and in equilibrium, then

$$MRT_{ij} = -(p_i/p_j).$$

In competitive markets, therefore, equilibrium for consumers and producers will be achieved when the marginal rate of transformation between any pair of products is equal to each consumer's marginal rate of substitution, and the value of both the MRT and the MRS will be equal to the negative of the ratio of the prices of the two products. This condition is equivalent to the statement that for each consumer and each product (i), in competitive equilibrium,

$$MV_i = p_i = MC_i.$$

The same equalities describe the equilibrium for market demand and supply, as well as the individual consumer and producer equilibria. The market demand for any good (say, beer) will be the total of individuals' demands at each price. But since the demand of every individual consumer for beer is equal to his marginal rate of substitution between beer and alternative consumption (held constant), the market demand curve will simply indicate the total amount of beer that will bring all consumers' marginal rates of substitution into equality with the ratio of the prices of beer and any alternative. Similarly, each competitive producer will produce beer as long as its market price is at least as great as its marginal cost, and the total amount supplied will be the sum of the amounts supplied by each producer. Along the market supply curve, therefore, the ratio of prices of beer and alternatives will be equal to the marginal rate of transformation between beer and alternatives. Market equilibrium, of course, is attained when the quantity demanded is equal to the quantity supplied at the going price. When this condition is satisfied, the common MRS of all consumers is equal to the common MRT of all producers.

"OPTIMALITY" AND "EFFICIENCY"

A graphical representation of the competitive equilibrium just described is presented in Figure 4.3. The curve CL denotes the economy's production possibilities between children's clothing and women's lingerie; its slope is MRT_{LC}, which rises in magnitude as L is substituted for C, causing the production possibility curve to be concave to the origin. Each of the three indifference curves, I_0, I_1, and I_2, shows the combinations of C and L that yield a representative consumer a particular (nonmeasurable) level of satisfaction. The MRS_{LC} at any point is the slope of the indifference curve through that point; thus, the diminishing MRS_{LC} accounts for the convexity of the indifference curves to the origin. Of course, the consumer prefers any point on I_1 to every point on I_0.

The competitive equilibrium described in the preceding section will be reached at the point (C_0, L_0) where the slope of the production possibility curve (the MRT) equals the slope of each consumer's indifference curve (the MRS). In Figure 4.3, this mutual slope is shown by the price line $p_C p_L$. If the economy is not initially at (C_0, L_0) but is at some other point on CL, such as (C_1, L_1), with a price ratio different from $p_C p_L$, consumers' preferences will bid up the price of C and drive down the price of L, shifting the economy toward the equilibrium point and moving consumers to higher levels of satisfaction. Only when the economy reaches the equilibrium point will consumers demand exactly the goods that producers are willing to supply.

Given the indifference curves in Figure 4.3, the equilibrium (C_0, L_0) represents the economy's optimal allocation of resources. If the economy is at any other point on its production possibility curve, all consumers could derive net benefits from a shift to the competitive

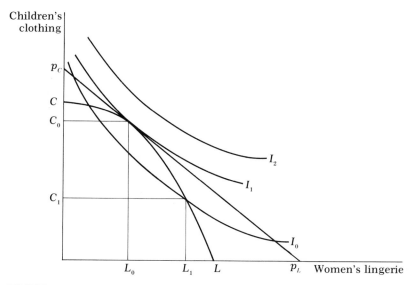

FIGURE 4.3 Competitive Equilibrium

equilibrium. Either such a move would provide every consumer with more utility, in which case none would resist the reallocation, or some would lose and others would gain. In the latter case, the fact that gainers were able to outbid losers in order to induce a reallocation to (C_0, L_0) suggests that gainers could compensate losers and still receive some net benefit from the reallocation. When such compensation was paid, however, no consumers would resist the reallocation, and some would still be made better off by it. These reallocations could continue until the competitive equilibrium was reached. At that point, there is no reallocation of resources that would permit a further improvement of anyone's utility without imposing a loss of utility on someone else. We know this to be true because at the competitive equilibrium no consumer or producer has any incentive to move the economy to a new position.

If we have allocated resources in such a way that it is impossible to increase anyone's utility without imposing a cost upon at least one other person, then we say that the allocation is Pareto optimal (after Vilfredo Pareto, the economist who developed the criterion). It is easy to see that except for (C_0, L_0), no point in Figure 4.3 on or inside the production possibility curve can be Pareto optimal, given consumers' indifference curves. We have already seen that other points on CL are Pareto inferior to the competitive equilibrium. If the economy were at an interior point such as (C_1, L_0), any point in the wedge-shaped area bounded by C_1, L_0, and the curve CL would be Pareto superior. Of those points, however, only (C_0, L_0) is Pareto optimal. The competitive equilibrium, therefore, is a Pareto optimal allocation of resources.

The competitive equilibrium (C_0, L_0), however, is not unique, for it depends on the location of consumers' indifference curves and implicitly on the distribution of income. If, for example, income were redistributed from a jet-set debutante with a preference for lingerie and given instead to a welfare mother with six children, there would be relatively more demand for children's clothing and less for women's lingerie. The price of children's clothing would be bid up, that of lingerie would fall, and the economy would move to a new competitive equilibrium somewhere between (C_0, L_0) and point C on the vertical axis. This movement would occur because of a change in society's preferences and hence a shift to a new set of indifference curves. Under this new distribution of income, however, the resulting competitive equilibrium allocation of resources would again be Pareto optimal.

This example can be generalized to the following proposition: every point on society's production possibility curve is Pareto optimal for some distribution of income. Moreover, there will be a different Pareto optimal allocation of resources for every distribution of income. Since we cannot make interpersonal comparisons of utility, we cannot judge whether one Pareto optimal allocation is preferred to any other. But we do know that if we are at a nonoptimal point such as (C_1, L_0), there is at least one Pareto optimal allocation such as (C_0, L_0) that would be preferred by society as a whole.

The concept of Pareto optimality is more general than that of pure competition. Whether or not the allocation of resources is competitive, Pareto optima will exist as long as resources are scarce and society's production possibilities are limited. For example, in a pure managed economy with all resources fully employed, the allocation of resources may be Pareto optimal although it will never be perfectly competitive. But we are concerned primarily with resource allocation in a market economy, and the important conclusion for our purposes is that, regardless of the distribution of income or welfare, the competitive allocation of resources will always be Pareto optimal.

The attractive feature of the criterion of Pareto optimality is that it does not require interpersonal comparisons of utility to judge whether one allocation of resources is preferable to another. If we can identify reallocations that are Pareto superior to one that now exists, then clearly we should try to reach one of the new allocations, since it will improve the well-being of at least one consumer while harming none. Discovering Pareto optimal (or superior) allocations, however, requires us to know the distributional consequences of allocation decisions and to be sure that any reallocations are accompanied by tax and transfer policies to compensate those who lose from the reallocation. In other words, we must know both the economy's production possibilities and the distributional effects of every allocational alternative in order to find a Pareto optimum.

A somewhat simpler criterion that examines only the production conditions is that of efficiency. In general, if the allocation of resources is efficient, it is not possible to increase the production of any good without decreasing the production of at least one other good. Efficiency is really a criterion for evaluating the ways in which producers use factors of production. Not only must all factors be fully employed (in the sense that at the going price for each factor of production the demand for the factor must equal its supply), but factors must be equally productive (at the margin) in all industries. If factors' marginal productivities were not equal in all industries, producers in different industries could exchange factors and increase the total production of all outputs. Although we have not discussed factor markets, it should be clear that in the model of perfect competition the mobility of factors of production among industries ensures that factor prices will be equal in different industries and therefore that factor marginal productivities must also be equal. In other words, the allocation of resources will always be efficient if the markets for factors of production are competitive.

There are many different efficient allocations of resources, each corresponding to a different point on the production possibility curve. The criterion of efficiency does not offer us any basis for choosing among these alternative points. To make such a choice, we must have some mechanism for evaluating the different goods produced. If all goods are sold in markets, then their prices offer us just such a mechanism, and we can expand the criterion of efficiency into that of Pareto optimality.

In one special case, the two criteria are equivalent. Let us assume that consumers' preferences are reflected perfectly by the market price ratio, p_c/p_L (the line $p_c p_L$ in Figure 4.3). In this case, the only efficient point is (C_0, L_0), for at any other point on the production possibility curve the opportunity cost of a factor of production is greater than the value of its marginal product. (That is, we could increase the value of total output by moving to the competitive equilibrium point.) Given the constancy of product prices, therefore, we are no longer indifferent among points on the production possibility curve. This special assumption will not often be justified, but it is appropriate if changes in the level of production of the goods we are studying are small enough not to affect either their prices or the prices of other goods. As long as we limit ourselves to marginal analysis, therefore, we can use the terms efficiency and Pareto optimality interchangeably. In general-equilibrium analysis, however, we must recognize explicitly that efficiency is not a complete criterion because it ignores the indirect effects that one good's allocation has upon the prices and quantities of other goods.

Finally, it is worth noting that in the special case of marginal analysis, the criteria of efficiency and Pareto optimality can be stated in terms of either one good or two. If the market price ratio adequately expresses consumers' preferences, then

$$MRS_{LC} = -(p_L/p_C).$$

Pareto optimality generally requires that MRS be equal to MRT, so in this case, as in the more general one, when the Pareto optimum is reached,

$$MRT_{LC} = -(p_L/p_C).$$

Efficiency demands that factor marginal value productivities, the value of the output produced by the marginal unit of a factor of production, be equal for all industries. In children's clothing, for example, the marginal value productivity of labor is $MP_C p_C$, and in women's lingerie labor's marginal value productivity is $MP_L p_L$. If these quantities are equal (and production is efficient), then

$$MP_C p_C = MP_L p_L,$$

and therefore

$$MP_C/MP_L = p_L/p_C.$$

But as we saw in the preceding section,

$$MP_C/MP_L = MC_L/MC_C = -MRT_{LC}.$$

Thus, the two-good statements of the optimality and efficiency criteria are identical. To derive the single-good condition, we can consider good C to have a price identically equal to unity. The optimality and efficiency conditions then become

$$MC_L = p_L = MV_L,$$

where MV_L is the marginal value of L (the single-good analogue of the marginal rate of substitution). We will use both of these conditions extensively in the chapters that follow.

THE EFFECTS OF IMPERFECT COMPETITION

Many kinds of market imperfections may prevent the economy from allocating its resources in the Pareto optimal fashion. For one thing, consumers may not all pay equal prices for the same goods and services due to price discrimination. Lawyers' and doctors' fees frequently depend on the client's or patient's ability to pay. Recent studies of the economics of poverty and black ghettos have indicated that the poor probably pay higher prices than the well-to-do for furniture, appliances, and food. Rigidities in factor markets are another source of market imperfection. An example of the unwillingness of some labor unions to accept the effects of shifts in consumer demand or technology is the demand of railroad workers that technologically obsolete firemen be retained on diesel locomotives. The mix of capital and labor in newspaper typesetting is inefficient (in the sense that the total cost of factors of production is higher than the minimum attainable under existing technology) largely because members of typesetters' unions have refused to permit the introduction of modern equipment and the consequent reduction in the number of typesetters.

These imperfections in the allocation process may have major impacts on efficiency and optimality, but they are not of great interest to us because governments do not usually have economic weapons to use against them. Legislation against price discrimination has been popular in the past, and we have usury laws, minimum-wage laws, and (more recently) laws requiring the full disclosure of effective interest rates on time purchases (one of the principal techniques used by ghetto merchants to inflate real purchase prices). But the chief characteristic of such laws is that they place constraints on the market's allocation of resources without necessarily attaining the spirit of their objectives. Thus, economists generally agree that minimum-wage laws merely eliminate those jobs in which workers' productivity is less than the wage floor and thereby lead to higher unemployment rates instead of more high-paying jobs. In contrast, governments have been reluctant to introduce programs that increase the productivity of unskilled, low-paid workers, although productivity increases offer the only long-run solution to the problem of poor workers. Similarly, laws requiring full disclosure of interest charges will result less in lower interest rates than in a smaller supply of credit. The real solution to the problem of price discrimination, increased knowledge on the part of consumers and the mobility to take advantage of the additional information, is difficult for any government policy to achieve.

In factor markets, too, governments have no panacea for market imperfections. Recent years have seen strikes by public employees in many different occupations against the officials who manage public programs: strikes in New York City by teachers, garbage collectors, and transit workers, and strikes in many other cities by firemen, policemen, hospital workers, and other civil servants. The federal government has been embroiled in labor disputes with postal workers and air traffic controllers. Teachers occasionally have carried their grievances to the steps of governors' mansions and state legislatures. These incidents merely stress the point that the public sector is no more able than the private sector to respond quickly to changing demand and technology.

A third source of nonoptimal allocation in the private sector is the price and output policies of producers who are not perfect competitors. (We will defer the discussion of the monopolist's allocation and public policy to Chapter 5.) The familiar graphical equilibrium for the imperfect competitor is shown in Figure 4.4. The producer's objective of profit maximization leads him to try to equate marginal cost and marginal revenue and thus to produce q_0 and sell it at p_0. Since the imperfect competitor can exert some influence over the market price for his product (by definition of imperfect competition), he is not driven by the forces of competition to produce at the point where p is equal to MC (that is, at q_1 and price p_1), and the allocation of resources will not satisfy the condition that the consumer's marginal rate of substitution equals the producer's marginal rate of transformation. In this case, therefore, resource allocation must not be optimal, for there are consumers who would gladly pay a price greater than the marginal cost of production in order to consume the incremental output $q_1 - q_0$. The allocative cost of this market imperfection is that the market price is too high (p_0 instead of p_1), the equilibrium quantity produced is too small, and too few resources are devoted to producing this good (so that too many resources are used to produce other goods).

There is some reason to believe, however, that the cost of the imperfection is too small to justify public intervention. If the firm really has only a little control over the market price, the demand curve is likely to be very elastic (although not perfectly so), and marginal revenue will be very little less than the market price. If the firm succeeds in equating marginal cost exactly to marginal revenue, therefore, its profit-maximizing output will be very close to the optimal output, and the cost of the imperfection will be small. Moreover, the high elasticity of the demand curve will prevent the firm from earning substantial monopoly profits, so the distribution of income probably will not be very different from that under perfect competition.

In practice, imperfect competitors do not behave precisely as described in this model. The price and output decisions of real-world

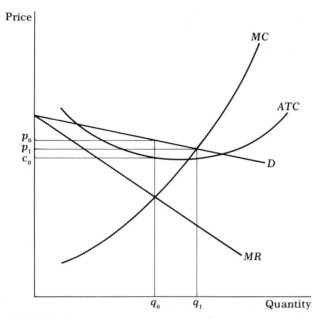

FIGURE 4.4   Imperfect Competition

producers are not as exact as economists would make them, and instead of a unique profit-maximizing output q_0 and a unique optimum q_1, there is probably a range of indeterminacy that includes both q_0 and q_1. In this case, the best policy for the government to follow is probably to leave the imperfect competitor alone and to accept a small deviation from the theoretical optimum (p_1, q_1) as part of the price of living in the real world instead of in an economist's graph or mathematical model.

5 Efficiency and Private Goods

The title of this chapter introduces a new concept, one that will recur throughout most of the rest of our discussions of the activities of the public sector. Most goods and services offer utility only to the consumer who buys and uses them and do not affect the well-being of other members of the economy. Certainly this description is true of the goods used as examples in Chapter 4, beer and ale, women's lingerie and children's clothing. Although it is possible to construct situations in which one person's consumption of any of these goods could affect someone else's level of utility, in the normal course of events the decision that any consumer makes to buy food or clothing has no direct impact upon any other consumer's allocation decisions.

Goods satisfying this condition, that they benefit primarily the direct consumer, are called "private goods." An important characteristic of private goods is that the decision to consume them is made by the individual consumer, in response to his desire to maximize his own utility. Whether these goods are produced privately or publicly, therefore, the equilibrium output of a private good is that which equates the marginal cost of production to consumers' marginal valuation of the good. Another way of stating this condition is that if an additional consumer decides that he wants to consume a private good, or wants more of the good he is now consuming, then more of the private good must be produced to satisfy his additional demand. Looked at in this way, private goods are goods that are consumed exhaustively: if one person buys a glass of beer, then that same glass of beer is not available to satisfy someone else's demand.

Anticipating Chapter 6, we may note in contrast that public goods are those goods not consumed exhaustively by individual consumers, goods that confer utility on many consumers simultaneously, goods that are not supplied in response to the demands expressed by individuals. Between these two polar types, pure private goods and pure public ones, are many goods and services that offer utility primarily to the direct consumer but also affect the utilities of some other consumers. Before discussing these goods, however, we will study the role of the government in two cases in which pure private goods are not supplied efficiently by the private sector.

MONOPOLY

In Chapter 4 we saw that even if the requirements for pure competition are not met exactly, the inefficiency in allocation may not be great enough to justify remedial governmental action. If there is some reason to believe that each firm in an industry faces a rather elastic demand curve and if the possibility of entry of new producers exists, then the potential benefits of government policy probably will be small, and the uncertainties always present in the real-world behavior of producers and consumers are likely to be greater than the inefficiency in allocation. Although government policy is unnecessary in this case, there may be a reason for corrective action if the firm's equilibrium deviates enough from the competitive norm.

Suppose that the producer can exercise a substantial degree of control over his market price; that is, suppose that he is a monopolist or imperfect competitor facing a rather inelastic demand curve, as shown in Figure 5.1. Under the assumption that the producer is still interested in maximizing his profits, the firm's equilibrium position in an unregulated market will be at point (p_0, q_0), where marginal cost equals marginal revenue. At this point the producer will be making substantial profits, equal in amount to $(p_0 - c_0)q_0$. It is clear that this equilibrium is not efficient from the economy's point of view, since marginal cost is much less than price, and consumers' marginal rate of substitution will be much greater than the producer's marginal rate of transformation.

The first point to notice about Figure 5.1 is that it depicts a short-run equilibrium, since the producer's cost curves reflect a given, constant stock of plant and equipment (capital). In the long run, the firm will not be able to maintain its equilibrium position (p_0, q_0) if new producers can enter the industry. If entry is a possibility, then new firms will shift the old producer's demand curve downward and to the left, and the greater elasticity of demand will lead to a closer correspon-

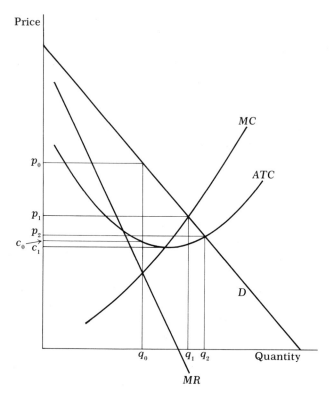

FIGURE 5.1   Monopolistic Industry

dence between demand, marginal revenue, marginal cost, and price, as shown in Chapter 4. In summary, there may be no need for remedial government action even if the producer faces a short-run demand curve like that in Figure 5.1, *as long as the possibility of entry will bring his long-run equilibrium position close to the competitive norm.* That is, for government action to be justified, the firm's short-run monopoly position must be accompanied by long-run restrictions on entry.

Restricted entry will characterize an industry that is either primarily monopolistic or oligopolistic, with a few potentially competitive producers preferring to maximize joint profits in response to a recognition that competitive behavior would reduce everyone's profits. Monopolistic firms are usually identified by economists as those that can seek their profit-maximizing outputs without worrying about the possibility that other producers will undersell them. Oligopolists, in contrast, are willing to accept an equilibrium output somewhere to the right of q_0 (in Figure 5.1), where profits are lower than maximum, price is lower and output is higher than at the profit-maximizing point, and the firm's profits are not high enough to encourage potential entrants or to generate pressures for government regulation and antitrust activities. Nonetheless, if the producer is either a monopolist or an oligopolist, he will be able to earn monopoly profits in both the long run and the short run.

The other point to notice about Figure 5.1 is that the efficient production point (p_1, q_1) is at a point where MC exceeds ATC, so that if the firm were to produce at the efficient level it would still make some profit in the short run. If the firm somehow can be induced to move near (p_1, q_1), therefore, it will nonetheless be able to continue to produce its output. For such a producer, the efficient production point is viable in the sense that the firm will not be driven out of business if it is forced to produce there.

Figure 5.1 shows the two costs that monopoly (or oligopoly) imposes upon consumers, compared to the efficient point (p_1, q_1). The allocation cost is shown by the under-allocation of resources to producing the good in question and the resulting level of production q_0 instead of q_1. Alternatively, the allocation cost is reflected in the divergence between consumers' MRS at the monopolist's equilibrium and the MRS at the efficient point, and between the monopolist's MRT at q_0 and his MRT at q_1. The allocation cost of monopoly can be seen in the inability of consumers to obtain as much of the good as they would like, given the monopolist's production possibilities and consumers' preferences.

Monopoly or oligopoly also imposes a distribution cost upon the consumers who consume the q_0 units actually produced. If the market price were p_1 instead of p_0, consumers' surplus on these q_0 units would rise by $(p_0 - p_1)q_0$, nearly the amount of the monopolist's profits. Each consumer who buys one of the q_0 units of the good at a price of p_0 is in equilibrium, in the sense that he is maximizing his own utility subject to the prices that he faces (one of which is p_0 instead of p_1). But if resource allocation were efficient, these same consumers would find their real incomes larger, since they could receive the same utility at a lower total cost. Thus, the effect of monopoly is to redistribute income from consumers to the monopolistic or oligopolistic producers, as well as to prevent some consumers from obtaining as much of the good as they would like (or, indeed, any at all).

The allocation and distribution costs of monopoly offer a justification for remedial governmental action, for the impossibility of entry prevents the market allocation from approaching the competitive optimum (p_1, q_1). The question is, what is the appropriate policy and how is it to be implemented. Three alternative policies are available: encouraging entry, regulating the producer, and taxing the producer.

Encouraging Entry. Governments can encourage entry in different ways. The approach most frequently discussed is to require firms already in the industry to divest themselves of some productive facilities, in effect thereby generating "instant competitors" in the form of the independent producers "spun off" by the monopolists. An example of this policy was the federal government's suit to break up the Standard Oil trust in the early twentieth century, which led to the formation of several independent oil refiners including Standard Oil of California, New Jersey, Ohio, and New York, and other producers. The degree of competition fostered by this antitrust suit might well have been sufficient to ensure competitive behavior if the federal government had not introduced other tax and import policies that limited the opportunities for competition among these and other oil refiners.

A second way to encourage entry is for the government to establish productive facilities itself and then offer them to a private firm in competition with the dominant monopolist in an industry. During the Second World War, the federal government constructed several factories for producing aluminum and aluminum products that were operated by the Aluminum Corporation of America (Alcoa), then the monopolist in the industry. After the war, the government refused to sell the facilities to Alcoa, but instead accepted a much lower price from a firm (Kaiser Industries) that previously had had no interest in the aluminum industry. A similar story concerns facilities owned by the German chemical trust, I. G. Farben, and seized by the federal government during the Second World War. Rather than sell the facilities (which manufactured photographic materials) to Eastman Kodak, the dominant American monopolist, the government created a private firm (Ansco) to produce at the I. G. Farben works. In both cases, the policy of fostering new competitors entailed a sizable loss of revenue.

Other methods of encouraging entry involve removing or lowering the barriers that new producers must overcome. One barrier in many industries is the extensive patent holdings of established producers, which prevent potential entrants from using up-to-date production techniques. This barrier may be overcome by a requirement that licenses be obtainable for all patents. New firms thus can compete at the price of reimbursing the patent holder for the cost of the research and development activities leading to the patent. Extensive capital requirements present another barrier to entry. As mentioned in Chapter 4, they may take the form of high initial (or continuing) advertising costs or expensive fixed plant and equipment. The appropriate public policy may be low-cost loans (for example, through the Small Business Administration) or antitrust activities designed to break up concentrations of capital (for example, the anticonglomerate merger activities of the Department of Justice).

In cases where the technological conditions of production are compatible with competition, the policy of encouraging entry is likely to yield good results. Among the advantages of this policy are that it does not involve the government in the production of private goods and that it creates an allocation of resources comparable to that reached in other competitive industries. Once the new producers are able to enter into competition, the government can let the normal operation of the market move toward an efficient production point.

Regulation. Regulation in this discussion is the "classical" regulation of price and quantity as practiced by federal agencies such as the Department of Agriculture, the Interstate Commerce Commission, and the Civil Aeronautics Board. The regulation of competitive practices, as administered by the Federal Trade Commission, the Food and Drug Administration, and the Antitrust Division of the Department of Justice, is not included in this discussion. This latter type of regulation is more properly considered as a form of stimulating the entry of new producers.

There are industries in which the policy of encouraging entry may not be effective for any of a number of reasons. Barriers to entry in the form of product identification may be too high to be overcome by new competitors. Given the scale of demand, the technologically efficient production technique may entail a level of production so large that one firm must dominate the industry. (This situation is treated at length in the next section of this chapter.) Or particular factors of production required to produce a good may be so scarce that they can supply only a single producer. In cases where new producers could provide a policy alternative, regulation may also be a politically motivated solution. The impact of regulation is felt quickly and is highly visible and thus offers two political advantages not available with a policy of encouraging new entrants. Regulation will also be attractive if (as is often the case) there is doubt about the ability of new producers to compete effectively.

If regulation is accepted as the preferred governmental policy for correcting the inefficiency of monopoly, the regulator must choose the (p, q) point to impose upon the firm and industry. If the monopolist's profit-maximizing position (p_0, q_0) is objectionable enough to lead to the passage of regulatory legislation, then the regulator must require the producer to move to some point to the right of q_0 (and in the case of oligopoly, to a point farther to the right of q_0 than the oligopolists had initially chosen). It is easy to see that if the regulator requires the producer to sell q_1 at a price p_1, then the regulated solution will enable consumers and other producers to achieve the Pareto optimal allocation of resources. In fact, if the regulator administers a price of p_1, then the monopolist's profit-maximizing behavior will lead him to the efficient production point, since the regulated marginal revenue curve will be perfectly horizontal at a level of p_1 and will intersect the marginal cost curve at q_1, the efficient point.

The trouble with this policy is that it usually cannot be carried out. Regulators (and frequently producers) do not know what the firm's marginal cost curve is or where the demand curve is or where the optimal point lies. Competitive firms may reach a point near (p_1, q_1) by a kind of exploratory groping around the equilibrium prices established by other firms, comparing different combinations of price and quantity sold to see which yields the greatest profit. Monopolistic or oligopolistic producers go through a similar process to reach (p_0, q_0) or their preferred equilibrium positions. But without explicit information about the firm's marginal costs and the demand curve it faces, and with no competitive forces driving the firm to seek the economically efficient production point, regulators will have no way of knowing where (p_1, q_1) is, even if they have the power to force the firm to produce there. Their alternative is to allow the firm to recover its total cost of production, including some allowance for the return to invested capital, and to require the price the firm charges to be no higher than necessary to cover average total cost. In effect, the firm thus regulated will go to (p_2, q_2) since at that point the firm's average total cost equals its average revenue or price.

At first glance, the regulated output (p_2, q_2) seems to be superior to the efficient output (p_1, q_1) from the consumers' point of view. After all, the regulated price is lower than the efficient price, and the regulated output (that is, the output that will be produced if the price is set equal to p_2) is greater than the efficient output. This conclusion is correct only in the short run and only with respect to consumers of the regulated industry's output. Even in the short run, the marginal cost of the q_2nd unit of output will be higher than the price paid by consumers, and so the optimality condition that MRS is equal to MRT must be violated. Too many resources are being used to produce the regulated industry's output; stated another way, the opportunity cost of the q_2nd unit of output (and, in fact, of all units beyond the q_1st) is greater than the value of that unit to consumers. If the industry is at (p_2, q_2) and all other industries are reasonably competitive, then a Pareto superior allocation of resources would occur if the regulated industry moved to (p_1, q_1). The gain in welfare to those consumers who would benefit from the move would be large enough for them to compensate the consumers who would be hurt by it, while still leaving the beneficiaries with a net gain.

In the long run, the average-cost rule is equally pernicious. If the regulatory agency could set p equal to MC, the fact that monopoly profits could be made at the efficient point (p_1, q_1) would serve as an inducement either for more firms to enter the industry or for each existing firm to expand its productive capacity and lower its marginal cost curve. In both cases, the long-run equilibrium price would lie below p_1, and under reasonable assumptions about the firm's production function the equilibrium price would be c_1, the minimum point on the average total cost curve.[1] Consumers obviously would prefer c_1 to any other attainable price, since it is lower even than p_2. But c_1 can never be reached if the regulated price is set at p_2, because at the regulated price firms are not making monopoly profits and there is no incentive either for them to expand production or for new firms to enter the industry. Thus, the policy of setting the regulated price equal to the average cost of production leads to a long-run as well as a short-run inefficiency.

It is hard to overstate the harm done by the policy of setting the regulated price equal to average cost. In addition to the inefficiencies in both the long and the short run, average-cost regulation offers no incentive for the market to allocate resources properly during peak-load situations (when capacity is fully used and marginal cost is much greater than average cost) and discourages producers in the regulated industry from allocating their internal resources efficiently. If a monopolist is guaranteed a return of, say, 8 percent on his invested capital regardless of how efficiently he uses factors of production, then his incentive for using factors in the most productive ways disappears. Neither does he have any incentive for pursuing research and development activities or for introducing new technology when it becomes appropriate. Finally, average-cost regulation discourages entry by potentially efficient producers, who can see that the industry offers no reward for greater efficiency.

Taxation. Two families of alternative taxes can be levied on business enterprises: taxes related to the level of production, excises or sales taxes; and taxes that do not vary with the level of production, lump-sum taxes. Since the excise imposes an additional cost on the pro-

---

[1] The "reasonable assumptions" are that all firms have similar production functions or that each firm's production function exhibits constant returns to scale.

ducer for each unit sold, it simply shifts his marginal and average costs upward by the amount of the tax. Sales and profits (net of tax) both fall and the price paid by consumers rises, thus taking the consumer even farther from the efficient allocation point. That is, the excise shifts the firm's equilibrium output to the *left* of q_0, the profit-maximizing output, while economic efficiency can be attained only if the firm's output is shifted to the *right*. The excise may be beneficial to consumers on balance if the revenues collected are distributed to those consumers who suffered a loss of consumer surplus by buying at p_0 (or above) instead of p_1. For example, an excise on steel might be used to finance research on cheaper production methods, thus reducing prices in the long run. In summary, excises may yield a distributional gain compared to the monopolist's profit-maximizing output, but they necessarily worsen the allocation of resources.

The other type of tax is one unrelated to the level of production. Suppose, for example, that the monopolist is assessed an amount equal to $(p_0 - c_0)q_0$, the amount of his monopoly profits. This tax does not affect either his marginal cost or his marginal revenue schedule, and the tax consequently offers no allocational gain. (This kind of tax is discussed in more detail in Chapter 8.) As in the case of the excise, however, a distributional gain may result if the revenue collected with the tax is distributed to the consumers who paid p_0 instead of p_1 for the product. The same analysis applies to a profits tax (such as the corporation income tax), which varies with profits but not directly with the level of output.

Conclusion. Of the three policies available to the government to counter the inefficient allocation caused by monopoly or oligopoly, only encouraging entry offers uniformly beneficial results. Regulation would be effective if it were possible to require firms to produce at the efficient point; however, average-cost pricing rules introduce several distortions from efficiency in both the long and the short run. Taxation does not promise to improve resource allocation, and excise taxation upon the monopolist actually worsens the allocation compared to the profit-maximizing position. Taxation does, however, offer the prospect of distributional gains if the revenues are returned to the consumers of the monopolist's product. Encouraging entry is beneficial if enough new entrants are able to compete with established producers, but this policy does not help in cases where, for one reason or another, the industry's demand and production conditions cannot support more than one producer. In these cases, the only choices are alternative suboptimal policies.

DECREASING-COST PRODUCTION

One of the assumptions made in our development of the competitive model in Chapter 4 was that if firms set price equal to marginal cost, total revenue would be at least as great as total cost. In discussing the case of monopoly in the preceding section of this chapter, we retained this assumption; thus, in Figure 5.1, the monopolist's efficient point (p_1, q_1) is one at which price exceeds his average total cost of production. There are many cases, however, in which this assumption is not satisfied, and the efficient price falls short of average cost in either the long or the short run. In this situation, the unregulated behavior of private firms obviously cannot lead to efficient resource allocation, since efficiency in such a case implies that each producer must incur a loss.

A more systematic presentation of this problem is shown in Figure 5.2. The significant relationship, and the departure from the competitive model, is that the *firm's* average total cost curve lies above its marginal-cost curve at all levels of output up to the *industry's* demand curve. Because of the connection between marginal and average cost, this relationship requires that the average-cost curve be decreasing over the entire range of production (up to market demand). Thus, this case is called one of production under conditions of decreasing cost. Note that the firm's marginal cost does not have to decrease over the range of production; in Figure 5.2, for example, the marginal-cost curve is rising, although at a slow rate.

When an industry experiences decreasing costs of production, there will be a tendency for the number of firms to diminish. In Figure 5.2, suppose that there are initially many competitors, each satisfying a small fraction of market demand by producing an output less than q_0 and selling it at a price greater than p_0. The presence of many competitive producers encourages each to view his demand curve as being highly elastic and thus to move down his average-cost curve by increasing his level of output. The normal tendency of a competitive market to reach the minimum point of each firm's average total cost curve is frustrated, however, because the long-run equilibrium price (set by the intersection of each firm's marginal-cost curve and the industry demand curve) is one at which each firm can satisfy the entire market demand. At this price, therefore, there is an excess supply of output, and some of the many original competitors have to leave the market. As the number of producers falls, each remaining producer acquires more control over market price. Eventually, either a single producer will remain in the market or there may be a small

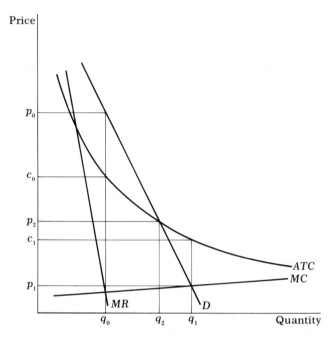

FIGURE 5.2   Decreasing-Cost Industry

group of mutually interdependent producers. In either case, decreasing-cost production is incompatible with a perfectly competitive equilibrium allocation of resources.

The Short Run. Decreasing-cost production can arise in either the short or the long run. In the short run, when capital stock is fixed, the decreasing-cost producer is characterized by a large fixed cost (and therefore a high average fixed cost) relative to his variable costs of production. Thus, up to the level of market demand, the reduction in average total cost from "spreading the overhead" exceeds the increase in average total cost resulting from the rising marginal cost of production. Some of the goods produced under this kind of short-run cost function are electricity, urban public transportation, bridge crossings (up to the bridge's capacity), other public utilities such as water and gas, and telephone calls.

   We may treat the case of short-run decreasing costs as an instance of an imperfection in the supply of factors of production. The nature of the imperfection is that capital goods are not infinitely divisible (at least not in the short run), so that a firm making an investment in capital equipment is "locked into" that capital stock in the short run.

This problem of capital-goods indivisibilities frequently arises when a firm undertakes an investment to provide enough capacity for expected future growth in demand, leaving itself with excess productive capacity in the short run, or when fluctuations in demand lead a firm to overinvest in order to have enough capacity to meet short-run peaks in demand. The result of the imperfection in the supply of capital goods is to create an allocation problem, because the short-run efficient price is incompatible with the firm's long-run survival.

Decreasing-cost production arising from indivisibilities in capital goods is unlikely to require government intervention to promote economic efficiency if new, efficient competitors are able to enter the industry in the long run. In Figure 5.2, the producer remaining in the industry after other competitors have been driven out will choose to produce at his profit-maximizing point (p_0, q_0). Suppose that competitors are able to adjust to this equilibrium by buying new capital equipment with which to produce q_0 units of output at an average cost of c_1, a cost formerly attainable only at a much higher level of output. Once this new equipment is installed, the initial producer will no longer be able to maintain his profit-maximizing output, for his competitors will drive down the good's price while increasing the total amount produced. In this example, the capital-goods indivisibility has vanished in the long run. Competition has taken its place, and the long-run allocation of resources can approach the competitive equilibrium.

If the indivisibility persists, however, competitors will not be able to undersell the surviving producer in the long run, and the short-run equilibrium at (p_0, q_0) will be stable in the long run. In this case, the short-run imperfection becomes a long-run one also, and there is no tendency for the industry to move away from the inefficient, profit-maximizing output toward an efficient one. Thus, if short-run indivisibilities in capital goods prevent the entry of competitors in the long run, government action is required to improve the efficiency of resource allocation. In most of the industries mentioned above as experiencing capital-goods indivisibilities, competitors have not been able to enter in the long run, and government intervention has resulted instead.

The Long Run. Persistent capital-goods indivisibilities are not the only (or even the major) source of decreasing costs in the long run. Industries without large capital requirements or factor indivisibilities may still experience economies of scale, increases in output that are accompanied by less-than-proportional increases in total costs. Economies of scale may arise due to increases in productivity accompanying a greater division of labor at higher output levels, or they may be due to savings in inventories in some industries such as retailing. Rapid rates of technological advance may lead to frequent shifts in the industry's production function, with the same effect as a decreasing average total cost curve. Or physical parameters in the production function may cause average total cost to fall as output rises. Electronic data processing is a good example of an industry that has benefited from rapid technological change, and electricity generation is one industry whose production function has offered economies of scale resting on physical laws.

In the long run, the decreasing-cost producer's cost curves will look like those in Figure 5.2. *ATC*, of course, is simply his long-run average total cost curve. *MC* is the cost of the most efficient way to increase output by one unit in the long run, when all factors (including capital goods) are variable. Thus, the long-run decreasing-cost producer will seek out the profit-maximizing point (p_0, q_0) in the absence of government action. At this point, he will make monopoly profits of $(p_0 - c_0)q_0$, price will not be equal to marginal cost, and the allocation of resources will be inefficient. It is worth noting, however, that the profit-maximizing output may not represent a point of profit for the decreasing-cost producer. If the demand curve in Figure 5.2 had been drawn so that the average cost were greater than average revenue at all points (that is, if the average total cost curve lay entirely above the demand curve), the profit-maximizing output would have been the point of minimum losses. In the monopolistic industry, in contrast, the intersection of demand and marginal cost to the right of the minimum average total cost makes it unlikely that the profit-maximizing output will cause the producer to incur a loss.

If an industry experiences long-run decreasing costs, the policy of encouraging entry obviously cannot force the producer to the efficient point. One alternative is governmental regulation, which is usually administered in the same way as for a simple monopolistic industry: the producer is allowed to recover his total costs of production, including a "fair" return on invested capital. The result is an equilibrium at the average-cost price p_2 and quantity q_2. This policy creates the same inefficiencies discussed in the preceding section of this chapter. Note that if the demand curve does not intersect the average-cost curve, average-cost regulation naturally is not an option for the government to pursue, for in this case there is no single price that will enable the firm to recover its total cost of production.

If price regulation is chosen as the government's policy, it is even more difficult for a regulatory agency to drive a decreasing-cost firm to the efficient point than for it to force a monopolist to price efficiently.

In the monopoly case, the efficient point offered the monopolist a net profit and was consistent with the firm's survival in business. In contrast, the efficient allocation under decreasing cost leads to a net loss for the firm and will tend to drive it out of business, since the producer will never be able to recover his outlays on capital equipment. Thus, a regulatory body must consider both efficiency at the margin (as in the case of monopoly) and the overall profitability of the industry, which is not an issue in simple monopoly regulation. We may state these conditions as the double criterion for efficiency in the decreasing-cost case: production should be efficient at the margin, so that p is equal to MC, and the total revenue earned by the producer (an amount that cannot exceed the total value that consumers place on his output) must be at least equal to his total costs of production. Since a regulatory agency usually has only one instrument variable, the regulated price, it typically cannot satisfy both the marginal and total efficiency conditions.

An alternative to regulation of a private decreasing-cost producer is government operation of decreasing-cost firms, either directly or through some sort of semipublic corporation. Examples of public enterprises at the federal level are the Tennessee Valley Authority, which operates numerous electric power generation and distribution facilities, and the newer Communications Satellite Corporation (Comsat), established to develop and operate the commercial communications satellites made possible by the public development of space technology. As we noted in Chapter 2, state and local governments operate many such public enterprises, including power companies and water facilities. Since all the goods produced by these public corporations also are produced by regulated private firms, public operation in these cases is truly an option and not in any way a necessity occasioned by the peculiar economics of any of these industries. In terms of Figure 5.2, equilibrium for these public firms usually is established at (p_2, q_2), the average-cost price and output.

Direct government provision of decreasing-cost goods arises when demand conditions are such that no average-cost price exists, or when the average-cost price is deemed inequitable. For example, urban public transportation systems commonly fail to recover their total costs from the fares they charge riders. Moreover, attempts to reduce the deficit by raising fares often drive passengers to other forms of transit and actually increase the deficit. Other publicly produced goods, such as police and fire protection, are in fact private goods offering economies of scale in production. As a matter of equity, governments usually do not try to recover the costs of such services through direct charges levied on users (although certain taxes, notably real property taxes, sometimes are defended as indirect charges for services like these). There are many other instances of public production of decreasing-cost private goods where the price charged to users is lower than the average total cost of production.

Governments can set price below average cost because public operation offers the possibility of subsidization out of general revenues. This aspect of public enterprise was touched on in the discussion of non-exhaustive expenditures in Chapter 2, where it was pointed out that public enterprises generally either require subsidization or offer a net surplus that can be laid off against other government obligations at a saving in other tax revenues. Accordingly, public operation of decreasing-cost firms offers the possibility of reaching the efficient point (p_1, q_1), where price is equal to marginal cost and consumers' MRS equals the producer's MRT, if an adequate subsidy is available to recover the cost of capital equipment.

From Figure 5.2, we can see that the loss entailed by public operation and efficient allocation is $(c_1 - p_1)q_1$. Unlike the monopoly case, the efficient point results in more of the good being produced and a lower price being charged than at the average-cost point. The true measure of the gain in efficiency, however, must be found in a comparison of MRS and MRT. A shift from (p_2, q_2) to (p_1, q_1) obviously confers an allocation gain on all consumers, for it extends consumption to all those who value the marginal unit at more than its cost. The shift to (p_1, q_1) also yields a distribution benefit for the consumers of the good in question if the subsidy is paid out of general revenues. The resulting redistribution of income complicates the issue of whether the shift to the efficient point is desirable, for it raises a second allocation question: Should consumers of a decreasing-cost good be allowed to reach the efficient allocation point if, at that point, they fail to cover the total cost of production?

One possible answer is offered by the slope of the demand curve. As we saw earlier, total allocational efficiency requires that consumers' total valuation of output be at least as great as the total cost of production. Efficiency at the margin requires that price and marginal cost be equal. If the efficient marginal operation of a decreasing-cost firm leads to a deficit, total efficiency still can be attained if the government covers the deficit by levying a tax on consumers of the product.

To guarantee efficiency at the margin, such a tax must be nondistorting in the sense that it must not alter either the MRS of consumers or the producer's MRT. But if such a tax is to be levied on consumers without affecting their *marginal* rates of substitution, then it must only reduce the benefit they derive from their consumption of *inframarginal* units of output—that is, the first $(q_1 - 1)$ units, since the q_1st unit is the marginal one. The total amount upon which a tax can be levied is the total benefit derived from consumption of these q_1 units. But this taxable area is the total of consumers' surplus, the area below the demand curve and above the (efficient) price p_1. If the area that can be taxed is as large as the area of deficit, then it will be possible to recover the total cost of production by levying a tax on consumers without affecting their decisions at the margin. Thus, marginal efficiency theoretically will be consistent with total efficiency in a decreasing-cost industry if aggregate consumers' surplus is at least as great as the subsidy engendered by operation at the efficient price.

In summary, we have shown that the goal of total efficiency in a decreasing-cost industry conflicts with the industry's marginal efficiency. Total efficiency requires that consumers pay the full resource costs of the goods they receive, but marginal efficiency in such an industry can be attained only if the producer operates at a deficit. These two objectives can be reconciled, however, if the producer levies a surcharge or tax upon inframarginal units of output, thus forcing consumers to pay the full resource cost of their consumption while letting their marginal decisions equate MRS and MRT. Such a tax or surcharge can be levied if total consumers' surplus is at least as great as the deficit of the decreasing-cost producer.

There is no single "best" tax upon consumers' surplus. Any such tax will leave allocation unchanged except for the secondary effect of the change in income distribution, and there is no way to rank the distribution alternatives in order of "goodness" or equity. From Figure 5.2 it is clear that the revenue collected with the tax or surcharge must be equal to $(c_1 - p_1)q_1$. Since aggregate consumer surplus in this case is much greater than that amount, any of a large number of alternative tax plans will be equally efficient. Consequently, there must be an element of arbitrariness in the selection of one particular surcharge as the means of covering the deficit.

In practice, many producers (regulatory bodies or public enterprises) in decreasing-cost industries have adopted what is called a "two-part tariff" in order to reach the efficient point. Under this plan, a consumer of, say, electric power pays a large initial charge for the opportunity to buy more electricity at a price equal to (or near) marginal cost. In effect, the price of the first unit of electricity is very high and the price of subsequent units is much lower. As long as the initial charge does not deter consumers from buying electricity, a plan of this sort will be consistent with efficiency in both the long and the short run. Similar surcharges can be used in most of the industries that have decreasing costs: in telecommunications and public utilities, the initial connection charge could include deficit recovery; in urban transportation, either a lump-sum tax or (preferably) some kind of admission ticket could serve the same function. All these alternatives offer some possibility of distorting individual consumers' allocation decisions by discouraging initial use. Nonetheless, the net allocational effect of a two-part tariff probably is preferable to the average-cost pricing policies followed by most regulatory bodies.

Unfortunately, even a two-part tariff cannot offset all the disincentive effects of average-cost regulation. For example, technological change may enable a decreasing-cost producer to lower his average total cost curve without affecting either marginal cost or the efficient equilibrium. Normally, the force of competition would compel producers to install the new equipment. Regulation, even under a two-part tariff, makes no such requirement, because the producer will continue to be able to recover his full costs even if he does not adopt the new technology. This problem of providing adequate incentives to ensure efficient resource use by the public sector is widespread. Perhaps the simplest solution is for a regulatory agency either to threaten to reduce the recoverable deficit, or deliberately to permit producers to over-recover deficits for some period after the installation of new equipment, in effect offering the producer a monopoly profit. If the output of the decreasing-cost industry is produced by public enterprise, then a system of rewarding the agency for cost minimization, consistent with efficient allocation, must be adopted. Only through such schemes will industries with decreasing costs be given the incentives to react efficiently to changes in either demand or production conditions.

EXTERNALITIES

The goods produced by both the simple monopolist and the decreasing-cost firm share an important characteristic: they confer benefits (utility) only upon the direct consumer. Goods produced in both cases are private goods, for the level at which they are consumed depends on the allocation decisions of each individual consumer. We must now consider a third category of private goods for which the private sector allocation, in the absence of government action, will not be efficient. These goods can be supplied and demanded under the "normal" competitive procedures described in Chapter 4, but they differ from the output of other competitive industries in that they affect the allocation decisions of other individuals besides the direct consumer or producer. The secondary effects on others' allocation decisions are called "externalities."

Before stating this condition rigorously, let us examine a few examples of such goods. A classic example of an externality in production occurs when a chemical plant undertakes water purification measures in order to recapture useful by-products and thus enables another producer downstream to use river water in his own production process. In this case, the allocation decision of the chemical plant, to treat waste discharges into river water, causes another producer to alter his allocation decisions, eliminating expenditures on water purification as a result of the additional filtration by the chemical plant. As an example of an externality in consumption, consider the case in which a family installs a large air conditioning unit that vents its noise and exhaust toward a neighbor's living room. The neighbor may well have to install soundproofing material and an air conditioner of his own if he is unable to keep open a window that previously had provided him with adequate ventilation. Obviously, the first person's allocation decision will then have caused the second family to change its allocation decisions in some important respects.

From these examples it is clear that externalities can arise in the course of either production or consumption decisions. Producers' allocations can impose externalities on other producers or on consumers and vice versa. And although the examples involved external benefits in production and external costs in consumption, other examples could be constructed to show external costs in production and external benefits in consumption. For these reasons, it is not useful to differentiate between externalities in production and those in consumption. Moreover, the analysis of the inefficiency in the case of external benefits is symmetric with that of external costs.

It is important to differentiate between true externalities and the secondary price effects that always accompany every individual's allocation decisions. One family's decision to buy an air conditioner will always affect everyone else's allocation decisions by increasing the price of air conditioners and electricity, lowering some other prices, changing patterns of resource use, and thus altering the distribution of incomes. All these effects, however, take place *within* the market. Externalities affect allocation decisions *outside* the market, as in the air conditioner example, by changing the demands that other consumers express *without* any change in market prices or incomes. This statement is only another way of saying that externalities arise when one consumer's allocations affect another consumer's utility at the margin.

The requirement that secondary effects be felt at the margin is important, for unless there is an impact on the indirect consumer's utility at the margin he will not be led to change his allocation. In that event, the primary consumer's allocation choice would serve to reduce the secondary consumer's level of well-being and, in effect, reduce his income, but there would be no impact upon the allocation of society's resources.[2] Since we cannot rank alternative income distributions (that is, state unequivocally that one is better than another), there would be no basis for governmental action if allocation decisions were unaffected. The presence of externalities provides a rationale for governmental policy precisely because the allocation of resources is inefficient if externalities exist and individuals' production and consumption decisions are affected at the margin.

Let us now consider rigorously the case of a good that imposes an external cost on Mr. Beall when it is consumed by Mr. Aylward. For example, the good in question might be the use of Mr. Aylward's air conditioner. The cost of using the air conditioner is the sum of the cost of the electricity it uses plus the reduction in its future productivity (depreciation). Both of these costs can be assumed to rise with the intensity of use as shown by the marginal-cost curve, MC_A, in Figure 5.3. It should be clear that the supply curve to Mr. Aylward is his marginal-cost curve, for it indicates the prices at which he can obtain various hours of use of his air conditioner. Mr. Aylward's demand for hours of air conditioning is shown by the MB_A curve in Figure 5.3, which indicates the marginal benefit or utility that he derives from additional hours of use. Since the demand curve always shows the marginal utility of the good in question, Mr. Aylward's equilibrium use of the air conditioner will be h_0 hours, for which he will pay a price of p_0 and a total cost of $p_0 h_0$.

Mr. Aylward's air conditioner, however, also imposes costs on Mr. Beall. These costs include additional operation of Beall's air conditioner, more extensive (and expensive) soundproofing, and perhaps more meals eaten in restaurants to escape from Aylward's air conditioner. It is likely that these costs will rise with the level of use of Mr. Aylward's air conditioner, so that we can indicate the costs imposed on Mr. Beall by the MC_B curve in Figure 5.3. Although the point (p_0, h_0) is efficient for Mr. Aylward, it obviously is not efficient for Mr. Beall since at that point the marginal cost imposed upon him (t_0) is considerably larger than his marginal benefit (which is zero).

Another statement of this point may be made using the MC_T curve, the total marginal cost imposed on all members of society (Aylward and Beall, in this case) by Aylward's use of the air conditioner. At h_0

---

[2] This discussion assumes that the change in well-being (real income) is small and that no one good is especially affected by marginal changes in income.

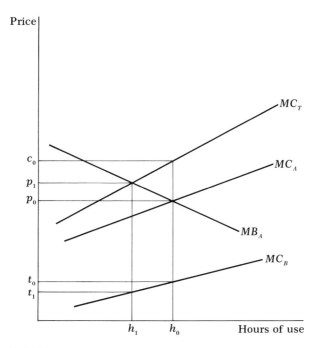

FIGURE 5.3   External Costs

hours of use, the total marginal cost to society is c_0, but the total marginal benefit (since only Aylward benefits) is p_0. Total marginal cost exceeds total marginal benefit, so it must be true that the allocation of resources is inefficient.

The efficient allocation will occur when total marginal cost equals total marginal benefit; that is, at point (p_1, h_1). The interesting aspect of this equilibrium is that Aylward will have no incentive to reduce his consumption to that point unless he is forced to compensate Beall for the costs he imposes, or unless Beall is allowed to pay Aylward to reduce his consumption. If Aylward is required to pay Beall, then he will gladly pay enough to induce Beall to let him consume the first hours of air conditioning, since the cost to Beall (MC_B) is much less than the difference between the benefit that Aylward derives (MB_A) and the direct cost that he must pay (given by MC_A). At h_1, however, the payment to Beall (t_1) is exactly equal to the surplus that Aylward derives from the h_1st hour, and beyond h_1, the payment to Beall for successive units is greater than Aylward's consumer surplus on the marginal unit. In the opposite case, when Beall must bribe Aylward *not* to use the air conditioner, exactly the same argument applies, so that Beall will pay Aylward to reduce his consumption from h_0 to h_1, but no farther.

Compared to the efficient allocation, a good that imposes external costs generally will be overconsumed if the externality is not taken into account. That is, if the consumer or producer whose allocation decision imposes an external cost does not compensate the victim of the externality or permit the victim to compensate him, then society as a whole will devote too many of its resources to producing the good. It is interesting, however, that once either compensation or bribes are introduced to take account of the externality, the efficient allocation results whether Beall pays Aylward or vice versa.

This conclusion follows from two key assumptions. First, the MB curves in Figure 5.3 are assumed to be independent of the income levels of Aylward and Beall. In other words, Beall's marginal-cost curve is the same, whether he pays Aylward not to use the air conditioner or whether Aylward pays Beall for permission to use it. If income effects are present, however, the direction of compensation will affect the allocation of resources. In cases where externalities impose large costs on indirect consumers, the necessity to pay compensation to a primary consumer will inevitably change the other allocation decisions of the victims of the externality.

The second assumption is that preferences are revealed accurately by all parties to the externality. For example, if Beall is able to overstate the cost he incurs from Aylward's use of the air conditioner, Aylward's ultimate use of the machine will be less than optimal. The direction of compensation may not be independent of participants' ability to conceal their preferences. Aylward may choose to run his air conditioner more than h_1 hours for the specific purpose of inducing Beall to pay him compensation. On the other hand, if Beall has the right to be free of Aylward's air conditioner, he may engage in nuisance suits to force Aylward to pay (or overpay) him. In practice, the direction of compensation is usually decided on moral (or at least noneconomic) grounds. There appears to be no basis for believing that any particular direction of compensation will lead to a more accurate revelation of preferences than the alternative direction.

A similar argument applies to the case of a good that yields external benefits. Suppose that the chemical plant previously mentioned has the option of installing a new filtering system that will increase the recapture of some valuable by-products, thus enabling the plant to produce more efficiently. The improved filters may also benefit a downstream pulp and paper factory, which needs clean water for its own production process. As shown in Figure 5.4, the chemical firm's demand for additional filtration is MB_C, and the supply curve for more filtration is given by MC_C, the marginal cost that the chemical plant must incur. The resulting equilibrium, in the absence of transactions between the two companies, is at (p_0, f_0), where the chemical firm is equating the marginal cost and marginal benefit of additional filtering of its wastes. At f_0, however, the paper firm derives a marginal benefit denoted by b_0. Since the filtration process bestows this external benefit as well as the direct one to the chemical plant, the total benefit derived by society is equal to b_1, the sum of p_0 and b_0. Total social benefit is greater than the total cost incurred, and efficiency requires that the level of filtration be increased to f_1, at which point the sum of the benefits accruing to both the direct and the indirect users is equal to the cost.

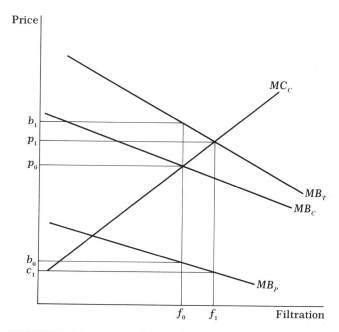

FIGURE 5.4   External Benefits

As in the earlier example, the chemical plant will not buy the additional $(f_1 - f_0)$ filters unless the pulp and paper company pays it to do so, with a payment equal to c_1 on each of the $(f_1 - f_0)$ additional filters. We also can identify another compensation possibility if it is determined that the pulp and paper firm has a right to perfectly clean water. In this case, the chemical plant might compensate the pulp and paper company in return for the latter's holding its demand for additional filtration down to $(f_1 - f_0)$. The MB_P curve shows that the pulp and paper firm would continue to derive benefits from much greater levels of filtration, but at f_1 the chemical company's cost of compensating the pulp and paper firm is equal to the net cost of additional filters. At lower levels of filtration, the chemical company would prefer supplying the filters to compensating the other company. As in the first example, the allocation of resources to filtration is unchanged by the direction of compensation, under our two assumptions about the absence of income effects and the accurate revelation of preferences. As a moral judgment, society might refuse to give the chemical company the right to pollute. The chemical company then would either have to buy additional filters or pay cash compensation to the pulp and paper firm if the externality is recognized. In this case of external benefits, however, the cost of ignoring the externality is to *undersupply* the good in question (at f_0 instead of the efficient level f_1) and to devote too *few* resources to its production.

Both these examples have assumed that the externality was imposed (or conferred) by one economic unit upon one other. There is no reason why externalities cannot be much more general. In the air conditioner case, not only Mr. Beall but also Mr. Cass, Mr. Denchy, and Mr. Eddington could have been affected by Mr. Aylward's allocation. The chemical plant's filters may benefit not only the pulp and paper mill, but also other downstream producers and even residents of downstream cities who will have lower water-purification expenses if the chemical plant installs additional filters. In fact, the same activity might impose both external costs and benefits, as would occur if the more effective waste filtration entailed the emission of noxious fumes in the immediate vicinity of the chemical plant.

Generalizing from the preceding examples, we know that the nature of the misallocation under externalities is that indirect benefits or costs are ignored, since the primary producer or consumer allocates on the basis of only his own costs and benefits. The allocation criterion for the direct user of the good may be stated

$$MB_D = MC_D.$$

This criterion conflicts with that for socially efficient allocation,

$$MB_T = MC_T,$$

where the subscript refers to total costs and benefits. Since the difference between these conditions is the indirect effects of the externality, we must modify the first criterion to yield

$$MB_D + MB_I = MC_D + MC_I.$$

In the case of external costs only, MB_I is zero. This condition is frequently stated, "Marginal private costs plus marginal social costs must equal marginal private benefits plus marginal social benefits." This statement of the efficiency condition is perfectly adequate if it is remembered that "social" means "indirect," *not* "to all members of society."

The ability of the economy to overcome the tendencies toward misallocating resources caused by externalities depends heavily on how many producers and consumers are affected by the externality and on the determination of the direction in which compensation is to be paid. Suppose that only Mr. Aylward and Mr. Beall are involved in the air conditioner case. Since Beall is the injured party, he may follow either of two courses of action. The simpler is to discuss directly with Aylward the possibility of compensation, leading to a reduction in Aylward's hours of use. Or, if Beall believes that the law is on his side, he may sue Aylward to force him to reduce his use of the air conditioner. If Beall wins, Aylward will then seek to compensate Beall in order to increase his hours of use, leading to the same eventual allocation. Matters are not so simple if Beall is not the only neighbor affected by Aylward's air conditioner. The possibility of voluntary compensation becomes more remote as the number of parties to the agreement increases, for Beall, Cass, Denchy, and Eddington all will try to understate their own willingness to compensate Aylward in the hope that each of the others will thus pay a larger fraction of the total compensation.

Voluntary compensation may be a more likely alternative if Aylward is forced to compensate his neighbors, for he may then reach an independent agreement with each of them. But Aylward probably will not be put in this position, for no one of his neighbors may have a strong enough incentive to take him to court, and collective action is no easier if Aylward is sued rather than compensated. Voluntary action to compensate for externalities is an important possibility only in small-numbers cases, although it is somewhat more important if the direct consumer or producer is required by law to compensate those upon whom the external effect is imposed.

When an externality is widespread, the misallocation it entails can be corrected only through some kind of governmental action. In theory, the appropriate policy is easy to determine. Since the nature of the misallocation is that the costs and benefits that the primary producer or consumer faces do not reflect the true social costs and benefits, the government must merely alter the private costs or benefits to make them conform to the social ones. In terms of Figure 5.3, if the external cost is widespread, the government should levy upon the private beneficiary (Mr. Aylward) an excise tax schedule corresponding to the schedule of external costs that he imposes. At h_0 hours of use, the tax should be t_0; at h_1 hours, the tax should be only t_1. The effect of this tax, of course, would be to shift the private marginal cost curve from MC_A to MC_T, since the private outlays per hour of air conditioner use would now include payment of the excise tax. Conversely, in Figure 5.4, the government should offer subsidies (negative excise taxes) to the chemical plant for additional filtration according to the MB_P schedule, in effect transforming the private benefit schedule from MB_C to MB_T. In both cases, the excise tax would lead to the socially efficient allocation.

Both of these policy prescriptions imply that the government is prepared to enforce a particular set of property rights. For example, we have assumed that Aylward's neighbors have the right to undisturbed peace and quiet and that Aylward cannot operate his air conditioner without their consent. In the filtration case, we have assumed that the downstream plants do not have the right to unpolluted water and that they must express their demand for waste removal by inducing the government to offer the chemical plant a subsidy. If the rights of either Aylward or the downstream users of water were reversed, then the appropriate government policy would also be reversed.

Another point to notice about the policy prescription is that it is incomplete unless it includes a discussion of how the revenue collected with a tax is used or how a subsidy is financed. If only Aylward's neighbors are injured by his use of the air conditioner, then it clearly would be inefficient to use the revenues collected by taxing him to do anything except compensate his neighbors, either in money or in kind. Unless each of the neighbors actually receives the amount t_1 in Figure 5.3, the conditions for efficiency will not be reached. But the tax on Aylward should be equal to the sum of the damages inflicted upon his neighbors, so that the total revenue collected will exactly equal the amount needed to compensate them. Similarly, the subsidy to the chemical plant must be paid by the downstream users, not by the general public, if the efficient amount of filtration is actually to occur.

In summary, the appropriate governmental policy in the case of externalities is a combined tax and subsidy program. The subsidy is to be paid to the consumer or producer whose property rights are violated by the externality. The tax (in an amount equal to the subsidy) must be levied on the producer or consumer whose action imposes the externality. The effect of such a policy will be to make the prices the primary consumer or producer faces reflect the indirect benefits and costs as well as the direct ones.

There are at least two major difficulties with this policy. One is that the determination of the level of the tax and subsidy may be extraordinarily difficult, for the normal means of evaluating goods and services—market prices—are not available with externalities precisely because the externalities do not occur in the market. In practice, economists frequently use surrogate or partial measures of external costs and benefits, such as the change in property values that can be attributed to the externality. But there is no generally correct way to measure the value of externalities, and the ability of the government to correct the private sector allocation must vary from instance to instance. In Part Five we shall discuss some attempts to evaluate external costs and benefits.

The second problem is that different levels of government should respond to different externalities. In the air conditioner example, it would be inappropriate for the federal government to intervene, levying a special tax on Mr. Aylward and distributing special transfers to his neighbors. Instead, a municipal ordinance probably would be the appropriate policy, levying a tax on all users of air conditioners and distributing transfers to all property owners or residents. (Although such a policy almost certainly would not lead precisely to the efficient allocation, a more flexible policy probably is beyond the reach of any government.) In the filtration case, however, the external benefit would extend at least over the entire downstream length of the river, perhaps crossing state lines and requiring either an interstate agreement or federal action. Political difficulties frequently arise during such attempts at intergovernmental coordination.

In general, higher levels of government will be called upon to respond to more widespread externalities. But the presence of externalities never entails a public determination of the efficient allocation of resources. Instead, the role of the public sector is limited to expressing the demands or costs that allocation in the private sector fails to take into account. When these demands are expressed, the private sector is free to reach the efficient allocation without government dictation. Externalities require not government production or consumption but only a modification of the private sector price mechanism. As externalities become more widespread, however, the *unexpressed* costs and benefits become more important compared to those expressed in private sector decisions, and the private sector allocation deviates more and more from the socially efficient one. The limiting case, in which all benefits accrue externally, is the special case of public goods discussed in the next chapter.

6 Efficiency and Public Goods

The characteristic of private goods is that they confer enough benefits or utility to induce consumers and producers to demand them in private markets. In the case of goods that exhibit externalities, however, we saw that the expression of demand in the private market was incomplete, for it ignored the benefits (negative ones in the case of external costs) that accrue at the margin to producers or consumers other than the primary demander. In the case of a good that confers externalities on a small number of indirect consumers or producers, the costs of incorporating the externality into the utility function of the primary demander may be small, so that it may be possible to adjust the private sector equilibrium rather easily to "internalize the externalities." If a good spreads externalities over a large number of secondary consumers, however, the costs of adjusting the private sector equilibrium are much higher because the externality affects the equilibrium allocations of so many different people.

As the antithesis of a private good, we can imagine a good that offers only insignificant benefits to the primary consumer and instead confers external benefits impartially on all members of society. Since the externality is general, one unit of such a good will offer one unit's worth of utility to *every* consumer. The primary consumer's use of the good does not reduce the ability of the good to provide utility to everyone else, and so we say that this good is consumed non-exhaustively. If a good is consumed non-exhaustively, the cost of allowing one more

94

person to benefit from the good must be zero.[1] Thus, another way to state that a good is consumed non-exhaustively is to say that the opportunity cost of extending consumption to another person is zero.

Since a good with the characteristic of non-exhaustive consumption is the opposite of a purely private good, we call it a "public good." It is public because it confers benefits or utility publicly, upon the economy at large rather than upon particular individuals. Goods that exhibit externalities usually restrict their benefits (or costs) to particular groups of consumers (Mr. Aylward's neighbors or the firms down-stream from the chemical plant, in the examples of Chapter 5). True public goods, however, offer benefits to all consumers, regardless of their incomes, residences, other allocations of income, and any other characteristics.

Public goods are public also because the demand for them must be expressed publicly. Even if the allocation of resources to private goods is not efficient (due to the factors discussed in Chapter 5), the appropriate policy for the government is to adjust the equilibrium determined by private sector demand and supply. In the case of public goods, however, the benefits accruing to any one individual typically are much smaller than the cost of production, so that the private sector equilibrium output of public goods will be zero. The government's role with respect to public goods is to aggregate consumers' demand for these goods and express it to private sector producers. If there is no public expression of demand, there will be no production of public goods.

It is important to note that the "publicness" of a public good depends on economics, not on technology. It may be physically possible to exclude additional consumers from receiving the public good unless they pay for it, in the same way that consumers are excluded from receiving private goods that they do not pay for. This possibility arises with radio and television signals, where unscrambling devices can be rented out to recover the costs of programming and transmission.[2] This practice clearly is economically inefficient, however, for the marginal cost of offering the signal to another consumer is zero. Even though it may be technologically possible to restrict consumption of the public good, economic efficiency requires that it be made available

---

[1] If the cost of extending benefits were greater than zero, the externality would not be truly general. An additional consumer would receive less than the utility of one full unit of the good, for he would have to incur a resource cost to obtain the good.

[2] Subscription or "pay TV" is an instance of the commercial use of unscrambling devices.

to all consumers at a zero price since the opportunity cost of extending consumption is zero.

Since public goods all share the characteristic of non-exhaustive consumption, it is obvious that public goods must be intangibles, services available to all members of society if they are available to anyone. With respect to citizens of the United States, for example, foreign aid provided to underdeveloped countries is a public good because the presumed benefits derived from it accrue to each citizen of the donor country (although perhaps not to each resident of the recipient nation). An interesting aspect of foreign aid as a public good is that different U.S. citizens are likely to place different evaluations upon it, based in part on their personal feelings of altruism or fear of revolution, or perhaps reflecting the likelihood that they will travel abroad in underdeveloped countries. Even though *evaluations* differ, however, the *good itself* is provided equally to all U.S. citizens.

Foreign aid is one of many government programs providing a good or service that is equally available to all members of society. Another is national defense, if we think of its unit of measurement as the reduction in the chance of being involved in war, or as the ability to protect the United States from external enemies. Again, the value of this good may vary widely among individuals, but all residents receive the same number of units of defense. The fact that these units are difficult or impossible to measure is not a *conceptual* problem with public goods theory. The important point is that a given level of "production" of defense confers utility on each member of society and that each person is able to evaluate the benefit that he derives from that "amount" of defense.

The same argument applies to the "good" of space exploration. The benefits that individuals receive may be increased feelings of national pride or greater knowledge about the earth and other planets. But whatever is the nature of these benefits, space exploration confers them equally on all members of society. Since the ability of a geophysicist or an astronomer to benefit from the knowledge obtained in the course of the space program presumably is much greater than that of a poet or an economist, the scientists should place a much greater *value* on the benefits they receive. The availability of knowledge, however, is equal for all.

Not all public goods confer benefits on a national level. Benefits may be localized in a region, as is the case under a program of flood control where the beneficiary area is the floodplain that faces a reduced chance of being inundated. All residents of the floodplain receive the same reduction in the probability of flood, although not all will place the same value on that benefit. Benefits may be confined to a particular industry or occupation, as when a government undertakes a program of research with the objective of improving productivity in a particular industry. A case in point is the extensive research program of the U.S. Department of Agriculture, which has developed plant and livestock strains and improved methods of cultivation and fertilization and has made this information available to all farmers. (If agriculture is a competitive industry, however, the benefits from agricultural research will be passed along to consumers in the form of lower prices for agricultural products.) Another instance of public industrial research is the space program, which its advocates claim has resulted in many technological advances with applications in the production of private sector goods. If this claim is correct and the beneficiary industries are not purely competitive, then these research activities will benefit only particular industries, their stockholders, and perhaps the consumers of their output.

SUPPLY AND DEMAND FOR PUBLIC GOODS

Now that we have identified some examples of public goods, let us determine the efficient level of production of such goods. Suppose that the public good in question is the service provided by a lighthouse that warns fishing boats away from a treacherous rock. Although this service is not provided to all members of society, it should be clear that it is nonetheless a public good for the fishing-boat owners, since if the service is provided to any one fishing boat then it is available to all others at an opportunity cost of zero. Different levels of service can be offered: the lighthouse might install a brighter light, thus giving warning over a greater distance and in different weather conditions, or a horn or bell could be added for use in foggy weather. Consequently, we must examine the supply curve as well as the demand curve for the public good.

Let us define the good provided by the lighthouse as "warning" and express the amount of the good supplied as "the probability of being warned of nearness to the dangerous rock." This unit of measurement has the right characteristics: if there is no lighthouse, then there is no warning, and the probability of warning is zero; but if there is a tall lighthouse equipped with a powerful beacon, a loud horn, and even a radio signal that permits boat captains to judge their distance from the rock, then the probability of warning will be close to one (that is, each captain will be nearly certain to be warned about the rock at all times and in all weather conditions). Higher probabilities of warning are costly, for they entail spending resources on additional equipment or structural changes in the lighthouse. There is no reason to suppose that higher probabilities of warning can be obtained under decreasing-cost conditions, so we can draw the supply curve of warning as the marginal cost curve (MC) in Figure 6.1.

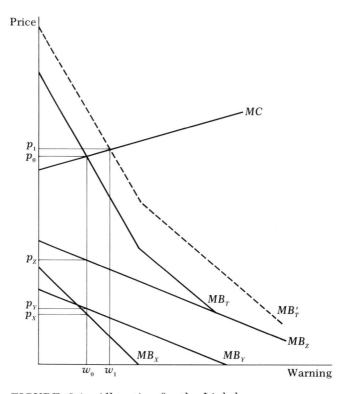

FIGURE 6.1   Allocation for the Lighthouse

Since the lighthouse is an elaborate facility with expensive equipment, the marginal cost of the services it provides may be high relative to the benefit received by any one fishing-boat owner. Suppose that there are only three fishing boats, owned and operated by captains Xavier, Yates, and Zamorra. Their marginal benefits derived from higher probabilities of warning are shown in Figure 6.1 by MB_X, MB_Y, and MB_Z, under the assumption that the only loss suffered from a wrecked fishing boat is the cost of replacing the boat, and that no loss of life or personal injury is involved.

Captain Xavier's demand curve reflects his ownership of an elaborate fishing boat that he uses only in fair weather. He will benefit greatly from a simple beacon because the replacement cost of his boat is high, and he will not benefit at all from foul-weather warning equipment. Captains Yates and Zamorra, in contrast, are all-weather fishermen. Captain Yates's small investment in his fishing boat causes his demand curve for warning to be low, but Captain Zamorra will place a greater value on the same amount of warning because his boat is a more expensive one. This example, therefore, illustrates the problem of allocating resources to the production of public goods when different consumers place different valuations upon these goods.

Since all three captains benefit from the service provided by the lighthouse, the total benefit to society will be the sum of their individual benefits. At the level of warning w_0, Captain Xavier receives a marginal benefit of p_X, Captain Yates a marginal benefit of p_Y, and Captain Zamorra a marginal benefit of p_Z. The marginal benefit to society is p_0, the sum of the marginal benefits to each of the captains. We can derive the other points on the MB_T curve by adding vertically the other points on the three captains' demand curves. MB_T, therefore, is the demand curve of society for the services provided by the lighthouse, and the intersection of the marginal-benefit and marginal-cost curves for society determines the efficient point (p_0, w_0) for the supply of the public good.

This model for resource allocation in the case of the pure public good is closely similar to that for a good conferring external benefits. In the externalities case, direct and indirect benefits are summed vertically to indicate social benefits, and the private equilibrium is adjusted to take indirect benefits into account. The same procedure is followed for the public good, with the difference that the private equilibrium in this case is at the zero level of production (since each individual's demand curve lies below the supply curve over the entire range of production). The efficiency criterion in the case of the pure public good is that the benefit to all members of society from the marginal unit of production must equal the marginal cost to society. This criterion can be stated as

$$MRS_T = MRT_T,$$

the social marginal rate of substitution must equal the social marginal rate of transformation, for the social MRS is the sum of p_X, p_Y, and p_Z, and the social MRT is the marginal cost of the public good. This statement of the efficiency criterion, of course, is identical to that in the case of externalities.

It is one thing to state the efficiency condition, however, and quite another to achieve it. In Chapter 5 we saw that inefficiency in the private sector allocation of goods with externalities could be overcome by either voluntary transactions (in the small-numbers case) or government action (in the case of a more general external effect). The public good, lighthouse services, will be produced only if a government undertakes to express demand so that private producers can respond to it. In the case of the lighthouse, the appropriate level of government may be the municipality in which all the fishing-boat owners live (although if we wish to adhere rigidly to our definition of public goods as accruing to all members of society, we should postulate an association of fishing-boat owners that has the power to tax its members). The efficient allocation can be reached only if each consumer pays an amount for the public good that reflects his marginal valuation of the benefits he receives, for only in this case will each consumer's MRS equal his own MRT (his MRS being the valuation of benefits and his MRT being his payment for the public good). At the efficient point (p_0, w_0) the valuations that the three captains place on the public good are p_X, p_Y, and p_Z, so these are the charges that must be assessed against the fishing-boat owners if all consumers (including those who do not benefit from the lighthouse) are to be in equilibrium.

This model of resource allocation in the case of public goods is called the "voluntary exchange model" because it leads to the conclusion that each beneficiary should pay an amount for the public good equal to the price that he would be willing to pay if the same good were available in the market. Under the assumption that the marginal cost of the public good is nondecreasing, it is reasonable to believe that this set of charges on beneficiaries will also yield enough revenue to cover the cost of producing the public good. If revenue does not exactly equal cost, then the voluntary exchange approach will lead to a redistribution of income, either to beneficiaries (if the public good is produced under decreasing-cost conditions in the long run and beneficiaries do not pay an additional lump-sum tax on consumers' surplus) or to the general population of nonbeneficiaries (if the excess revenue is used to reduce other tax rates). Under either increasing- or decreasing-cost production, however, the voluntary exchange approach makes public goods directly analogous to private goods. Consumers' marginal rate of substitution is equated to producers' marginal rate of transformation, so that economic efficiency is achieved. The cost of production of inframarginal units of output simply determines whether income is redistributed toward the consumers of the public good (if costs are decreasing) or away from them toward either producers or the general public.

One conclusion emerging from the voluntary exchange model is that the optimal level of production of public goods, like that of private goods, depends on all the production and consumption decisions in the economy. This conclusion is not initially apparent. On the contrary, we might think that the optimal level of production of each public good would depend only on the preferences of those consumers who stand to benefit from it and on the conditions of production, for there is likely to be only one intersection of the social MRS and the MRT, as at point (p_0, w_0) in Figure 6.1. But the consumer preferences described in Figure 6.1 by the individual *MB* curves are determined by many other factors in addition to the price of the public good. Some of these factors, mentioned in Chapter 4, were the prices of other goods, the level of each consumer's income and wealth, and personal tastes (which may not be predictable but which most certainly are not unchangeable). The optimal level of production thus depends on these other factors as well as on the production conditions. As in the case of private goods, the optimal level of production of public goods is determined by the general equilibrium conditions in the economy.

To see how production of the public good depends on the distribution of income, for example, suppose that Captain Yates has a lucky day at the racetrack and wins $10,000. (Suppose, furthermore, that there are five thousand losers, none of whom alters his allocations as a consequence of his unsuccessful $2 bet.) Captain Yates may use his winnings to invest in a more luxurious fishing boat similar to that of Captain Zamorra, with the result that Yates's demand for the services of the lighthouse will rise since he now stands to lose more if his boat is wrecked. If Yates's *MB* curve now becomes identical to Zamorra's (for simplicity), the MB_T curve for all three captains will shift upward to MB'_T and the optimal level of warning will rise from w_0 to w_1. At this level of warning both Xavier and Zamorra will refuse to pay as much as before (per unit), for their marginal benefit will have declined, but Yates's increased demand will make up the difference and lead to the new total payment per unit, p_1.

The voluntary exchange model illuminates the question raised in the Downs and Galbraith models about "social balance," the division of resources between public and private sector goods. Except for public operation of utilities that produce private goods under decreasing-cost conditions, most government resource allocation involves the production of goods that have an element of "publicness," so that the opportunity cost of extending consumption is small (even though it may not be exactly zero). Clearly, there is no optimum size for the government budget, because the budget includes redistributional as well as allocative activities and thus affects consumers' preferences and producers' alternatives. Similarly, the question of social balance cannot be resolved because consumers do not demand homogeneous private and public goods but rather must choose among individual goods that happen either to be private or to have aspects of "publicness." The value of the voluntary exchange model is that it establishes the conditions under which the allocation of public goods will be efficient and consistent with the efficient allocation of private goods, both in unfettered private markets and in those cases when the government must intervene due to market imperfections.

The short-run allocation of pure public goods bears a close resemblance to the case of private goods produced under decreasing cost. Once the decision has been made to produce a given amount of the public good, the marginal cost of extending consumption to all members of society is zero, and the average cost of the given level of production thus falls as the number of consumers rises. The difference between the two cases is that the average cost for the private, decreasing-cost good refers to the average per unit of production, while the average for the public good refers to the cost per beneficiary. Since the short-run consumption of the public good is fixed and identical for all consumers, there is really no short-run allocation problem, unlike the case of the private, decreasing-cost good. Instead, if all consumers are charged according to their marginal benefit schedules, then the efficient amount of the public good will be supplied and each consumer will be in equilibrium. As long as the marginal cost of public goods exceeds their average total cost in the long run, equilibrium at the margin will also entail equilibrium overall, as we saw in Chapter 5. Later in this chapter we will discuss the mixed case of public goods produced under long-run decreasing costs.

THE VOLUNTARY EXCHANGE MODEL
IN THE REAL WORLD

Even though the requirement of efficiency and a zero price for extending consumption may not pose an analytical difficulty, it poses an important practical problem. If a public good confers benefits on all members of society (instead of only the three fishing-boat owners), any one consumer may refuse to pay his assessment, reasoning that even without his contribution the public good will be supplied in nearly the same amount. This consumer thus will make himself better off, for he will still receive some of the public good (because the government cannot or will not exclude him from consuming it as long as the cost of extending consumption is zero), but he will pay none of its cost. If only one consumer behaves this way, the inefficiency may not be great, although he may succeed in redistributing income in his favor. But everyone will have an incentive to refuse to pay for public goods, because each person believes (correctly) that he exerts only a negligible influence on supply.

This difficulty with the voluntary exchange model is known as the "free rider" problem. Each consumer of a public good is analogous to a train passenger who believes that the total cost of the train will be the same whether or not he is aboard. Thus he feels that he is entitled to a "free ride" since his presence adds nothing to the cost of the train. Similarly, each consumer, looking only at his own private-good consumption possibilities and his impact on the amount of public goods available, believes that he will continue to be able to consume the public goods even if he refuses to pay for them—that is, he will get a "free ride" with respect to his consumption of public goods. As long as this possibility is open to him, each consumer will try to conceal his demand for public goods, and the government will not be able to determine what price he would be willing to pay if the goods were offered in private sector markets. Unfortunately for the voluntary exchange model, this kind of consumer behavior is perfectly rational as long as the number of beneficiaries of the public good is large, for whether or not any one person is aware that others are concealing their preferences, it will still be true that *his* effect on the level of supply is insignificant. Moreover, the "free rider" problem will characterize every public good that is priced efficiently (at zero), since consumers cannot be penalized for their refusal to pay for the public good.

The "free rider" problem is most likely to apply to public goods that confer benefits generally, for as the number of beneficiaries falls each consumer becomes more cognizant of his own influence over the level of supply. When the number of beneficiaries is small, as in the fishing-boat example, each consumer may realize that if he refuses to pay for the public good it will not be produced. But even then he will try to convince the other beneficiaries that his demand for the good is low and that he should be charged only a small price for it. In no case will a consumer willingly reveal his demand for the public good. Public goods, therefore, will tend to be undersupplied if the voluntary behavior of consumers is the basis for allocating resources.

Even if the government is able to discover what consumers' preferences are and to allocate resources accordingly, to the production of public goods, it may be unable to levy the efficient set of charges. This is not a theoretical argument, but it is a practical difficulty unique to public goods. Efficiency can be achieved only if each consumer's marginal rate of substitution is equated to the price he pays for his consumption. But if the price is collected through a tax, the government must be able to vary the tax rate in response to variations in income, occupation, residence, and all the other factors that affect each consumer's MRS for each public good. As a practical matter, of course, such extensive variation in taxes is impossible. Moreover, taxes usually are levied on the basis of the taxpayer's ability to pay, rather than as a price for the benefits that he receives from consuming public goods. The tax system must serve many purposes, and even though many tax instruments are available, tax policy rarely seems to be directed at achieving efficiency in the supply of public goods.

Intertwined with the question of how much different consumers pay for public goods is the problem of aggregating their preferences into an expression of overall demand. If the voluntary exchange approach does not lead consumers to contribute toward the production of public goods, some nonmarket determination of preferences must be substituted. In making such a nonmarket evaluation of the strength of demand for public goods, the government may not even be able to rely on the imperfect evaluations prevailing in other markets, for there are no close substitutes for many public goods like national defense and space exploration. Thus, the government must substitute some other decision rule for the market-oriented expression of demand. In the absence of a market, there are as many methods of expressing demand for public goods as there are forms of government: under dictatorship, the preferences of the dictator are imposed on the rest of society; under aristocracy and other forms of limited franchise, only the preferences of those who vote are considered; under democracy, all members of society have an equal chance to determine the level of production of public goods.

VOTING AND PUBLIC GOODS

Our concern is with the different ways a collective decision can be reached in a democratic society—that is, with the different voting mechanisms that may be used. The three we will consider are the unanimity rule (that a public expenditure requires the consent of *all* voters), the simple majority rule, and the weighted majority rule or point voting. Although voting for public expenditures does not entail the use of resources (except for the minor costs of the balloting itself), it is important to remember that a vote for a public good is implicitly a vote for a higher level of taxation, since the production of the public good requires the use of real resources whose opportunity cost is greater than zero. Thus, equal weights for all citizens' preferences in the mechanism for making a collective decision may not imply that all voters pay equally for the public good. And even if voters do pay equally, there is no assurance that the resulting tax burden will correspond to the evaluations that different people place on the benefits of the public good. Consequently, an assessment of how nearly alternative voting mechanisms lead to efficient allocation cannot be separated from a consideration of how the tax structure is linked to the benefits of public goods.

Unanimity. Suppose that we are not at a Pareto optimum and that reallocation to produce a public good would lead to an optimal position. Such a reallocation would require the net beneficiaries of the public good—those whose total benefits exceed their tax liabilities—to compensate any taxpayers who are made worse off by the additional taxes and production of public goods. (We assume that consumers are fully aware of the benefits and costs of the reallocation.) If the electorate is given the choice of retaining its present allocation or shifting to the new one, then no voter will prefer to remain at his present position, and some will vote in favor of the shift. Among those who express a preference, therefore, the vote in favor of changing the resource allocation will be unanimous. In the general case, when the benefits of the public good are widespread and no voter or consumer is left unaffected by the reallocation, all voters will prefer to shift to the Pareto optimum. The unanimity rule for collective decisions, therefore, is the counterpart of the criterion of Pareto optimality for individual allocations.

Collective decisions in the real world, however, are not made on the basis of unanimous consent. In the model, voters must be offered a choice between two allocations, only one of which is Pareto optimal. But the collective decisions that voters actually must make are between allocations that are all nonoptimal, for the tax structure never equates the tax each consumer pays with the benefit he receives. On the contrary, we saw earlier (and will discuss in Part Three) how taxes are assessed on the basis of the taxpayer's ability to bear the tax burden, not on the basis of what he would be willing to pay for the public services he receives. The unanimity rule would be valid as a guide to real collective decisions only if the schedule of marginal tax rates coincided exactly with the marginal benefit every consumer received from all public goods. (Even in this case, the secondary impact of taxes upon income distribution and allocation might render the unanimity rule inappropriate.) If the choice among allocations does not include a Pareto optimum, then any reallocation will harm at least one consumer (by definition of Pareto optimality), and no reallocation will be able to command the unanimous support of all voters.

Simple Majority. Once we eliminate unanimity as a feasible rule for collective decisions, we are left with the choice between simple and weighted majorities. If the decision to produce public goods is made by a simple majority vote, then the decision rule means, in economic terms, that society has decided to ignore the *amounts* of utility gained and lost by the voters. Instead, the decision is based on only the *numbers* of gainers and losers. This decision rule is unsatisfactory in terms of both efficiency and equity. We know that simple majority voting will not lead to the efficient level of production of the public good, where all consumers equate their marginal rates of substitution with their marginal tax cost, for if that were the case then there would be no votes against the public good. Since all voters have equal voice under the simple majority rule, the equity argument must be either that society is better off as long as the majority is better off or that gainers and losers all experience the same change in utility, so that the effect of the production decision is to increase total social well-being. (If the latter judgment prevails, then gainers must not be compensating losers, or else we would effectively have a unanimous vote for the public good.) In either case, the simple majority rule links the allocation decision to a redistribution of income.

Although this decision rule may be democratic, it can easily lead to individual cases of flagrant inequity. For example, suppose that the three fishing-boat captains are asked to vote on the proposal that a lighthouse be built and financed by a tax on the town millionaire, an invalid who needs the healthful sea breeze to survive. If all citizens who are unaffected by the proposal fail to vote, the lighthouse will pass by a vote of three to one, even though the utility lost by the rich invalid may be far greater than the gains of the three captains. The fear of just such a "tyranny of the majority" led many conservative political philosophers of the eighteenth and nineteenth centuries to inveigh against universal suffrage. Even today, policy proposals such as a high tax on wealth (as distinct from income) are rejected for this reason. An examination of the size distribution of income, however, shows that it has changed little during the twentieth century in most industrial countries. This fear of a majority of the electorate oppressing the minority appears not to have been well founded (at least insofar as income redistribution is concerned).

One of the reasons that simple majority voting leads to inequities is that it does not offer voters a chance to express their *degree* of preference. This shortcoming can create inconsistencies. Suppose that captains Xavier, Yates, and Zamorra must choose among three alternative lighthouse projects (light, bell, and radio), each of which will be financed by taxes levied on them alone. Under the existing tax structure, their rankings of the three projects may be as shown in Table 6.1. Two of the captains (Xavier and Zamorra) prefer the light to the bell, and two (Zamorra and Yates) prefer the bell to the radio beacon. We would like to be able to infer that the light is preferred to the radio beacon, but we cannot because a direct comparison reveals that Yates and Zamorra would vote for the radio over the light. In this example, the voters' preferences are not *transitive* ($L > B$ and $B > R$ does not imply $L > R$). The choice among the three projects will not be made on the basis of which one of the three is the most preferred alternative but will hinge instead on whether (for example) Yates can convince Xavier to vote for the bell over the light or whether Zamorra can induce Xavier to vote for the radio beacon rather than the light.

Of course, there are many other coalitions that might result from the preferences shown in Table 6.1. But none of the coalitions will be superior to any of the others in terms of either the allocation of resources or the distribution of income. If we base collective decisions on simple orderings of preferences, without including any description of the intensity of preferences, then we cannot expect the decisions to be consistent with those made in private markets where consumers express the intensity of their preferences with every "dollar vote."

TABLE 6.1   Lighthouse Simple Rankings

		PROJECT	
CAPTAIN	*L*	*B*	*R*
X	1	2	3
Y	3	1	2
Z	2	3	1

Point Voting. A voting mechanism that permits voters to express the degree of their preferences is point voting, under which each voter receives a certain number of voting points that he can allocate as he chooses among the alternative projects. To see how such a system works, examine Table 6.2, in which the rankings of all three captains for all three projects are based on a total of ten voting points per man. Captain Yates has a relatively weak preference for the bell and a still weaker one for the radio beacon as his second choice. Captain Xavier's preferences are more strongly expressed, and Captain Zamorra feels very strongly that the radio beacon should be provided but does not care very much about the choice between the bell and the light. If the three captains vote according to Table 6.2, then the radio beacon will be selected with eleven voter points, against ten for the light and nine for the bell. In this case, weighted or point voting has converted the ambiguity of the simple majority rule into a clear-cut decision.

TABLE 6.2   Lighthouse Weighted Rankings

| | | PROJECT | |
CAPTAIN	*L*	*B*	*R*
X	6	3	1
Y	2	5	3
Z	2	1	7

The main advantage of point voting is that it permits voters to relate the benefits or costs they incur from collective decisions to their expressions of preference. Table 6.2 tells us that Captain Zamorra expects his net benefits (the value of the public good minus the tax cost imposed upon him) to be nearly as great if the bell is chosen as if the light is selected but that he expects to benefit much more from the radio beacon. Point voting is not without its own ambiguities, resulting chiefly from the effect third and fourth choices have on the points that voters can allocate to their preferred alternatives. Another lighthouse alternative would cause all three captains to reallocate their ten points even though none of them might prefer the new option. As a result, the overall choice might change from the radio beacon to the light or even to the bell. Point voting also has the drawback of weighting all voters' total well-being the same (ten points in the example), so that Captain Xavier's net benefits from the radio beacon are given the same weight as Captain Zamorra's from the bell even though the dollar amounts may be very different and the utilities themselves cannot be measured. But on balance it seems likely that point voting will lead to an allocation of resources more nearly consistent with private resource allocation than will simple majority voting.

Point voting may seem to be an idle alternative to simple majority voting, but in the real-world political process it is really very common. Suppose that the three captains are participants in a real-world municipal decision to build a lighthouse and finance it through a tax on fishing boats. Captain Yates, having no strong preference, may cast his vote in favor of the bell. Captain Xavier probably will urge the other two to vote for the light, since his preference is strong enough for him to go to some trouble (expend some resources) to obtain the light rather than the alternatives. Captain Zamorra, however, will do even more. He may write to the mayor, publish handbills, engage in a get-out-the-vote drive, and try to influence the design of the three proposals that are submitted to the electorate. In short, he will do all the things that concerned citizens do in the real world to influence collective decisions. He may not succeed in changing the rankings of either of the other captains, but he may well induce them to moderate their criticism of the radio beacon, his preferred alternative, and in so doing to let him tip the social decision in his favor.

If the political system is less than completely open, Captain Zamorra may engage in other activities to obtain his preferred project. He may lobby with his Congressman, form a group to bombard his elected representatives with mail, or suggest legislative trade-offs in the manner described in the Downs model, with the result of increasing the overall size of the government budget. An example of such behavior in the case of a real public-good decision was the advertising campaign undertaken by Lockheed Aircraft for its supersonic transport aircraft design. Although Lockheed lost the competition (Boeing was the successful bidder), its advertisements show how one segment of the electorate that stands to benefit substantially from a government decision will expend resources to win others' support and to counteract adverse criticism.

Our discussion of real-world point voting reemphasizes the interrelationship of allocation and distribution. In the point voting example, all three captains were given the same initial endowment (ten points) and allowed to allocate it as they chose. In real political processes, however, each voter's ability to influence collective decisions depends on the amount of resources he can spend in the ways just described. Clearly, all voters will not have equal amounts of time and money with which to affect the political process; instead, a bigger voice in collective decisions will go to people at the upper end of the income size distribution. In public-goods decisions as well as private-goods ones, the rich are better able than the poor to express their preferences.

PUBLIC AND SEMIPUBLIC GOODS

It should be clear from the discussion of externalities in Chapter 5 and the examples of public goods early in this chapter that many public expenditures are "impure" public goods in the sense that the opportunity cost of extending consumption to another person is not truly zero. In other cases, goods that have the attribute of "publicness" also may confer private benefits, or "impure" public goods may exhibit decreasing costs of production. Most programs of public expenditures fall into one or more of these mixed categories rather than into any of the pure cases of market imperfection.

As an example of a private good that is usually supplied publicly, consider the services of police and fire protection. Although these goods are almost always treated as requiring public expression of demand (and usually public production), in fact the cost of offering, say, fire protection to a home or office building is not zero. To see this point more clearly, suppose there was a decision to provide fire protection to an entire neighborhood. Men and fire engines would have to be supplied, and even a new firehouse might be required. The additional demand posed by one more house is qualitatively identical to that of the entire neighborhood (although quantitatively much smaller). One justification for public supply of police and fire protection is the decreasing (but not zero) cost of extending consumption, since it offers economies of scale in production. Another justification is that these services may confer rather general external benefits, and thus would be undersupplied in the absence of governmental action.

Other goods may confer a benefit that is public while at the same time being useful to the direct consumer. In Chapter 16 we will examine education, which is frequently said to confer general benefits to society as well as specific ones to the student. While such general benefits obviously fall into the category of externalities, their widespread nature may require the government to treat the externality as a public good while trying to recapture from direct consumers some of the benefits that they derive. In such cases, the government will be forced to compare allocations that are less than optimal because of the "publicness" of the good, and it may be preferable simply to ignore direct benefits because of the high cost of making consumers pay for them. Goods with large-number externalities, conceptually similar to public goods, are very troublesome for economic analysis because of the difficulty of measuring the external benefit and the practical and political problems of reaching the efficient level of supply.

Public and semipublic goods may be produced under decreasing-cost conditions. Although decreasing costs do not affect the theoretically optimal level of supply, they may introduce another source of inefficiency since they cause a deficit that must be made up from other revenue sources. Classic examples of public decreasing-cost goods are bridges and tunnels used at less than their capacity and the television signal mentioned at the beginning of this chapter. For such goods, efficiency at the margin requires a zero price, so the sum of consumers' marginal valuations is zero. Thus, the marginal benefits derived from these goods offer no hint about the total benefits derived by consumers. The "publicness" of these goods is secondary to their decreasing-cost nature, and the long-run level of supply must be determined according to the principles set forth in Chapter 5.

An even more difficult problem arises when decreasing-cost goods yield benefits in the "gray area" between externalities and public goods. Examples of a good of this type may be education (if costs of production really are decreasing), medical care, and hospitalization. The determination of an even approximately efficient set of charges or taxes is difficult for these goods because the efficient price to charge for them is not zero. Education and medical care, for example, both yield large private as well as public benefits, and neither good can be consumed non-exhaustively. Efficient charges on direct beneficiaries, however, would not cover the total costs of these goods. Thus, some social decision must be reached about whether the semipublic benefits of such goods are great enough to justify public subsidies for their production. In practice, political questions of equity usually arise in these cases long before the allocation of resources approaches efficiency.

When public programs exhibit more than one of the attributes that make public sector allocation necessary, complicated methods of discovering voters' preferences and financing the public expenditures may be called for. Mixed benefits require mixed expenditure and revenue programs. It is important to identify the nature of the market imperfection—monopoly, decreasing-cost production, externality, or public good—that justifies public intervention in private markets, for intelligent decisions about the role of government can only be made once the shortcomings of the private sector allocation of resources are understood.

SUMMARY

Goods that confer benefits generally, rather than on the primary demander, are called "public goods." The criterion for goods to be pure public goods is that they must be consumed non-exhaustively, so that one consumer's use of the good does not reduce its availability to everyone else. For such goods, the opportunity cost of extending consumption to another person is zero. These goods require a public expression of demand, for no consumer derives enough benefit to demand them privately.

Efficiency in the supply of pure public goods requires that each consumer's MRS be equated to his MRT. For society as a whole, the sum of all marginal rates of substitution must be equal to the social marginal rate of transformation. The efficient level of production will result if each consumer is charged an amount equal to his MRS and the funds are used to produce the public good. Increasing-cost or decreasing-cost production may cause a redistribution of income if the efficient charges are used. This determination of the level of production is called the "voluntary exchange approach."

In the real world, the voluntary exchange model cannot be used because of the impossibility of setting tax rates to reflect the marginal benefits that each consumer derives from each public good. Voluntary payments will not be made because of the "free rider" problem—namely, that each consumer stands to benefit from refusing to reveal his preferences for any public good. The government must substitute some collective decision rule for the voluntary exchange model's determination of the efficient level of production. If tax rates could be set in a manner that permitted the economy to reach a Pareto optimum, unanimity would be the correct collective decision rule.

In practice, collective decisions usually are made by simple or weighted majorities. The simple majority rule is unsatisfactory from the standpoint of equity as well as of efficiency. Weighted majority voting permits individuals to express the intensity of their preferences, as well as their rankings of alternatives. Although weighted majority voting does not lead to a Pareto optimum, it is more nearly consistent with efficiency and consumers' expression of demand in private markets. Real-world weighted majority voting comes about because consumers expend resources to try to influence others' preferences. As in private markets, the rich have a larger voice than the poor in public-good allocation decisions.

Examples of government resource allocation rarely fit into any of the pure cases of decreasing-cost production, externalities, or public goods. Most government allocations respond to a degree of "public-ness," frequently a large-numbers externality that makes efficient allocation difficult to achieve. Semipublic goods may be produced under decreasing-cost conditions. In these mixed cases, efficiency can be achieved (if at all) only if the compound nature of the misallocation is recognized and compound remedies are applied.

PART THREE Efficiency Considerations in Taxation

Taxation traditionally has been the primary concern of public finance economists, often to the exclusion of other aspects of public sector economics. In this part we examine the major types of taxes, primarily with reference to federal taxation except where states or local governments are the principal users of a tax. No attempt is made to describe different taxes in detail, but some of the most important features of current tax laws are discussed. The focus of Chapters 7 through 10 is on the effects that different taxes may have upon the twin goals of allocational efficiency and distributional equity. Individual provisions of tax statutes are mentioned only if they have a major impact on one or both of these objectives.

BIBLIOGRAPHY

A more detailed discussion of most of the taxes analyzed in this part can be found in Joseph A. Pechman's *Federal Tax Policy,* revised edition (Washington, D.C.: Brookings Institution, 1971). Pechman includes many tables indicating the importance of various provisions of the tax laws. His discussions of personal and corporation income taxes in chapters 4 and 5 are especially comprehensive.

For more extensive surveys of the literature on taxation, several monographs are available: Richard Goode, *The Individual Income Tax* (Washington, D.C.: Brookings Institution, 1964); John F. Due, *Sales Taxation* (Urbana: University of Illinois Press, 1957); Dick Netzer, *Economics of the Property Tax* (Washington, D.C.: Brook-

113

ings Institution, 1966); Carl S. Shoup, *Federal Estate and Gift Taxes* (Washington, D.C.: Brookings Institution, 1966); and Richard Goode, *The Corporation Income Tax* (New York: Wiley, 1964). For a review of recent contributions to the debate on the corporation income tax, see P. Mieszkowski's article "Tax Incidence Theory: The Effects of Taxes on the Distribution of Income" in *Journal of Economic Literature* 7 (December 1969): 1116–20. Employment taxation is discussed by Seymour Harris in part 2 of his *Economics of Social Security* (New York: McGraw-Hill, 1941); a comprehensive discussion of social security is *Social Security: Perspectives for Reform* by J. A. Pechman, H. J. Aaron, and M. K. Taussig (Washington, D.C.: Brookings Institution, 1968), especially chapters 4 and 8.

7 Personal Income Taxation

Personal income taxation in the United States dates from 1913, when the Sixteenth Amendment to the Constitution gave Congress "power to lay and collect taxes on incomes." In the years since then, the percentage of the population paying the federal income tax has expanded from about 1 percent to over 75 percent, and the income tax has become the largest revenue producer of all federal taxes. The maximum marginal tax rate (the rate levied on the highest income bracket) rose from 7 percent in 1913 to over 90 percent during the Second World War, before being lowered to 70 percent by the 1964 tax revision.

Income taxation has also been adopted by most states and many municipalities and is approaching equality with sales taxation as a revenue producer at the state level. Most state income taxes are similar to the federal tax, and some states simply compute income tax liability as a percentage of federal tax liability. Our discussion of the federal income tax, therefore, applies to most state income taxes as well.

ALTERNATIVE TAX BASES

The choice of income as a tax base reflects the judgment that taxes on the alternative broad bases—wealth, sales, and consumption expenditures—would lead to more inequities or a greater distortion of resource allocation.

Wealth. One argument against the taxation of wealth as a major revenue source was mentioned in Chapter 6: since the distribution of wealth is much more concentrated in the hands of the rich than is the distribution of income, a tax on wealth could be levied on a discriminatory or punitive basis. The highest-income 1 percent of families and individuals receives about 6 to 8 percent of total personal income, but owns 25 to 30 percent of total wealth. Conversely, the lowest-income 90 percent of families and individuals receives 70 to 75 percent of personal income, but the lowest-income 90 percent of families controls less than 20 percent of total wealth.

Another problem with a wealth tax is that a taxpayer's cash flow may not correspond at all well to his tax liability, even though the tax rates may be small relative to his total assets. This difficulty would be especially severe if wealth were computed on an accrual basis, measured by the current value of illiquid assets such as common stocks or physical capital equipment, instead of on a realization basis including only the cash realized from the actual sale of capital assets. These inequities also arise under income taxation, but they are unlikely to be as severe for most taxpayers since tax liability is related to income flow.

Sales. For many years, sales taxation (in the form of customs duties) provided the major revenue source for the federal government. Sales taxes are still the most important revenue source for most state governments, yielding nearly half of all state-raised revenues (excluding local taxes and federal grants). Sales taxes may be either general taxes on sales of all goods or excises on particular commodities. Neither a general sales tax nor specific excises will be as broadly based as an income tax, however, because of the difficulty of taxing personal services such as housing, repairs, and medical care. In addition, some economists believe that sales or excise taxation distorts resource allocation more than an income tax of equal yield, so that income taxation is preferable on efficiency grounds even if the two taxes are distributionally equivalent. We will discuss this issue and some of the alternative forms of sales taxation in Chapter 9.

Expenditures. In many ways the most intriguing alternative to income taxation is a consumption or expenditure tax. Expenditure taxation is similar to sales taxation, with the difference that the tax is levied on each person's total consumption expenditures, not on his consumption of taxed items. Whereas sales taxation must be proportional to total sales, an expenditure tax may be levied with progressive rates. Thus, a person whose consumption expenditures totaled $5000 might pay at the rate of 10 percent, while someone who spent $10,000 on consumption goods might pay at 15 percent.

One argument against expenditure taxation is that it is difficult to administer. Consumers do not ordinarily keep records of all their purchases, and they buy from such a large number of different sellers that it would be expensive for each seller to keep track of each buyer's expenditures. The alternative is for each taxpayer to estimate consumption as the difference between income and saving. This procedure would raise as many questions as wealth or income taxes about the valuation of capital assets, while imposing additional bookkeeping requirements on the taxpayer.

Proponents of expenditure taxation claim that consumption expenditures are the best measure of the taxpayer's ability to pay, since illiquid assets are excluded from the tax base. Another advantage is that, relative to income taxation, an expenditure tax encourages saving and thus promotes a faster rate of growth. Under an income tax, each taxpayer may consume or save his disposable income after paying his income tax. When he saves, he is then taxed on the interest he earns. An expenditure tax, however, does not tax him on his initial saving and thus increases the amount he may save, although when he eventually consumes the income he earns by saving, he will have to pay a tax on it. In effect, the expenditure tax exempts saving and thus makes it more attractive relative to current consumption.[1]

The net impact of the expenditure tax on growth, compared to the income tax, is not so simple, for it depends on what other incentives the income tax law may offer to savers. In view of the additional administrative complexities that an expenditure tax would entail and the uncertain magnitude of its effect on the rate of growth and investment, most economists believe that income taxation is preferable.

ELEMENTS OF THE FEDERAL INCOME TAX

Adjusted Gross Income. The federal income tax is defined by a series of marginal tax rates, each levied on a certain bracket of taxable income. Although the tax is called an income tax, taxable income bears little relation to an economist's notion of factor returns or personal income. In the National Income and Product Accounts, personal income is the sum of returns to factors of production owned by the income recipient, plus transfer payments from business and government. Social security taxes are deducted by accounting convention. Under the tax law, however, the basic income concept is Adjusted

---

[1] In addition, an expenditure tax will fall more heavily on taxpayers with high consumption propensities. The importance of this effect depends on how much difference there is among different peoples' propensities to consume. Most empirical studies conclude that this difference is small.

Gross Income (AGI), which consists of all income earned by the income recipient (including social security tax payments), plus realized changes in the value of capital assets (which are excluded from the definition of personal income because they represent no change in productivity or output produced). Interest received from state and local bonds is excluded as a subsidy to these levels of government. Most transfer payments are excluded from AGI on equity grounds, and most income in kind and miscellaneous labor income are excluded as too difficult to measure. Other credits and exclusions are items such as sick pay and nonreimbursed moving expenses related to employment. The result of these major differences and of many minor ones is that AGI averages about 85 or 90 percent of personal income, with the exact percentage varying from year to year.

Exemptions and Deductions. Once the taxpayer determines his AGI, he derives his taxable income by subtracting a series of exemptions and deductions. Exemptions are allowed for each person supported by the taxpayer (himself and his dependents), with additional exemptions permitted for old age and blindness. Under the 1969 Tax Reform Act, the allowance for personal exemptions will rise from $600 to $750 by 1973. In addition to his exemptions, the taxpayer is offered the choice between itemizing his deductions or simply subtracting a "standard deduction." Before 1970, the standard deduction was computed as the greater of 10 percent of AGI or $200 plus $100 per exemption. The 1969 act increased the AGI percentage to 15 percent by 1973 and introduced a "low-income allowance" designed to eliminate the tax liability of poverty-level families. The low-income allowance is, in effect, a *minimum* standard deduction. The *maximum* standard deduction will rise from $1000 to $2000 by 1973, making it more attractive than itemizing for many middle-income taxpayers.

There are many different allowable deductions, but they fall into four main families. The first type is for emergency or hardship and includes the medical deduction (in excess of about 3 percent of AGI) and the deduction allowed for casualty loss such as fire and theft. A second type includes subsidies for particular kinds of economic activity, particularly home ownership and installment purchases of consumer durables (since all interest paid is deductible) and private philanthropy (since charitable contributions up to 50 percent of AGI are fully deductible).[2] A third type of deduction is for taxes paid to state and municipal governments. Since many state and local officials argue that the federal government has "preempted" potential rev-

[2] The 50 percent ceiling applies after 1974, under the 1969 Tax Reform Act.

enue sources by levying high taxes on personal and corporate income, this family of deductions represents an attempt by the federal government to restore state and local revenue capacity. In return, some states exempt federal income tax liability from state income taxation. The fourth family of deductions includes the costs of earning income: items such as union and professional dues, nonreimbursed travel related to one's employment, and child-care expenses for low-income families.

Income Splitting. An important special feature in the federal income tax is income splitting, the practice by which a married man filing a joint tax return is allowed to impute half of his total taxable income to his wife. Couples filing jointly thus pay much lower taxes than single people at the same income levels. Under the Tax Reform Act of 1969, single taxpayers' additional tax liabilities were reduced to 17 or 20 percent above the tax liabilities of married couples filing jointly. Unmarried heads of households also received a reduction, to about 8 or 10 percent greater liability than married couples. In part, the income-splitting provision merely compensates for the inadequate level of personal exemptions, which discriminates more heavily against married couples and families than against single taxpayers.

Capital Gains. A subject worthy of separate mention is the federal tax treatment of capital gains, changes in the value of capital assets. Capital gains are taxed only upon realization (that is, the actual sale of an asset whose price has changed) and then receive preferential treatment compared to other types of income. First, half of all capital gains realized from holding assets more than six months are excluded from taxation. (Other, short-term, capital gains are taxed as ordinary income.) Those capital gains included in AGI and eventually in taxable income received an additional preference prior to the Tax Reform Act of 1969, when they were taxed at a maximum marginal rate of 50 percent. Thus, the effective maximum marginal rate on long-term capital gains was 25 percent. The 1969 tax reform modified this preference, limiting the 25 percent effective maximum marginal rate to the first $50,000 of long-term capital gains and raising the effective rate on additional long-term gains to the "normal" 35 percent (half of the maximum marginal rate of 70 percent on ordinary income) by 1972.

Before the reforms of the 1969 act, the 25 percent tax rate on capital gains created a major incentive for income recipients to distort their resource allocations in order to earn capital gains rather than other forms of income. Several provisions of the 1969 law modified or reduced this incentive. One was that "earned" income (wages, salaries, and other compensation for personal services) is taxed at a maximum rate of 50 percent, rather than the 70 percent applying to other forms of income (primarily dividends and interest). Another is the "minimum tax" of 10 percent levied at high levels of excluded or "preference" income: the excluded 50 percent of long-term capital gains, depletion and accelerated depreciation (discussed in Chapter 8), and other smaller items. Thus, a taxpayer with large capital gains could pay a marginal tax rate of 45 percent on his capital gains (35 percent on included capital gains and 10 percent on the excluded portion), compared to the 50 percent maximum on earned income.

The effect of these provisions of the 1969 tax reform is to reduce the net marginal tax benefit from capital gains over $50,000, from 45 percent (70 percent minus 25 percent, pre-1969) to (1) 35 percent if noncapital gains income is not "earned," (2) 25 percent if capital gains are subject to the minimum tax, (3) 15 percent if no minimum tax is paid but all other income is "earned," or (4) 5 percent if all other income is "earned" and the minimum tax must be paid on preference income. The impact of these changes on resource allocation will not be known for several years, but some tax analysts believe that there will be a substantial reduction in "avoidance behavior." Although the number of taxpayers affected by these provisions is small, the increase in their tax liability may well be significant.

Tax Liability. When the taxpayer has calculated his AGI and then subtracted exemptions and deductions, he is left with taxable income. The magnitude of exclusions, exemptions, and deductions is so large that taxable income is little more than half of AGI (counting the fraction of AGI—about 10 percent—that is unreported due to ignorance, low incomes, or lack of compliance on the part of the taxpayer). As recently as 1965, taxable income amounted to less than half of AGI, and aggregate taxable income still is less than half of the personal income total in the National Income and Product Accounts.

The calculation of each taxpayer's tax liability is performed by applying the series of marginal tax rates to taxable income. Under the Revenue Act of 1964, the first $500 of a single taxpayer's taxable income is taxed at 14 percent, the second $500 at 15 percent, the second $2000 (from taxable income levels $2000–$4000) at 19 percent, and so on to the maximum rate of 70 percent levied on all taxable income in excess of $100,000. Each taxpayer's total tax is thus the sum of the taxes that he pays on each part, or bracket, of his taxable income. No taxpayer will pay a tax equal to 70 percent of his total taxable income, for the tax rates on his first $100,000 of taxable income are less than

70 percent. The marginal tax rates, therefore, do not give us a clear indication of how total tax liability is related to total income.

The relationship between tax liability and income may be progressive, proportional, or regressive. These concepts apply to all taxes, not only to the income tax. If tax liability grows more rapidly than income, then the ratio of tax to income is a rising one, and we say that the tax is progressive. If the ratio of tax to income remains constant as income grows, then the tax is said to be proportional; and if the ratio falls as income grows, the tax is regressive. In all cases, progressivity and the other measures refer to the particular income aggregate used. Thus, since income tax liability grows more rapidly than taxable income (as it must, given the schedule of marginal income tax rates) the income tax is progressive *with respect to taxable income.*

Due to exclusions, exemptions, and deductions, however, taxable income is not a good measure of a taxpayer's gross income. A better measure consistent with the income definitions used in the income tax law would be AGI plus excluded capital gains. This income measure still excludes "hardship" transfer payments but includes all capital gains in the calculations of the taxpayer's cash flow. (The "gross income" measure used below also includes two smaller items, excluded sick pay and excluded dividends, that are not counted as part of AGI.)

If we applied the marginal tax rates to AGI plus excluded capital gains, we could derive a schedule of the average tax liability at each level of income. This tax schedule would tell us whether the *nominal* tax rates—those specified in the income tax law—were progressive with respect to "gross income." Obviously, this schedule of nominal tax incidence would be highly progressive, ranging from a low average tax rate of 14 percent on the income up to $500 to a high average tax rate approaching 70 percent for incomes well in excess of $100,000.

No taxpayer, however, pays tax at this nominal rate, for taxes are calculated on the basis of taxable income. To compare the actual incidence of the tax law with the nominal incidence, we may calculate each taxpayer's average *effective* tax rate, the ratio of his actual tax liability to his "gross income." The effective tax rate for low-income taxpayers is zero, for no tax liability is incurred until "gross income" exceeds the minimum exemption and deductions. The effective tax rate for wealthier taxpayers is much higher, but it never approaches the maximum marginal rate of 70 percent because of the availability of deductions and the special treatment of capital gains. Pechman has shown that before the tax reforms of 1969, the effective tax rate rose from zero (at about $900 of "gross income") rapidly to about 6 percent (at $2000), then more slowly to about 10 percent at $10,000, and eventually to a maximum of about 30 percent at $200,000 of "gross income."[3] Beyond the $200,000 level, the average effective tax rate actually declined slightly, due entirely to the very rapid increase in the share of "gross income" received as capital gains (and thus subject only to low tax rates). Thus, effective tax rates (in contrast to the nominal ones specified in the income tax law) were mildly progressive over most of the range of incomes but exhibited regressivity at very high levels of income.

THE CASE FOR PROGRESSIVITY

There is no conscious policy decision underlying these effective tax rates, for the effective rates are the result of the nominal rate schedule and the (largely unpredictable) response of taxpayers to the nominal rates and the other provisions of the tax law. After the fact, however, we have observed that the tax law is progressive over most of the range of incomes. We must decide whether there is any foundation for progressivity in either the allocative or distributional effects of the personal income tax.

Since the personal income tax is the principal source of revenue for the federal government and a major one for most states, it is an important contributor to the provision of public goods and other benefits derived from public sector resource allocation. One basis for a progressive tax structure, accordingly, might be that the benefits of public expenditures accrue disproportionately to high-income taxpayers. As we saw in Chapter 6, however, we can never find out how much benefit individual consumers derive from pure public goods, since public goods are always available at a zero price and consumers have an incentive to conceal their preferences. Using Galbraith's argument, we might reason that the value of public goods to high-income taxpayers would be greater than their value to the poor since the opportunity cost (the utility of private consumption goods) is much lower for the rich. But even if we accept this argument (and to do so involves making interpersonal comparisons of utility), it offers no basis for deciding *how much* progressivity there should be in the tax system.

Other categories of public expenditures do not help us resolve this question. In the case of most transfers (non-exhaustive expenditures), benefits are received disproportionately by low-income consumers. To the extent that public sector funds are used to produce decreasing-

---

[3] J. A. Pechman, "Individual Income Tax Provisions of the Revenue Act of 1964," *Journal of Finance* 20 (May 1965): 265.

cost goods or to control monopoly, there is no reason to believe that benefits accrue primarily to high-income taxpayers. On balance, then, the benefit theory of taxation does not justify a progressive tax structure. And even if we could use the benefits of public expenditures to justify progressive taxation, we could not base any particular set of tax rates on the distribution of benefits.

Another argument for progressive taxation is that the progressive personal income tax acts as an "automatic stabilizer" upon the level of income and employment. Since the tax is progressive, its revenues rise faster than personal income during business cycle expansions, causing fluctuations in disposable income and consumption to be proportionally smaller than fluctuations in personal income and GNP. In recessions, likewise, tax revenues fall proportionally more than personal income, so disposable income and consumption remain relatively stable. Thus, the level of aggregate demand is stabilized by the progressivity of the tax structure, and fluctuations in income and employment are mitigated.

Studies of automatic stabilizers have concluded that they contribute significantly to stabilizing the level of aggregate demand. Nonetheless, this benefit is not adequate to justify progressive taxation. For one thing, many alternative stabilizing instruments (such as corporation income taxes or social security transfers) are available to the government. It is by no means clear that progressive taxation is an efficient stabilizing device: perhaps other stabilizers could dampen economic fluctuations equally well and at a smaller resource cost to taxpayers. In a complex economy, moreover, it is difficult to identify the stabilizing effect of one particular instrument such as the progressive personal income tax. And the tax rates levied under the income tax law certainly are not those that would maximize the stabilization potential of the tax.

A popular argument among early utility theorists was that progressive taxation would minimize the reduction in total utility associated with obtaining the revenue needed for public expenditures. According to this argument, if society has a choice between collecting revenue from a tax on the rich and one on the poor, it should choose a tax that is equitable in terms of the utility sacrifices imposed upon taxpayers. Although economists no longer believe it possible to make interpersonal comparisons of utility, progressive taxation necessarily embodies just such comparisons, and thus it is worth looking at this sacrifice argument in a little more detail.

Actually, there are two major variants of the sacrifice approach. In the first, the objective of tax policy is to exact the same average sacrifice from each taxpayer, so that the rich man would sacrifice the same percentage of his total utility as the poor man. To translate this equi-proportional sacrifice principle into a set of tax rates, utility theorists made the assumption that all taxpayers had the same marginal utility schedule for income. Thus, the rich man and the poor man might not have equal marginal utilities at their present income levels, but it was assumed that if their incomes were equalized then their marginal utilities would also become equal. Under this assumption, the last dollar of a rich man's income would yield a smaller proportion of his total utility than the last dollar of a poor man's income. For this marginal utility schedule to yield a progressive tax structure with respect to income, it is necessary that the marginal utility of income decrease fairly rapidly. The details of the analysis are not important, since the basic assumptions upon which the theory rests—interpersonal comparisons or identical utility functions and measurable utility—are unrealistic. What matters is the concept, that if one's equity ideal is to require the same proportional sacrifice from all taxpayers then the resulting tax structure may well be a progressive one.

The second variant on the sacrifice theory of taxation was to minimize the total loss of utility to society. We can attain this objective by making the marginal sacrifice equal for all taxpayers, for if one taxpayer's marginal sacrifice is greater than another's, total sacrifice can be lessened by reducing the former's tax and increasing that of the latter. This sacrifice theory, equimarginal sacrifice, always leads to progressive taxation if all taxpayers have the same schedule of marginal utility for income and if marginal utility is decreasing. Equimarginal sacrifice does not offer a guide for the design of actual tax rates for the same reasons as equiproportional sacrifice, but it illustrates how a slightly different equity objective can lead to progressivity.

Although we cannot translate sacrifice theories into a real-world tax rate structure, the political process of determining tax rates seems to have an objective akin to minimizing the burden of raising a required amount of revenue. The objective is most often expressed as taxing on the basis of "ability to pay," a phrase with two meanings. One sense of the phrase is that of sacrifice theory, that the rich are better able to give up their income than the poor and that the overall tax structure should be progressive. The other meaning of "ability to pay" refers to the fairness of imposing equal tax rates on taxpayers in different circumstances (although at equal income levels). For example, a married man with three dependents may be less well able to pay taxes than a bachelor with the same income. But if the married man's entire income is received as wages and the bachelor's is capital gains realized in an exchange of real estate, then some adjustment must be made for the additional costs to the bachelor of borrowing against his illiquid assets in order to pay his tax bill. It is this concept of equity, as well as the practical difficulties of measuring many types of income, that underlies some of the special provisions of the income tax law.

As the result of these two different kinds of equity, the tax rate structure growing out of the "ability to pay" doctrine is a patchwork. There is no single determination of equity; instead, the tax law is modified when inequities become so blatant or injurious that they generate enough political pressure for change to occur. For example, after economists and political figures spent many years publicizing some of the inequities in the tax law, enough public outcry was produced to pass the Revenue Act of 1969. This act attempted to close some of the most aggravating loopholes in the tax law, including the operation of private foundations, the oil depletion allowance (to be discussed further in Chapter 8), and the ability of some of the very rich to escape taxation completely. But many other loopholes remain because tax reform is difficult, time consuming, and expensive, and because victimized taxpayers do not know enough about the details of the tax law.

TAX SHIFTING AND INCENTIVES

Any tax has a distorting effect upon the allocation of resources as long as it changes the taxpayer's ability to do some of the things that he did before the tax was imposed. An excise tax makes the taxed goods more expensive relative to the untaxed ones; an estate tax makes it difficult to bequeath large sums; a wealth tax lessens the attractiveness of holding assets compared to flows of income. The extent to which these taxes actually alter the allocation of resources depends on how well the people who pay the tax are able to shift the burden of the tax to others. We say that a tax is shifted completely if the real income of the statutory taxpayer (the one named in the law) is not changed by the tax.

Whether the statutory taxpayer is able to shift the tax or not, the tax burden must eventually come to rest on some economic unit (a consumer or producer), who thus becomes the actual taxpayer. The actual taxpayer will reallocate his resources in response to the tax, reflecting the higher costs that the tax imposes on some of his allocations. The tax thus provides a disincentive for him to continue his former allocations or, conversely, offers an incentive to change them. The actual taxpayer's utility loss depends on how powerful these disincentives are. If we could design a tax that reduced taxpayer's incomes without causing any reallocation, we would have an allocatively neutral tax that altered only the distribution of income. In fact, any tax will affect allocation, if only through the income effect on the taxpayer, but one of the desirable properties of a tax is that it should cause as little reallocation as possible.

Work Effort. One of the effects of the personal income tax is that it reduces the net utility that the taxpayer receives from a marginal dollar of income. If the tax is progressive, the reduction in marginal utility is higher at high income levels, for an increasing share of the marginal dollar is taxed away as income rises. This is the source of the argument that the income tax will discourage work effort and thus reduce the level of national income and its rate of growth.

Figure 7.1 depicts this situation. Employers' demand for labor is shown by demand curve D and is unaffected by the imposition of the tax. Workers' supply of labor initially is S_1, yielding an equilibrium number of hours of work N_1 and a wage rate w_1. The income tax shifts workers to a new supply curve S_2, and the progressivity of the tax makes the difference between the old and new supply curves an increasing function of the number of hours worked (and thus of the workers' income level). Since the disutility of work has not changed, workers now supply only N_3 hours at the old wage rate. Alternatively, they would demand a wage rate t_1 to supply N_1 hours of work, since the average tax rate is t_1 minus w_1, and the net wage would then be w_1, the same as before the tax. Employers, however, refuse to pay t_1 and instead reduce their demand for labor to N_2, at a wage rate of t_2. At this point, part of the tax has been shifted by workers, for employers have been forced to reallocate their resources. Part of the tax is being paid by workers, for their incomes have fallen from w_1N_1 to w_2N_2. Employers may find that their wage bill has increased, for they will now pay workers a total of t_2N_2 instead of w_1N_1, but they will certainly have to pay a higher wage cost per hour. Thus, they will try to raise prices, and they may be forced to buy more capital goods to substitute for the reduction in labor.

This shifting mechanism depends on the elasticities of the demand and supply curves for labor. We may expect the demand curve to have a negative slope and a fairly high elasticity, so that higher wage demands will cause employers to reduce their purchases of labor. The slope and elasticity of the supply curve, however, are much more in question.

For one thing, income is not the only reward for work. Many jobs carry nonmoney compensation, including power, prestige, and even the personal satisfaction that comes from providing some vital ser-

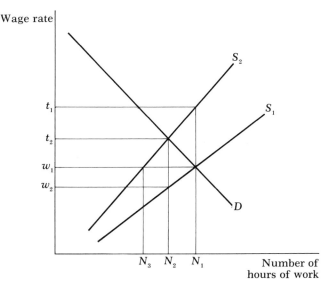

FIGURE 7.1   Work Disincentives

vice. These nonmoney rewards are especially prevalent among high-income jobs, the ones in which we might expect work effort to be most affected by the progressive income tax. Several studies of the response of high-income professional personnel to progressive income taxation have indicated that these nonmoney compensations are dominant and that the disincentive effects of progressive taxation are insignificant for these professions. Among the occupational groups covered by these studies are business executives and financial consultants, lawyers, accountants, and surgeons.[4]

At lower income levels, the effect of taxation upon the worker's total income may outweight its effect upon his marginal work effort. In Figure 7.1 the shift of the supply curve to S_2 led to a reduction in total labor income from w_1N_1 to w_2N_2. Workers may not be able to tolerate such a fall in their incomes, however, for they may have fixed obligations such as mortgages, automobile payments, families to feed and clothe, and other taxes to pay. These circumstances may lead workers to have *negatively* sloped supply curves, so that a fall in their net wage forces them to *increase* their supply of work effort. This income effect conflicts with the desire to substitute leisure for work since the

---

[4] See G. F. Break, "Income Taxes, Wage Rates, and the Incentive to Supply Labor Services," *National Tax Journal* 6 (December 1953): 350–51; and T. H. Sanders, *Effects of Taxation on Executives* (Cambridge, Mass.: Harvard University Press, 1951).

marginal return to work is lower due to the tax, but the income effect may well be stronger than the substitution effect at low levels of income. Studies of both British and American low- and middle-income workers have suggested that the net disincentive effect of income taxation is insignificant.[5]

For technical reasons, such as few respondents and the lack of control groups, these studies of both high- and low-income workers are not conclusive. But they indicate strongly that neither the very high marginal rates that the U.S. income tax levied on high incomes prior to 1964 nor the generally high levels of income taxation in the United Kingdom has led to much of a reduction in the supply of work effort. As an empirical matter, therefore, most economists agree that the income tax is not shifted by workers to employers or consumers and that the tax has little effect on work effort. With respect to the supply of labor, the income tax seems to be very nearly neutral.

Saving and Investment. Another charge leveled against progressive income taxation is that it restricts the *amount* of capital formation and reduces the average *return* on investments, thus retarding growth in two ways. This is a complicated argument, for it involves the impact of the income tax upon saving, risk-taking, and the composition of new investment. Several different features of the tax law are relevant, in addition to the general disincentive effects of income taxation.

SAVING. The effect of the progressive income tax upon saving stems from two sources. First, income taxation makes saving less attractive, relative to consumption, than either a broad-based sales or an expenditure tax.[6] Under the consumption taxes, the taxpayer's options (say in year 1) would be consumption and the payment of a tax, or saving and no tax. In year 2, the taxpayer could consume all his year 2 income plus the interest on his savings from year 1 while paying a tax on the total, or he could again elect to save some of his total income and pay no tax on it. Under an income tax, however, all his income in year 1 would be taxed, and he would have less income to allocate to consumption and saving. When he chose to save, he would still pay a tax on the interest in later years. Saving thus is greater under a consump-

[5] See G. F. Break, "Income Taxes and Incentives to Work: An Empirical Study," *American Economic Review* 47 (September 1957): 529–49; and Royal Commission on the Taxation of Profits and Income, *Appendix I to the Second Report* (London: H. M. Stationery Office, 1954), pp. 91–124.

[6] In the following discussion, we assume that the additional desired saving under sales or expenditure taxes is not offset by lower interest rates stemming from an increase in the supply of funds.

tion-based tax than under an income tax because the saver has the added incentive of earning interest on the taxes that he avoids by deferring consumption from year 1 to year 2. In addition, the net rate of return to savers (measured by the consumption that must be foregone in year 1 for additional consumption in year 2) is higher with a consumption tax than with an income tax, and we may expect a higher rate of return to elicit some additional savings. Compared to consumption taxation, therefore, income taxation reduces the amount of saving both by decreasing savers' incomes and by lowering the rate of return they can earn.

The second effect of progressive income taxation upon savings stems from its different impact at different income levels. If the marginal propensity to save (MPS) were equal for all income levels, the progressivity of the income tax would not affect total saving more than an equal-yield proportional income tax. Both taxes would reduce total personal income by the same amount, and since the MPS was equal for all taxpayers, total saving would be reduced by the same amount in both cases. Many economists, however, believe that the MPS is an increasing function of income. If the marginal propensity to save is, in fact, increasing, then the progressive income tax reduces aggregate saving more than a proportional tax since the reduction in wealthy families' incomes is larger than under a proportional income tax.

There is some evidence that neither of these effects—the substitution of consumption for saving or the higher tax on heavy savers—is of major empirical importance. Using the highly progressive marginal tax rates of 1950 (when the maximum marginal rate was over 80 percent), Goode and Musgrave have estimated that a proportional income tax would reduce savings by 1 to 4 percent more than a flat-rate tax on all consumption expenditures.[7] The effect of progressivity is somewhat greater and depends on one's assumptions about how rapidly saving increases with income. Goode's estimate, based on a slowly increasing average propensity to save, was that in 1950 progressivity reduced saving by about 5 percent more than a proportional income tax would have. Musgrave's estimate was higher, derived from his assumption that marginal and average propensities to save rise over the entire range of incomes. This assumption is at variance with the conclusions of several recent studies of consumption and saving be-

[7] Richard Goode, *The Individual Income Tax* (Washington, D.C.: Brookings Institution, 1964), appendix C, pp. 335–37; and R. A. Musgrave, "Effects of Tax Policy on Private Capital Formation," in *Fiscal and Debt Management Policies,* Research Studies for the Commission on Money and Credit (Englewood Cliffs, N.J.: Prentice-Hall, 1963), pp. 65, 68.

havior, on the basis of which Goode's estimate must be preferred. In total, therefore, the net reduction in saving due to progressive income taxation (compared to a proportional tax on consumption expenditures) probably is less than 10 percent, and perhaps no more than half that, or between $2 billion and $4 billion of gross saving per year. Using 4 percent as the long-run growth rate, the retardation of economic growth thus is between 0.04 percent and 0.16 percent. Goode concludes that even this low estimate overstates the impact of progressive income taxation on growth.

RISK-TAKING. When producers invest in new productive facilities, they do so in the expectation of earning a return on the capital they have invested. If all investors were perfectly rational and had perfect knowledge about the chances of success in every investment opportunity, the expected return from any investment would equal that from any other. Different investments, however, would not all offer equal chances of success. For high-risk investments (with low probabilities of success) the return in the event that the investment paid off would have to be very high in order to yield the same expected return as other, less risky, investments. In the real world, all investors are not perfectly rational and do not have perfect knowledge but usually prefer not to undertake risky investments if a secure investment offers the same expected yield. This kind of behavior is called "risk aversion." As long as investors are risk averters, risky investments will have to offer a higher return—a risk premium—to induce investors to undertake them.

A numerical example may illustrate this point. Suppose that Mr. I. N. Vestor has two options, to buy safe government bonds that guarantee a return of 3 percent or to invest in Fly-by-Night Enterprises, with a probability of failure of 50 percent and a return of 8 percent in the event of success. If Vestor is indifferent between these two investments, then in effect he is demanding a 33.3 percent reward for risk-taking since the expected return to Fly-by-Night bonds is 4 percent. The imposition of a 50 percent proportional income tax now will reduce the net return on government bonds to 1.5 percent. The net return on Fly-by-Night bonds will fall to 4 percent in the event of success, for an expected return of 2 percent.

We cannot predict the net effect of the proportional income tax on overall risk-taking. Some investors will try to recoup their loss in net income by undertaking more risky investments. Others may respond to the reduction in the absolute risk premium by choosing less risky investments. The former effect is the income effect, since it is the change in income that influences some investors. The latter is the substitution effect, since the reduction in the reward for risk-taking (the lower absolute risk premium) causes a substitution between risk and expected return. Without empirical information about the magnitude of these effects, we cannot forecast the tax's effect on investors' preferences.

We do know, however, that a progressive tax will be more inimical to risk-taking than a proportional tax. In the foregoing examples, the higher dollar income that Vestor will receive if Fly-by-Night is successful may be taxed at, say, 75 percent. Then the expected yield from Fly-by-Night will be only 1 percent, since the net return in the event of success is only 2 percent, and Vestor clearly will prefer the safer, lower-yield government bonds. In general, a progressive tax will deter risk-taking more than a proportional tax will. We still cannot predict, however, whether a progressive tax will reduce risk-taking in comparison to the pretax allocation, since the income effect still may dominate the substitution effect.

The cost to the economy of this effect is the lower rate of growth that results from investors' unwillingness to take risks, given the returns available to them. In the example, I. N. Vestor initially was indifferent between the government bonds that offered him—and society—a rate of return of 3 percent and the Fly-by-Night bonds that offered an expected social rate of return of 4 percent. Vestor's risk aversion thus would cost society 1 percent in all cases in which he chose the safe bonds over the risky ones. The progressive income tax, however, made the government bonds much more attractive, since they offered higher expected yield and lower risk. Thus, the progressive tax imposed a cost on society in the form of a lower rate of return and a slower rate of growth.

To some extent, this disincentive effect can be reduced by loss offsets, which allow investors to deduct their losses from unsuccessful investments against their other income. In the preceding example, suppose that I. N. Vestor buys $1000 of Fly-by-Night bonds and loses all his money when the company goes bankrupt. If he can offset his loss against his other income, then his total tax liability will fall by $500 (under a proportional, 50 percent income tax). The net amount of capital that he has risked will be only $500, for he stands to gain $500 in reduced tax liability even if he loses the full $1000 investment. The 0.5 percent net risk premium that he receives on his $1000, however, amounts to a 1 percent premium on the $500 that he stands to lose. Thus, there is no reduction in the reward for risk-taking under a proportional tax with full loss offset. The income effect should increase overall risk-taking, since there will be no substitution effect to decrease investors' willingness to take risks. In other words, a proportional income tax with full loss offset will lead society as a whole to prefer more risky investments than before the tax.

Loss offsets may not stimulate risk-taking under a progressive income tax. The higher rates applied to higher incomes cause a reduction in the net risk premium (and, thus, a substitution effect) even if all losses can be offset against other income. Moreover, there is no guarantee that the investor will have other income against which to offset his losses. The federal income tax law contains liberal offset provisions allowing losses to be deducted from income over a nine-year period (three years before the loss and five years after, as well as the year in which the loss is incurred), but, even so, progressive taxation probably has some disincentive effect upon risk-taking. Before we can discuss the magnitude of this disincentive, however, we must examine some of the features of the tax law that offer incentives to particular uses of capital.

COMPOSITION OF INVESTMENT. Included in Gross Private Domestic Investment in the National Income and Product Accounts are the replacement of existing productive facilities, the creation of new productive capital stock, and some kinds of capital whose productivity is difficult to measure, such as private homes. The tax law affects these different types of capital unequally, principally through the capital gains provisions but also through some particular deductions.

As an empirical matter, capital gains seem most often to be received from investments in high-growth, relatively risky industries, rather than from industries with more conservative growth experience. Thus, the favorable treatment of capital gains increases the willingness of investors to accept high degrees of risk in return for better prospects of growth. To that extent, the capital gains provision counteracts the disincentive effect of progressive income taxation on risk-taking and leads to a faster rate of economic growth.

The positive incentive of capital gains, however, does not operate evenly on all investments. One effect is that firms are encouraged by their stockholders to retain earnings for reinvestment, perhaps leading to the inefficient operation of capital markets. Another problem is that capital gains can be earned from nonproductive investments as well as from productive ones. Ten thousand dollars invested in diamonds or in a fine watercolor may well earn greater capital gains than common stock of equal value, although neither the diamonds nor the painting contribute to economic growth in any real sense, while the stock makes funds available for productive investment. In addition, the long-term requirement that a capital asset be held at least six months serves in some cases to "lock in" investors and prevent their reallocating capital to attractive investments. A more powerful lock-in effect arises because capital gains are not taxed when assets are transferred at death. Instead, the legatee pays capital gains only on the appreciation occurring after he receives the assets.

The home ownership provisions of the tax law undoubtedly provide a major stimulus to home ownership and single-family housing, for the deductibility of mortgage interest and property taxes reduces the cost of private housing substantially compared to the cost of renting. As a result, taxpayers probably consume more private housing than is economically efficient, since the tax law in effect provides a subsidy, or negative excise. Too many resources thus are drawn into housing and away from producing other types of investment goods.

Finally, there is the uneven treatment of "human capital," investments that increase the productivity of labor. If a businessman buys a new machine, he can amortize its cost over its lifetime and deduct each year's amortization from his taxable income. A student in a vocational training course, however, cannot deduct the cost of the schooling over his lifetime or even over the duration of his next job. This differentiation makes investment in physical capital more attractive than investment in people and thus leads to overinvestment in physical plant and equipment. The cost of this misallocation in terms of foregone economic growth cannot be estimated. Many economists, however, have noted that trained, productive personnel are frequently in much shorter supply than physical capital, so that the rate of return on human capital may be substantially higher than that on physical capital.

Empirical evidence on the net disincentive effect of progressive income taxation is scanty. There is some indication that the disincentive effects on risk-taking do affect investors but that the low taxation of capital gains induces some offsetting increase in risky investment. Overall, however, the impact of the income tax on the level and composition of investment, and thus on the rate of growth, probably is small.

REFORM OF THE PERSONAL INCOME TAX

The importance of the capital gains provision in offsetting both the progressivity of income tax rates and their effect upon investment has led to many suggested reforms. Those involving the integration of the personal and corporate income taxes will be discussed in Chapter 8. Other proposals have concentrated on diminishing the inequities of capital gains taxation without reducing its stimulus for investment. Two desirable reforms might include lengthening the holding period, thus making it more difficult for speculators to receive capital gains treatment, and providing "free rollover" for investors who sell one capital asset in order to buy another. The "free rollover" provision applies to private housing (with some exceptions), so that a home-owner is not forced to pay taxes on capital gains realized from selling his house if he buys another house within a short time. Such a pro-vision would improve the functioning of capital markets, for it would eliminate the possibility of investors' being "locked in" during a period of changing market conditions. A related reform would elim-inate the "forgiveness" of capital gains transferred at death, thus im-proving both equity and the efficiency of allocating investible funds.

A reform discussed intermittently is substituting a simple propor-tional tax on AGI for the present complicated tax law. This proposal has much to recommend it from the viewpoint of administrative sim-plicity, savings to taxpayers in the form of lower costs of filing, and fewer misallocations caused by special features of the tax law. Its disadvantage is that it ignores the question of horizontal equity. Many of the special provisions in the present tax law compensate for cir-cumstances that affect one's ability to pay taxes. If a flat-rate tax were really to offer the advantage of simplicity, it would have to abol-ish most (if not all) of these special provisions. Although society as a whole might gain from the change, there would be many individual cases of inequity.

A simpler reform would take into account the cost of additional de-pendents by introducing variable exemptions. Under such a plan, the head of a household might be entitled to a $1000 personal exemption, his wife to $800, other adults to $600, and all children to $400. The justification for such a plan is that it would bring exemptions more closely into line with their original rationale, the cost of supporting a dependent. On the other hand, variable exemptions could decrease the progressivity of the tax structure since they would grant larger ex-emptions to the wealthy as well as to the poor. Among the alternatives to variable exemptions that do not have this defect are family allow-ances and tax credits. These plans would provide either income or deductions from tax liability on the basis of family size.

SUMMARY

A taxpayer's personal income tax liability is calculated by applying a set of marginal tax rates to his taxable income. Taxable income is equal to Adjusted Gross Income minus many categories of exclusions, exemptions, and deductions. The resulting pattern of tax incidence is mildly progressive with respect to "gross income" over most of the range of income but is slightly regressive at high levels of income (over about $200,000). Two of the major contributors to the difference between statutory and effective rates are income splitting, which favors married couples at the expense of single taxpayers and unmarried heads of households, and the treatment of capital gains, which accounts for virtually all the regressivity at high income levels.

Although there is some reason to believe that progressive taxation should decrease the supply of work effort (by making leisure relatively more attractive), empirical studies have concluded that the magnitude of this effect probably is insignificant. It is somewhat more likely that progressive income taxation reduces the rate of saving, relative to both proportional income taxation and consumption (sales and expenditure) taxes. Two estimates put the reduction in savings at from $2 billion to $4 billion per year (at current levels of income), for a rather small reduction in the overall growth rate in the economy.

Income taxation also affects investors' willingness to undertake risky investments. The effect of a proportional tax on risk-taking cannot be deduced without some empirical knowledge of the importance of income and substitution effects, but we know that a progressive tax will reduce the amount of risk-taking compared to a proportional income tax. This disincentive for risk-taking is reduced in the U.S. tax law by allowing loss offsets and offering favorable treatment for capital gains (which accrue largely from risky investments). Although the effect of the progressive income tax on aggregate investment and risk-taking probably is small, there may be distortions in the composition of investment as a result of the uneven treatment of owner-occupied housing, human capital, and the "lock-in" effects of capital gains provisions.

Most economists agree that the personal income tax is very nearly neutral in its effects on resource allocation. Some of the reforms proposed to increase equity include altering the definition of long-term capital gains and reducing the "lock-in" effects, substituting a simple proportional tax on AGI for the present, complex tax law, and improving equity at the lower end of the income distribution through variable exemptions, family allowances, or tax credits. Even without these reforms, the overall effect of the tax law is to provide a moderate degree of progressivity (vertical equity) while making allowances for differences in individuals' abilities to pay (horizontal equity).

8 Corporate Income Taxation

Perhaps the least-well understood of all major U.S. taxes is the one levied on the income of corporations. The corporation income tax was first enacted in 1909, four years before the personal income tax, and has been a major revenue source for the federal government ever since. In recent years, the tax has produced 20 to 25 percent of federal revenues, more than any other tax except that on personal income. Many states have adopted the corporation income tax, although the rates levied usually are low because corporations can easily change their legal place of business and thus avoid paying state taxes. Despite wide acceptance of the tax, however, there is no consensus among economists about how much and to whom the tax is shifted, what its effects are upon resource allocation, total investment, and growth, and whether the tax discriminates against certain types of income.

STRUCTURE AND RATIONALE

Since corporations are not individuals, for whom complicated questions of equity arise, the rate structure of the corporation income tax can be a very simple one. The tax consists of two parts, a "normal" tax, currently set at 22 percent, and a surtax of 26 percent. The current maximum marginal tax rate of 48 percent was established in the Revenue Act of 1964, which lowered the maximum marginal rate from the 52 percent level that had been in effect since 1952. (The highest marginal rate, in force from 1942 until 1949, was 53 percent on taxable income between $25,000 and $50,000. In addition, an excess-profits tax was levied during World War II.) As a concession to progressivity, since 1916 the corporation income tax has allowed either an exemption or a reduced tax at low levels of income. The current treatment is to exempt the first $25,000 of taxable income from the surtax, in effect making the marginal tax rate 22 percent of the first $25,000 of taxable income and 48 percent on the remainder. Although most corporations are subject only to the normal tax, roughly 90 percent of corporate taxable income is subject to both normal tax and surtax, so that the effective tax rate on taxable income (before credits) is about 45 percent.

The "taxable corporate income" upon which both normal tax and surtax are levied is the difference between a corporation's gross revenue and its costs of doing business. Although this definition of taxable income sounds very much like the economist's definition of "monopoly profits" (the difference between total receipts and the total cost of production), taxable income is defined to *include* the return to invested capital (usually paid as dividends). Economists would *exclude* this return on the grounds that it merely represents "normal profit," the competitive return to investment. There are many other divergences between the deductions from gross revenue allowed by the tax law and what an economist would view as the total cost of production. Many of these items offer an incentive for the corporation to misallocate its resources, as we shall see later in this chapter.

When the tax on the income of corporations was first enacted, it withstood a court challenge on the ground that it was not really a direct tax on income (then considered unconstitutional). Instead, it was argued, the tax was really an excise levied on the privilege of doing business as a corporation, a privilege extended by the government and carrying some very real advantages. Perhaps the greatest advantage of the corporate form of organization is limited liability. A stockholder's liability for corporate debts is limited to the amount of his investment (in contrast to a partnership, where each partner is legally liable for the debts of the entire business). The effect of this provision is to place a ceiling, or maximum, on the loss that any investor can suffer from purchasing stock. Accordingly, the returns investors demand as an incentive to invest are smaller for corporations than for other forms of business organization, and corporations have much easier access to capital than unincorporated enterprises do. The privilege of doing business as a corporation improves the firm's ability to raise capital and thus to grow.

Some of the other benefits of the corporate form of organization include perpetual life, greater liquidity for stockholders because shares can easily be marketed, and the possibility of arrangements with other corporations as an aid to growth. Although the market value of these advantages is hard to calculate, the original Supreme Court decision agreed that a corporation's profitability was a good measure of the benefits it derived from its favored status. Accordingly, the tax on corporation income was viewed as an excise on the value of benefits received. This approach is not, however, a true example of the benefit theory of taxation, for it ignores the use to which the government puts the revenue collected. Instead, it is really an application of the ability-to-pay principle, since it assumes that the privilege of corporate organization increases the corporation's ability to pay.

The view that corporations had an obligation to pay a tax was bolstered by the economic argument that a tax on the profits of corporations would be neutral with respect to allocation and would redistribute income from monopolistic corporations to the general public. This argument follows from the analysis of monopoly presented in Chapter 5. If corporations are interested in maximizing profits, they will seek the level of production at which marginal cost equals marginal revenue. The imposition of a tax will not affect either MC or MR, and thus the corporation's allocation will not be affected by the tax. Since the tax cannot be shifted by a reallocation of resources, its only effect will be to reduce the corporation's net earnings. Thus, the tax will reduce either the concentration of income (since corporations will have less income to distribute to wealthy stockholders) or the concentration of investible funds under the control of wealthy corporations. In either case, the redistribution will be desirable from the viewpoint of the electorate.

The main difficulty with this argument is that the real-world corporation income tax does not correspond to the economic model. Because of the incentives for misallocation supplied by particular features of the tax law, most economists agree that the tax is not neutral with respect to allocation. Moreover, a longer-run view of allocation raises the question of the effect that the tax has upon overall economic growth. Although there is a great deal of disagreement on the direction in which the tax is shifted, economists generally are convinced that the corporation income tax does not have the same effects as the "profits tax" of economic theory.

Despite the uncertainty surrounding its economic effects, the corporation income tax is an important and relatively stable element in the federal fiscal structure. The reason seems to be that at least politically, the net income of corporations is an attractive tax base. Although most corporations are "small," with taxable income less than $25,000, the public identifies corporations with large-scale production and control over resources and views the corporation income tax as a tax upon "bigness."

SHIFTING AND INCIDENCE

One reason economists are unsure about the direction and extent to which the corporation income tax is shifted is that the businessmen who manage corporations have refused to admit that it is a levy upon net, rather than gross, income. If corporations were all perfect competitors, economists could be confident that the market forces that bring other competitors to the point at which total revenue equals total cost would also apply to corporations. But the wide diversity of size among corporations, together with businessmen's protestations about how they actually respond to the tax, has led to a formulation of tax shifting under the assumption that corporate profits are *not* maximized.

In the words of one businessman: "Corporate taxes are simply costs, and the method of their assessment does not change this fact. Costs must be paid by the public in prices, and corporate taxes are thus in effect concealed taxes."[1] This statement fits well with the markup theory of pricing. According to this approach, businessmen set prices by calculating their average cost of production, and then apply a markup representing their desired profit (including the return on invested capital). The markup thus is a percentage of the average cost of production. The profits that businessmen expect to make are only occasionally realized, for their expected profits depend on their levels of production and their estimates of market demand. Actual production may either exceed or fall short of actual demand, and thus businessmen may have to lower or raise their prices in response to the demand conditions that actually prevail. In any case, their eventual equilibrium positions will not ordinarily be those of profit maximization.

This situation is illustrated in Figure 8.1. If the producer is faced with a demand curve D and marginal-revenue curve MR and production conditions described by his MC and ATC curves, his profit-maximizing output will be, of course, at (p_1, q_1) where his profit is $(p_1 - c_1)q_1$. If the producer is a markup price setter, however, he may simply apply a percentage markup to his ATC curve, leading to the ATC' curve as the basis for his output decision. Then, if he estimates market demand accurately, he will choose to produce q_0 and sell it at p_0. The position (p_0, q_0) is certainly not one of profit maximization, but it does enable the producer to earn his "target rate" of profit. It is important to note that he will earn his target rate only if he estimates demand accurately. If he overestimates demand, he will produce more than q_0 and will be forced to reduce his price in order to sell his

[1] E. M. Voorhees, U.S. Steel Corporation, reported in *The New York Times*, October 10, 1943.

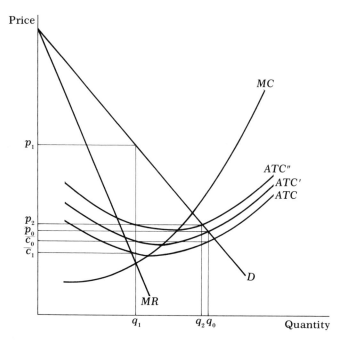

FIGURE 8.1   Nonmaximizing Behavior

output, thus earning less than his target rate. Conversely, he will earn a larger rate of profit than he expects if he underestimates demand. In general, however, not only will he fail to maximize profits but he may also fail to earn the profit rate he expects and desires.

Now suppose that a tax on monopoly profits is levied on the markup pricer. Even if there is no problem with identifying monopoly profits, the tax may not have the incidence economists predict. In theory, of course, the tax is supposed to be levied on an area like $(p_1 - c_1)q_1$. Even if the producer has chosen (p_0, q_0) as his equilibrium, he is still receiving monopoly profits measured by the area $(p_0 - c_0)q_0$. But when the producer is confronted with a tax levied on his monopoly profits, he may simply treat the tax liability as another fixed cost of production, not directly related to his level of output. He may then estimate his tax liability, add it to his other fixed and variable costs of production, and thus derive a new average-cost curve such as ATC''. On the basis of this average-cost curve, the producer will try to sell q_2 at a price of p_2, for this price includes not only his true average cost of production but also an allowance for his target rate of profit and for the tax liability that he *expects* to incur per unit of output.

In the attempt to incorporate his tax liability into the markup formula, the producer has shifted some of the tax to his consumers, for the price that they pay at (p_2, q_2) is higher, and the quantity that they consume is lower, than in the absence of the tax at (p_0, q_0). Whether or not *all* the tax is shifted depends on several factors, including the producer's elasticity of demand and his accuracy in estimating his tax liability. It is much harder to estimate "average tax liability" than average fixed cost, for total fixed cost is constant over wide ranges of output while total tax liability varies greatly. But if all producers try to shift 100 percent of their tax liability, we may expect some of them to shift more and some to shift less. The reason is that, just as in the case of markup pricing with no tax, not all producers will forecast equally well. Those who greatly overestimate their tax liabilities and accordingly make large increases in their prices may shift more than 100 percent of their actual tax liability. Those who forecast smaller tax liabilities or overestimate demand will shift less than their full tax.

This kind of shifting is called "short-run shifting," since it hinges on the firm's ability to vary its equilibrium price and output in response to the tax. The firm's optimum mix of factors of production and its access to capital need not be affected by the tax, so there will be no change in its (long-run) conditions of production. Short-run shifting will be *forward*, to consumers, for the producer avoids his tax burden only if he is able to raise prices. In order to raise prices, the producer must either be a monopolist or one of many competitors who all use the same markup pricing formula. In the latter case, moreover, all producers would have to make similar forecasts of tax liability if all were to raise prices equally. Since this event is rather unlikely, forward shifting will most probably be limited to monopolistic or oligopolistic industries.

Most economists are skeptical about the possibility of forward shifting, since a producer could shift his tax burden to consumers only if he were a monopolist or oligopolist facing an inelastic demand curve and preferred markup pricing to some attempt at profit maximization. An attempt to estimate the extent of forward shifting empirically was made in 1963 by Krzyzaniak and Musgrave, who concluded that the degree of shifting was *over* 100 percent for all industries and that an increase in tax liabilities of $1.00 per unit of capital stock would increase pre-tax profits by $1.35 per unit of capital.[2] This remarkable result has been attacked by a number of other economists on the basis that Krzyzaniak and Musgrave ignored important variables and included others that biased their results.[3] Several other authors have

[2] M. Krzyzaniak and R. A. Musgrave, *The Shifting of the Corporation Income Tax* (Baltimore: Johns Hopkins Press, 1963).

[3] Some of the counter-attacks are Richard Goode, "Rates of Return, Income Shares, and Corporate Tax Incidence," in M. Krzyzaniak (ed.), *Effects of Cor-*

estimated the degree of short-run shifting (that is, shifting with a given level of capital stock) as not significantly different from zero. Although the controversy still has not been resolved, later work has largely negated the initial impact of the Krzyzaniak and Musgrave study. Most economists now would agree that short-run shifting to consumers is unlikely to be near 100 percent in most industries.

If short-run shifting is not widespread, then firms probably are producing near their profit-maximizing outputs, and the prices that consumers pay in the short run are not very different from what they would have paid in the absence of the tax. In the long run, however, the corporation income tax may affect the rate of return on capital invested in corporations. Changes in the corporate rate of return will cause *long-run* shifting through changes in aggregate investment, the composition of investment among industries, and the incentives of savers to hold different kinds of assets.

Even if the corporation income tax did not differentiate between dividends and interest (the latter is deductible from gross income but the former is not), the tax would affect the rate of return to investors. Suppose that before the tax is imposed, I. N. Vestor decides to buy common stock in Fly-by-Night Enterprises (instead of the bonds that he bought in Chapter 7). He does so expecting to earn a rate of return of 4 percent, greater than the safe 3 percent he would receive from buying government bonds. The 1 percent differential is just sufficient to compensate him for the extra riskiness of the Fly-by-Night stock. If Vestor is an average stockholder and Fly-by-Night an average company, he will receive two kinds of income: dividends on the stock that he holds and capital gains (or losses) when he sells it. As long as Fly-by-Night is making profits and paying less than all its profits as dividends, the company's net worth will rise, and the price of its stock will rise also.[4]

Now suppose that a corporation income tax is imposed on Fly-by-Night's profits. If the company keeps its dividend payout constant, Vestor will receive smaller capital gains because some of Fly-by-Night's addition to net worth is taxed away. If the company increases

---

poration Income Tax (Detroit: Wayne State University Press, 1966); R. J. Gordon, "The Incidence of the Corporation Income Tax in U.S. Manufacturing, 1925–62," *American Economic Review* 57 (September 1967): 731–58; and J. G. Cragg, A. C. Harberger, and P. Mieszkowski, "Empirical Evidence on the Incidence of the Corporation Income Tax," *Journal of Political Economy* 75 (December 1967): 811–21.

[4] Capital gains may also result from increases in expected earnings. But the corporation income tax will affect anticipated earnings in the same way as actual ones, so the analysis is valid for the general case as well as for the models without expectations.

its dividends, Vestor will have to pay a higher tax on the return on his investment (because capital gains are taxed at a rate no more than half of the rate on dividends), so the net return on his investment will still fall. In addition, Fly-by-Night's internal resources for investment and expansion will be depleted, so the market value of the firm's stock will suffer, and Vestor's capital gains will fall. No matter how the firm responds to the corporation income tax, the effect of the tax must be to reduce the net rate of return to investors in corporations.

This conclusion rests on the assumption that corporations will not be able to avoid a reduction in the after-tax rates of return that they pay to investors. One way that this outcome could be sidestepped would be for corporations to raise prices to consumers, thus increasing their pretax profit rates and keeping their after-tax rates of return constant. As we have seen, however, the balance of empirical evidence suggests that corporations are not able to shift their entire tax liabilities forward while keeping their capital stock constant. Another possibility would be for corporations to shift the tax backward to employees in the form of lower wages, but this alternative is implausible for two reasons. In view of the presence of strong unions in many industries, to assume that corporations—*all* corporations, not just the giants—have the power to lower wages at will is unrealistic. Moreover, an attempt to reduce wages would enable unincorporated businesses to hire labor away from corporations. It is difficult to escape the conclusion that the eventual incidence of the corporation income tax must be a reduction in the rate of return on capital invested in the corporate sector.

Even a well designed corporation income tax, therefore, will make investment in corporations less attractive than other allocations of resources. In the next section we will examine some of the distortions of allocation introduced by the present federal corporation income tax, which is not "well designed" because of its treatment of interest, capital consumption, and other particular allocations of resources. Now, however, let us trace the impact of a corporate profits tax upon the level and composition of aggregate investment.

Figure 8.2 indicates how the profits tax will influence both corporations and unincorporated enterprises. Part A shows the situation of Fly-by-Night Enterprises and I. N. Vestor before and after the tax. Fly-by-Night's ability to offer Vestor a return on his investment is shown by the company's marginal efficiency of investment (MEI_c) curve, which indicates the rate of return the firm will receive on increments in its capital stock. Vestor's willingness to supply funds depends only on the net rate of return he expects to receive, and thus his supply curve is not affected by the imposition of the corporation income tax.

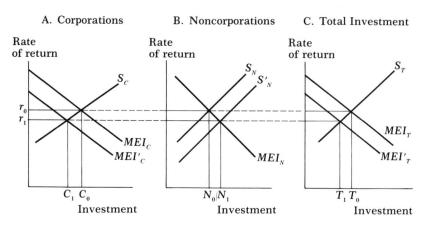

FIGURE 8.2   Effect of Corporation Income Tax on Investment

Before the tax, Fly-by-Night invests C_0 of Vestor's capital and pays him a rate of return r_0. After the tax, however, Fly-by-Night can no longer offer Vestor the same rate of return, for its total profits are reduced by the amount of its tax liability. Accordingly, its MEI shifts down to MEI'_C, the difference between the two schedules representing the company's tax liability. At this lower schedule of rates of return, Vestor finds himself less willing to invest in Fly-by-Night, and he reduces his level of lending to C_1 where he receives a rate of return r_1.

How much of an impact the tax has on the level of corporate investment depends on both the tax rate (the shift in the MEI curve) and the interest-elasticity of Vestor's supply curve. As long as the firm is earning *some* return on invested capital, the tax rate is greater than zero and the MEI must shift in response to the tax. And unless Vestor's supply schedule is perfectly inelastic (that is, vertical), the reduced profitability of investment leads him to cut back on his supply of funds. Thus, the tax must lower the level of investment in the corporate sector.

One reason that Vestor's supply schedule to the corporate sector may not be perfectly elastic (horizontal) is that the alternative uses of his investment funds may not offer him very high rates of return. If Fly-by-Night is typical of the entire corporate sector, then the rate of return on all corporate investment falls as a result of the corporation income tax, and investors find that no corporation is able to offer r_0 as the rate of return on C_0 of new capital. As shown in Figure 8.2C, the MEI curve for all businesses (corporate and noncorporate) must fall as a result of the corporation income tax, since the corporate MEI falls and the noncorporate MEI is unchanged.

The alternatives to investing in the corporate sector are consumption and investing in unincorporated enterprises. Although the supply schedule of savings is not affected by the tax, the reduced rate of return leads to a reduction in the amount of funds that consumers are willing to divert from current consumption. Accordingly, total investment falls (from T_0 to T_1) in response to the lower rate of return that investors receive on their capital (r_1 instead of r_0). One effect of the corporation income tax, therefore, is to reduce the amount of new capital formation and retard the rate of economic growth.

In addition to reducing the level of aggregate investment, the corporation income tax distorts the allocation of investment funds between corporate and noncorporate businesses. This effect is shown in Figure 8.2B. The profitability of noncorporate investment is unaffected by the corporation income tax, and so the MEI_N curve in part B does not shift as a result of the tax. But the reduction in the rate of return that investors can earn in the corporate sector may increase their willingness to supply funds to the noncorporate sector. In other words, the opportunity cost of noncorporate investment falls due to the imposition of the tax. (Even if we consider increased consumption as an alternative to corporate investment, we can expect some of the reduction in the level of corporate investment to trickle into the noncorporate sector). Thus, investors may increase their supply curve to noncorporate firms from S_N to S_N'. The level of noncorporate investment then rises from N_0 to N_1, where the rate of return in the noncorporate sector is exactly equal to its opportunity cost, the rate of return in the corporate sector.

Although this reallocation of his investment portfolio is profitable as far as each individual investor is concerned, it is inefficient from society's viewpoint. The rate of return each investor receives on all his capital is r_1, but society receives a return on corporate investment that is higher by the amount of the tax on corporate income. When an investor shifts some of his assets from corporate to noncorporate investment, the social rate of return on the amount of capital shifted falls from r_0 (at the margin) to r_1. Since the same argument applies to all investors in corporate and noncorporate assets, the corporation income tax will impose two allocation costs on the economy: (1) a reduction in total investment and a lower growth rate, and (2) a misallocation of resources from (socially) profitable corporate investment into less (socially) profitable noncorporate investment. This conclusion does not make a value judgment about corporations' investments. It simply says that if capital was allocated among investments efficiently (or nearly so) before the corporation income tax was imposed, then the post-tax allocation is socially inefficient.

Empirical evidence on the cost of the long-run shifting of the corporation income tax is rather scanty. One reason is that the magnitude of the revenue yield forces us to consider the cost of the tax compared to alternative taxes, rather than to estimate the cost as a deviation from a zero-tax norm. Since the tax is levied on capital in the corporate sector, the alternatives we may consider are a tax on all capital and a tax on all output.

As long as producers are able to substitute one factor of production for another if their prices change, the corporation income tax distorts allocation in two ways. Capital flows from the corporate sector into unincorporated enterprises, so that the social rate of return on capital falls (Figure 8.2C). Producers are unable to use resources efficiently, and the marginal rate of transformation is distorted. Moreover, prices of corporations' products rise relative to those of goods produced by unincorporated firms, and consumers' marginal rates of substitution are not equated with even the distorted marginal rate of transformation.

Using the assumptions that the elasticities of demand among products and of supply between factors are unity, Harberger has made crude estimates that these distortions caused by the corporation income tax impose a net cost to society of about 4 percent of the total return to capital.[5] About 20 percent of national income, or $160 billion, accrues as capital income. Using Harberger's estimate, the excess cost of the corporation income tax, compared to a uniform tax on all types of capital, is $6.4 billion. The meaning of this estimate is that if the corporation income tax were replaced with an equal-yield uniform tax (of about 30 percent) on all capital income, the gain that society would receive from the reallocation of resources would be as great as if national income increased by $6.4 billion with no change in taxes.

A different estimate is reached if producers cannot substitute at all between one factor of production and another. In this case, the excess cost of the corporation income tax is smaller because society does not realize new production possibilities from removing the tax on corporate capital. Instead, a tax on capital is equivalent to a tax on total output, with the difference that a tax on corporate capital is levied at a higher rate on corporations that use capital extensively. Thus, the corporation income tax is, in effect, a discriminating output tax levied at the highest rates on capital-intensive corporations and at the lowest rate (zero) on noncorporate producers. Replacing the corporation income tax with a general tax (of about 8 percent) on the value of each firm's output and including unincorporated businesses as well as corporations would yield a benefit to society that Harberger estimates as

    [5] A. C. Harberger, "The Corporation Income Tax: An Empirical Appraisal," in U.S. House of Representatives, Ways and Means Committee, *Tax Revision Compendium* (1959), pp. 231–50.

0.1 to 0.2 percent of national income, or between $800 million and $1.6 billion. The only benefit is that consumers' marginal rates of substitution can now adjust to the value that the marginal rate of transformation had before the tax rather than after it.

Factor substitutability differs from industry to industry. For the economy as a whole, it probably lies between the two extremes (zero and unity) for which we have estimated the excess cost of the corporation income tax. If we take a middle value from our range of estimates, the cost of the misallocation of investment caused by the tax may be from $3.5 billion to $4 billion, or about 10 percent of the tax yield ($36.7 billion in 1969). This estimate includes the cost of the specific disincentives discussed in the next section of this chapter.

To estimate the effect of the tax on aggregate investment requires some assumptions about saving. About one-quarter of gross investment is financed by personal saving, with business saving—undistributed profits and capital consumption allowances—accounting for the other 75 percent of invested funds. Personal saving usually is thought to be rather interest-inelastic, so that the supply of savings curve (Figure 8.2C) might be nearly vertical if it were drawn to show the responses of personal savers. The corporation income tax should reduce business saving through a reduction in undistributed profits, but there is no evidence of falling business saving. One reason is the progressive liberalization of depreciation (discussed in the next section) that has increased the supply of investible funds to corporations. Another reason is that high corporation income tax rates have generally been accompanied by high personal income tax rates. The favorable capital gains provision is even more favorable when marginal tax rates on personal income are high, and stockholders are more willing to let corporations retain their earnings in order to reap future capital gains.

Although theory tells us that the corporation income tax must reduce the level of aggregate investment, changes in the tax law apparently have offset this tendency so that total investment has not, in fact, been reduced. Nonetheless, the distortions in the allocation of investible funds between corporate and noncorporate sectors may be very costly. In terms of Figure 8.2C, the difference between T_1 and T_0 apparently is very small. But the difference between r_0 and r_1 causes misallocations of investment whose cost may be $3.5 billion per year.

RESOURCE ALLOCATION

Interest and Dividends. The federal corporation income tax is not the ideal instrument whose effects we examined in the preceding section. One of its principal incentives for misallocation is the deductibility that it extends to interest payments but denies to dividends. The result of this differential treatment is that corporations have an incentive to use debt financing rather than equities to pay for new investment. This provision favors large corporations, which have better access to bank funds than smaller corporations. Most corporations (and most other businesses), however, are reluctant to use debt financing because the fixed interest charges increase the firm's vulnerability to fluctuations in its cash flow over the business cycle. As well as discriminating in favor of large corporations, therefore, the deductibility of interest fails to remove the growth disincentive of the tax.

Capital Consumption. A second distortion is introduced through deductions for capital consumption. Since changes in capital productivity are virtually impossible to measure and the lifetimes of capital goods cannot accurately be predicted, the tax law specifies alternative patterns of depreciation and the service lifetimes over which each item of capital equipment is to be depreciated. These specifications are important because capital consumption allowances provide the largest single source of investible funds for most corporations. The trend in the tax law has been toward accelerated depreciation (that is, depreciating larger proportions of the initial cost of a capital good in the early years of its productive life) and shorter service lives (with larger amounts of depreciation per year).[6]

One effect of this liberalization of capital consumption allowances has been to reduce the effective corporation income tax rate by several percentage points. Another effect has been to encourage the substitution of capital for labor, since the cost of capital is reduced by both accelerated depreciation and shorter service lives. A further substitution of capital for labor was encouraged by the investment tax credit in force between 1962 and 1969. This credit allowed corporations to deduct from their tax liability (*not* their taxable income) 7 percent of the cost of their new capital equipment with service lives of eight years or more. Structures were excluded and smaller credits applied to shorter-life equipment and utilities.

In addition to affecting factor proportions, accelerated depreciation, shortened service lives, and the investment tax credit probably have increased the level of corporate investment. The magnitude of the

---

[6] The Tax Reform Act of 1969 reduced allowable accelerated depreciation from the rates prevailing before 1969, but corporations are still allowed to use a variety of accelerated depreciation methods. The value of accelerated depreciation is that it allows firms to postpone their tax payments, earning interest in the meantime. Thus, accelerated depreciation has the same effect as interest-free loans to producers.

increase is still the subject of a great deal of controversy among economists. Early studies indicated that a substantial increase in investment had occurred. Later work, however, has concluded that little substitution of capital for labor has taken place and that the income effect (the increase in corporations' investment funds) also has been small.[7]

Mineral Depletion. As a corporation "uses up" its capital stock in the course of production, it is allowed to deduct from its taxable income an amount that supposedly represents the cost of the capital equipment used. If the capital asset is not a machine or a building but is instead an oil well or a coal mine, the firm still should be allowed a deduction related to the decline in the value of its asset. This deduction is in fact offered under the tax law and is called a "depletion allowance."

While there is little disagreement over the principle behind depletion, there is a great deal of controversy over the appropriate level of the depletion allowance. At present, depletion is computed as a percentage of gross receipts and ranges from a high of 22 percent for oil and gas (under the tax reform of 1969, reduced from 27.5 percent in earlier years) to 5 percent for gravel, sand, clay, stone, and certain types of shells. The maximum amount of the depletion allowance is not permitted to exceed half of the property's net income.

The economic basis for depletion, the decline in the value of a capital good, would be more nearly met if depletion were computed as a fraction of investment rather than of sales. In oil and gas, for example, the current allowance amounts to estimating the useful life of an oil pool or natural gas field at between four and five years (using straight-line methods; somewhat higher if accelerated depreciation methods are used). Clearly, this practice confers an enormous subsidy when compared with the actual useful life of many discoveries. (The Alaskan North Slope has been estimated to contain enough oil to satisfy *all* U.S. demand for thirty years.) The result of current percentage depletion allowances is to subsidize overinvestment in high-depletion industries and thus to create a substantial misallocation of resources.

Research and Development. Most businesses recognize that research frequently is a profitable investment. If a firm is unable to increase its own profitability as the result of its research activities, it may none-

[7] For example, see the initial study by R. E. Hall and D. W. Jorgenson, "Tax Policy and Investment Behavior," *American Economic Review* 57 (June 1967): 391–414; and comments by R. M. Coen and R. Eisner, *American Economic Review* 59 (June 1969): 370–88.

theless be able to patent its discovery and capitalize on it in that way. The deferred nature of the benefits makes research directly comparable to other investments. But unlike other investments, a corporation is allowed to deduct from its taxable income all its current outlays on research and development. The result is to divert too many resources from other investments into research activities and to subsidize industries in which research is a principal investment. The misallocation caused by the deductibility of research and development, however, may be offset by a tendency to undervalue their future benefits. As we saw in the Downs model, uncertainty and remoteness in time will lead to undervaluation of benefits, no less in the case of private research and development than in that of many public programs.

Advertising. Corporations are allowed to expense advertising outlays in the same manner as research and development costs. There is some evidence, however, that advertising builds up corporations' "good will" and thus leads to higher profit rates. In this sense, therefore, advertising is analogous to any other capital expenditure (or research), and outlays on advertising logically should be depreciated, rather than expensed. Weiss has estimated that about one-third of the purchasers of many consumer goods would switch brands in the absence of continued advertising, although the fraction varies widely among industries.[8] The tax provision that lets advertisers write off all their costs, rather than only one-third of their total outlays, thus leads to an estimated subsidy (reduction in tax revenues) of about 6.4 percent of total advertising investment. The subsidy is even higher for industries that advertise very heavily.

Charitable Contributions. Corporations are businesses and are not allowed the exemptions and deductions permitted under the personal income tax. The one exception is corporate charitable contributions, which are fully deductible in the same manner as personal charitable contributions. One reason for the deduction is that the alternative to private philanthropy is public support of charitable activities, and on this basis the corporate deduction is as valid as the personal one. In the case of private contributions, however, we may argue that taxpayers would express their preferences through voting if they could not deduct the cost of private charity. Our voting system gives no weight to corporations' preferences, and there is some question as to

[8] Leonard W. Weiss, "Advertising, Profits, and Corporate Taxes," *Review of Economics and Statistics* 51 (November 1969): 421–30.

whether their preferences among charities should be encouraged by the tax law.

INTEGRATING CORPORATION
AND PERSONAL INCOME TAXES

The corporation income tax imposes a kind of double taxation on dividend recipients. First their rate of return on investment is reduced by the corporate tax, and then they must pay personal tax on the income they receive. Thus, the double tax creates a horizontal inequity between dividend recipients and taxpayers receiving other kinds of income (wages, interest, etc.). In addition, the double tax is levied at a higher rate on the poor than on the rich because the tax liability of the poor on their dividend income would be zero without the corporate tax but is 48 percent with it. Thus, double taxation provides a disincentive for low-income groups to invest in dividend-paying assets and thereby misallocates resources.

The attempt to eliminate this double taxation in the current tax law is through the $100 dividend exclusion. Under this provision, a taxpayer is allowed to exclude the first $100 of dividends received (up to $200 for a joint return) and thus reduce his taxable income. For wealthy taxpayers, the value of this exclusion is minuscule (a maximum of $140). Moreover, the value of the exclusion depends on the taxpayer's marginal tax rate and benefits the rich substantially more than the poor. The dividend exclusion fails to remove the excess burden that the corporation income tax levies on dividend recipients.

There are two analytically correct methods of eliminating this excess burden: the deduction by the corporation of dividends paid (or, alternatively, treating part of the corporation tax as withholding on personal incomes) and considering all corporate profits as accruing proportionately to stockholders.

Deduction of Dividends. The excess burden on dividend recipients would be reduced if corporations were allowed to deduct from their taxable income the full amount of their dividend payout. This provision would place dividends more nearly on a par with interest, although the capital gains received from increases in corporate net worth still would be reduced by the corporation income tax. Corporations would have an incentive to distribute larger dividends (and stockholders would demand them), and the increased payouts would benefit poor stockholders more than rich ones due to the difference in marginal tax rates. The deduction of dividends would reduce the double taxation of the poor by the same fraction as the double taxation of the rich, unlike the current dividend exclusion that benefits the rich more than the poor.

The trouble with deducting dividends is that it may hamper the growth of corporations, since most investment is financed out of internal funds (capital consumption allowances and retained earnings). To enable corporations to retain the same amount of earnings and thus foster growth, a method equivalent to deducting dividends is to treat part of the corporation income tax as withholding on stockholders' dividend income. Each stockholder would include in his computation of taxable income the amount of the tax that the corporation was considered to have paid and then would deduct that amount from his tax liability. Since the rich pay a higher tax than the poor on the additional income represented by the corporation's "withholding," the net deduction from tax liability would be worth less to the rich, and the net effect would be to reduce the "double taxation" burden by the same proportion for taxpayers at all income levels. In this case there would be less demand for corporations to distribute dividends because taxpayers would benefit from the credit even if the corporation had to pay some income tax.

Distribution to Stockholders. This method of integrating the corporation and personal income taxes is frequently called the "partnership method" because it is equivalent to making stockholders full partners in the assets of the corporation. Under this approach, the corporation income tax would be abolished, and total corporate income would be apportioned to stockholders on a per-share basis. Each stockholder would then have to pay personal income tax on the amount of his apportioned income from the corporation. Presumably the tax would be due whether the stockholder actually received his share of the corporation's income or the corporation retained a portion of its profits. Conceptually, the partnership method makes great sense, and under the current tax law it can be used by "closely held" corporations with fewer than ten stockholders. For larger corporations, however, it presents a dilemma. Either stockholders would demand that earnings be distributed to help them meet their tax liabilities, in which case the corporation's investment and growth would be hampered, or individual stockholders would have to juggle their asset positions to obtain enough cash to pay their taxes. The advantage of the partnership method is that it would simplify the measurement of capital gains (since one of the major determinants of stock prices, changes in net worth, would automatically be included in stockholders' income). But the disincentive for corporate saving and the inequity to individual stockholders are strong arguments against this approach.

SUMMARY

Originally levied as an excise tax on the privilege of doing business as a corporation, the corporation income tax has been popular with the general public largely because it is viewed as a tax on "bigness." Economists initially thought that the tax would not affect resource allocation and would only redistribute income away from corporate investors. Monopolistic or oligopolistic corporations, however, may be able to shift the tax to consumers in the short run by raising their prices and maintaining their net rates of return at pretax levels with no reduction in capital stock.

If corporations cannot shift the tax to consumers or employees, then the tax will eventually come to rest on investors. As a result, rates of return will fall for all investment (noncorporate as well as corporate), and some investment funds will shift to unincorporated enterprises. Prices of goods produced by the corporate sector will rise relative to the prices of noncorporate goods, and the allocation of resources will be inefficient. One estimate of the cost of this distortion of resource allocation is about $3.5 billion, or 10 percent of the revenue yield of the corporation income tax. There is no evidence that the tax has reduced aggregate investment. The theoretical disincentive that the tax creates apparently has been offset by specific incentives.

Among the particular provisions in the tax law that lead to resource misallocation are the deductibility of interest but not dividends, the liberalization of capital consumption allowances, the favorable treatment of mineral depletion and research and development, and the deductibility of corporate charitable contributions. Integration of the personal and corporation income taxes would require either the deductibility of dividends (or equivalent treatment) or the general use of the "partnership method" now used to allocate the assets of corporations with only a few shareholders.

Our discussion of the corporation income tax has indicated (but not resolved) some of the areas of uncertainty about the effects of the tax on allocation, distribution, and growth. Although many economists believe that the adverse effects of the tax are substantial, the corporation income tax is likely to remain a part of our revenue structure precisely because its excess costs cannot clearly be shown or measured.

9 Sales and Excise Taxation

Taxes on consumption have been one of the most popular sources of revenue at all levels of government for many years. Before 1913, when passage of the Sixteenth Amendment permitted Congress to levy taxes directly on income, taxes on particular goods and imports provided nearly all federal revenue. Even though the federal government has recently lowered its rates on most taxed commodities, excise taxes and customs duties were projected to yield 10 percent of federal revenues through fiscal year 1971, compared to about 13 percent ten years earlier. Sales taxation is the primary revenue source for most state governments and is being used increasingly by local governments to supplement the yield of the property tax. Sales taxes yield a steady 25 to 30 percent of the total revenues of state and local governments.

There are two major types of taxes on consumption. Excises are taxes levied on particular goods or allocations of resources. They are used primarily by the federal government, although many states levy some excises in addition to more general taxes. Sales taxation is levied on a broader base than excises: either total consumption expenditures (in the case of an expenditure tax, discussed in Chapter 7) or the total revenue or output of certain businesses. Most states and some local governments levy sales taxes; the federal government does not do so at present, although there has been some discussion of adding a form of sales tax, the value-added tax, to the federal tax structure.

EXCISE TAXATION

A bewildering variety of excises is levied by both the federal government and many states and localities. The chief federal excises are those on liquor (including wine and beer), tobacco, and gasoline, but even after the excise tax reductions of 1969 some of the remaining taxed commodities included matches, tires, firearms and ammunition, air travel, gambling, dairy products, and narcotics. In addition to taxing many of these same goods and services, state and local governments typically levy excises upon real estate transactions (in the form of recording deeds), automobile registration, particular occupations, and the gross receipts of particular industries including communications and utilities. Many state and local (and some federal) services are paid for by revenues collected from the beneficiaries: refuse collection, transportation facilities, and public utilities are some examples. Closely related to excise taxes on private sector goods, these charges for public sector goods are called "user charges."

One of the most ancient forms of excises is customs duties. In the United States, import duties (for example, the stamp tax) were levied by the British government before the Revolutionary War, and after independence was won the new government relied on tariffs as a major revenue source. Import duties were so prolific a source of revenue that they were reduced toward the end of the nineteenth century because the federal government was embarrassed by its large budgetary surplus. More recently, however, the revenue yield of tariffs has become insignificant compared to that of the personal and corporate income taxes. The principal function of excises on imports now is to encourage particular reallocations of resources, such as the purchase of domestic rather than foreign investment or consumption goods.

The statutory incidence of excises usually is on the producer or seller, but most economists believe that the effective incidence of most excises is shifted largely to consumers of the taxed commodities. Producers treat excise taxes as a cost of production that varies with the level of output, whether the tax is levied *ad valorem* (as a percentage of the value of output) or as a certain amount per unit of sale. Most excises are levied on an *ad valorem* basis, but some—including the important federal excises on liquor, tobacco, and gasoline—impose a charge per unit of output. In either case, the excise simply shifts the producer's cost curve, forcing him to charge a higher price in order to recoup his total cost of production (including the tax).

Given the definitions of shifting cited in Chapter 8, we can say that an excise will be completely shifted forward, to consumers, if the

product's price rises by the full amount of the tax, so that only consumers are forced to reallocate their resources. Complete backward
shifting can occur only if the product's price remains unchanged despite the imposition of the tax and factor incomes fall as a result of
either lower factor prices or reductions in the levels of employment of
factors of production. At any intermediate degree of shifting, both the
producer and some other economic units are forced to reallocate their
resources as a result of the tax.

These cases are shown in Figure 9.1. In part A, demand is perfectly
inelastic with respect to price, so that consumers demand q_0 of output
no matter what the price is. The imposition of a per unit excise tax
shifts the producer's supply curve from S_1 to S_2, forcing him to charge
a higher price per unit of output (p_2 instead of p_1). The amount of tax
revenue is $(p_2 - p_1)q_0$, and total expenditures on the product rise by the
full amount of the tax. Thus, the producer's after-tax revenue is equal
to his total revenue before the tax was imposed. While it is unlikely
that any good exhibits a perfectly inelastic demand curve over the
range of all possible prices, the demand for many goods probably is
highly inelastic for fairly small price changes.

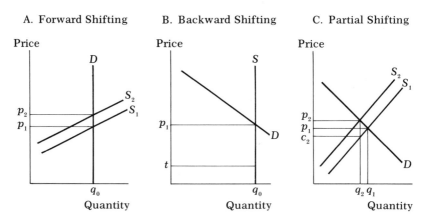

FIGURE 9.1   Excise Tax Incidence

In part B, the opposite case is shown. Here the marginal cost of production is effectively zero up to q_0, and then it becomes infinite. Imposition of an excise tax shifts the marginal cost of the first q_0 units up
to t but does not affect the supply price of additional units of output.
Since the demand curve does not shift, the after-tax price and quantity are the same as the pretax ones. The only difference is that the
producer's profit (in the short run, the excess of revenue over the vari-

able costs of production) falls from $p_1 q_0$ to $(p_1 - t)q_0$. This case is even less likely to occur than the inelastic-demand case. The only goods exhibiting such a supply curve would be those naturally available in fixed amounts. For such goods, the producer's return is pure economic rent, since rent is defined as the excess of market price (p_1 in the diagram) over the supply price of the good (zero, up to q_0, in the diagram). To the extent that land satisfies the condition of fixed availability at a zero price, an excise on the return to land is allocationally neutral. (We will return to property taxation in Chapter 10.)

Two parallel cases not shown in Figure 9.1 are those of perfectly elastic supply and perfectly elastic demand. In a perfectly competitive industry with a constant average total cost of production, the imposition of an excise tax will shift the (horizontal) industry supply curve vertically by the amount of the tax. If the demand curve is not perfectly inelastic, the equilibrium quantity demanded will fall, and some firms will leave the industry. The equilibrium price will rise by the full amount of the tax, and thus this case will be one of complete forward shifting. Conversely, if the industry should face a perfectly elastic demand curve, the imposition of an excise will simply shift the after-tax demand curve downward by the full amount of the tax, leading to a reduction in factor incomes and complete backward shifting. Local businessmen frequently claim that city or county excise taxes would have this effect.

The most probable case is shown in part C, where both the demand and the supply curves exhibit some price-elasticity. Here, the imposition of the (per-unit) excise drives the supply curve from S_1 to S_2. At the higher price consumers reduce the quantity demanded from q_1 to q_2; the equilibrium price thus rises from p_1 to p_2. Consumers are worse off because they have lost consumer surplus in the amount of the trapezoidal area bounded by p_1, p_2, the vertical axis, and the demand curve. Producers are worse off because their rent has fallen by the trapezoidal area bounded by p_1, c_2 (the marginal cost of q_2), the vertical axis, and supply curve S_1. The amount of tax revenue, however, is only $(p_2 - c_2)q_2$. Thus, the total loss in welfare exceeds the amount of revenue by the triangular area bounded by q_2, the demand curve, and supply curve S_1. This argument leads to the conclusion that consumers would be better off if they paid a tax of $(p_2 - p_1)q_2$ levied on consumers' surplus, and producers would prefer a tax of $(p_1 - c_2)q_2$ levied on their profit or rent. Thus, excise taxation apparently imposes an allocative cost, or burden, in excess of the revenue yield. We will return to this point in the next section of this chapter.

Shifting need not stop with the product market. Figure 9.2 shows the possible effect of an excise tax on a factor of production, labor.

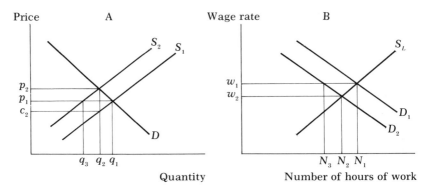

FIGURE 9.2   Excise Tax Shifting to Factors of Production

Part A reproduces Figure 9.1C, the case of partial shifting. When the tax shifts the supply curve from S_1 to S_2, the producer intends to reduce his level of production from q_1 to q_3 at the price (p_1) then prevailing in the market. If he makes no adjustments in prices or wages, his demand for labor will fall from N_1 (in Figure 9.2B) to N_3, the number of hours of labor he needs to produce q_3. Thus, his demand for labor shifts from D_1 to D_2 as a result of the excise tax. Eventually the product market equilibrium adjusts to (p_2, q_2), and the labor market equilibrium becomes (w_2, N_2) after the tax. Workers are also bearing some of the burden of the tax, for their income has fallen from $w_1 N_1$ to $w_2 N_2$, and their "rent" (the excess of wages over the price necessary to call forth that amount of labor) has been reduced by a trapezoidal area bounded by w_1, w_2, the vertical axis, and the labor supply curve.

Certain principles about elasticities and shifting emerge from this discussion. If product demand is inelastic or if product supply is elastic, shifting to consumers may approach 100 percent. If product supply is inelastic or if product demand is elastic, shifting to consumers will be close to zero. In intermediate cases, the larger the price-elasticity of supply is relative to the price-elasticity of demand, the greater will be the degree of shifting to consumers. The same principles apply in the factor market. If product demand is fairly elastic or if product supply is rather inelastic, so that producers are unable to shift the burden of the excise to consumers, the reduction in factor prices will vary directly with the elasticity of demand for the factors and inversely with their elasticity of supply.

Given these conclusions about elasticity and the degree of shifting, any estimate of the extent of shifting in the real world must rest on some estimates of the price-elasticities of demand and supply for taxed commodities. Most economists agree that demand is quite price-inelastic for many of the most important taxed commodities, including liquor, tobacco, and gasoline. For many other products, demand is thought to be inelastic over the range of the tax; that is, adding 5 percent to the price of an airline ticket or 6 cents to the price of a gallon of lubricating oil probably does not induce the consumer to substitute another good for the taxed one. Consumers presumably will decrease their demand for taxed goods (and untaxed ones) because the tax will reduce their incomes and thus reduce their ability to allocate resources overall. But this effect is not limited to excise taxation, so an excise cannot be said to rest on the producer if it only reduces demand through a reduction in consumer incomes. Thus, if demand for taxed goods is price-inelastic, excises will tend to be shifted completely to consumers, with allocative effects similar to those of an income tax.

If the tax is not shifted completely to consumers, the burden of an excise must eventually come to rest upon entrepreneurs and factors of production. The supply curves of factors are likely to be rather elastic for single industries, as opposed to factor supplies in the economy as a whole. Unionization may increase labor's supply-elasticity in particular industries, and capital's high degree of mobility will lead to a similar result. Demand for both labor and capital, however, is less likely to be elastic with respect to price, especially if producers find it difficult to substitute one factor for another. Thus, if demand for a taxed commodity is elastic and the tax cannot be shifted to consumers, the result is likely to be a reduction in the level of factor use (rather than factor prices) in the taxed industry. An excise tax on a product with a price-elastic demand probably will lead to a reduction in the scale of production in the industry.

On balance, most excises probably are shifted to consumers due to their price-inelasticity of demand. In the long run, however, excises may encourage changes in patterns of allocation and consequent shifts in the industry composition of demand. These secondary allocation effects may be substantial and may impose major distributional costs on the factors of production employed in the taxed industries.

EXCESS BURDEN OF EXCISE TAXATION

An income tax is nearly neutral in its effects upon the allocation of resources, although as we saw in Chapter 7 it does discriminate against saving, compared to a tax on consumption expenditures. An excise tax is not neutral, because it makes the taxed commodity relatively more expensive than before the tax. The distortion of resource allocation caused by excise taxation can impose a cost on taxpayers over and above the revenue cost of the tax.

In Figure 9.3 the excess burden argument is presented for the simple case of one representative taxpayer and two goods: a taxed good, tobacco (T), and an untaxed good, uniforms (U). We assume that the government has decided to raise a certain amount of revenue and undertake certain programs that remove resources from the production of private goods. We are not concerned with the government's use of the revenue; our only interest is in the relative costs of raising it with an income tax or an excise.

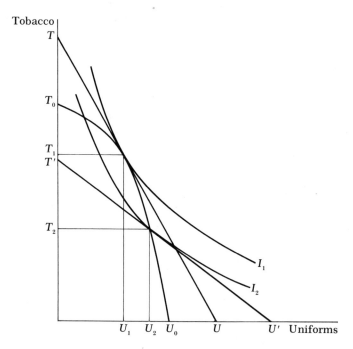

FIGURE 9.3   Excess Burden

Once resources are removed from private-good production, the remaining production possibilities may be shown by the transformation curve T_0U_0. If consumer preferences are given by the indifference curves I_1 and I_2, the equilibrium allocation of resources to the production of tobacco and uniforms will be at the point where the production possibility curve is tangent to an indifference curve (since that point represents the maximization of consumers' utility and producers' profits). The equilibrium ratio of the price of uniforms to the price of tobacco will be the (negative of the) slope of the tangent TU, and at equilibrium T_1 of tobacco and U_1 of uniforms will be produced. This allocation will be reached if the government obtains its resources by levying an income tax that leaves the relative prices of tobacco and uniforms unaffected.

Now suppose that the government raises the same amount of revenue and obtains the use of the same resources by levying an excise tax on tobacco. Since the net withdrawal of resources is the same as under the income tax, T_0U_0 still presents the production possibilities for tobacco and uniforms. Now, however, the price that consumers pay for tobacco has risen relative to the price of uniforms, so the price ratio (p_U/p_T) to consumers must fall, perhaps to the slope of $T'U'$.[1] Producers, however, continue to receive the prices net of the tax and produce at a point on the production possibility curve where the ratio of prices equals the marginal rate of transformation. Since producers' prices are net of the tax, the ratio of producers' prices (p_U/p_T) must be greater than the ratio of consumers' prices (the slope of $T'U'$). The new equilibrium, accordingly, must be somewhere to the right of (T_1, U_1) at a point such as (T_2, U_2).[2] At this equilibrium, consumers will be maximizing their utility subject to the tax, and producers will maximize their profits at the net-of-tax prices.

As long as indifference curves are convex to the origin, the equilibrium under the excise tax must lie on a lower indifference curve than the income tax equilibrium. Since the revenue yields of the two taxes are equal, it is clear that the excise imposes an extra cost, or excess burden, measured by the additional sacrifice of utility from I_1 to I_2. The excess burden arises because the excise forces the economy away from the efficient point. At (T_2, U_2) producers' marginal rate of transformation is equal to the slope of the production possibility curve, but consumers' marginal rate of substitution is given by the slope of the price line $T'U'$. Obviously, the excise causes the MRT to differ from the MRS, and thus the basic requirement for efficient allocation is violated.

The excess burden of the excise occurs because the allocation of resources under the income tax is distorted by the excise. In terms of our discussion in the preceding section, an excess burden arises only if the tax causes consumers to substitute between the taxed commodity and untaxed ones or if producers change their patterns of resource use, or both. If either product demand or product supply is perfectly

---

[1] In this case, U' is the X-intercept of the pretax transformation curve, since under the excise tax no revenue would be raised and no resources withdrawn from the private sector if only the untaxed good were consumed.

[2] Note that if the magnitude of the slope of $T'U'$ is less than that of TU and both price lines are tangent to indifference curves, I_2 must intersect the transformation curve from below, to the right of the tangency of I_1.

inelastic (Figures 9.1A and 9.1B), the quantity produced will not be affected, and the excise will be equivalent to an income tax on consumers (total shifting forward) or factors of production (total shifting backward).

Most economists have accepted the proposition that an excise is inferior to an equal-yield income tax because of the likelihood that the excise will impose an excess burden on consumers.[3] The magnitude of the excess burden may not be great if the degree of shifting of the excise is close to 100 percent, for in that case the effect on allocation will not be large. (A fully shifted excise, however, is a tax on the income of consumers *of the taxed commodity* and not necessarily on the incomes of all consumers. Thus, a fully shifted excise may still be unattractive on equity grounds.) But in some cases, a partly shifted excise may have desirable effects on the allocation of resources.

Monopoly. If producers do not behave as competitors, then they do not set their prices equal to (long-run) marginal cost and the MRS of consumers does not equal producers' MRT in the absence of an excise. In terms of Figure 9.3, the economy is not initially at point (T_1, U_1) before the excise is imposed. Instead, monopoly-produced goods are priced above marginal cost, and the MRS is greater than the MRT. Since resources are misallocated to begin with, excise taxation may actually increase efficiency. Unfortunately, an excise on the monopolist's output only aggravates the difference between MRS and MRT. Instead, a complicated tax must be levied to penalize the monopolist for earning monopoly profits and induce him to increase his level of output. The alternative is to tax the nonmonopoly good and use the revenue to subsidize production of the monopoly good. While this policy might have desirable allocative effects, it would serve to redistribute income from competitors to monopolists. This distributional inequity would be acceptable only if other taxes—especially the personal income tax—were able to compensate for it. Under the structure of the personal income tax described in Chapter 7, excises are not justified as a means of compensating for the presence of monopoly.

---

[3] Technically, the excess burden argument also applies to income taxation, for income taxes discriminate against a good, work effort, which is unaffected by excise taxation. If income taxation affects the amount of work and leisure, then we cannot differentiate the excess burden of excises on commodities from the excess burden of an excise on work. In practice, however, we may expect the supply of work effort to be inelastic with respect to income taxation, as we argued in Chapter 7. Thus, excise taxation will impose an excess burden whereas income taxation will not. For a good statement of both the excess burden argument and this defense of excise taxation see I. M. D. Little, "Direct Versus Indirect Taxes," *Economic Journal* 61 (September 1951).

Externalities. In Figure 9.3, the pretax equilibrium at (T_1, U_1) is efficient only if all costs and benefits are taken into account by consumers and producers. Suppose, however, that the production and consumption of tobacco impose external costs. The production externality may arise from the depletion of soil productivity resulting from growing tobacco. The consumption externality may be the costs that a smoker imposes on nonsmokers: discomfort and occasionally even illness. Either of these external costs causes social cost to exceed private cost and private consumption to be greater than optimal. If an excise is levied on tobacco in an amount equal to the external cost imposed by consumers and producers, then the social MRS can be brought into equilibrium with the social MRT. In this case, excises can increase economic efficiency.

The major federal excises were originally levied without the benefit of the foregoing argument; tobacco and liquor were merely convenient revenue sources. More recently, excises on these goods have been justified as sumptuary taxes, levies on the use of morally or socially undesirable goods. The economic basis for these excises, however, is the *economic,* not moral or even social, harm that they impose on others than the primary consumer or producer. Excises on other goods imposing external costs are similarly justified. For example, pollution taxes designed to compensate for the costs that polluters impose upon the rest of the economy have been discussed by the U.S. Senate. Excises may well represent an effective technique for dealing with general external costs if the amount of the cost can be determined.

Other Taxes. The excess burden argument applies to a very simple case: two goods, one representative consumer, and an efficient economy. In reality, however, excises are part of a structure that includes many other taxes. In a situation where excises are being levied on other goods, we cannot say unequivocally that still another excise on still another good is allocationally inferior to an income tax yielding equal revenue. Since the allocation of resources is already distorted by the existing excises, we do not know whether the new tax would cause further deterioration or whether it might compensate for some of the other excises. The answer to this question depends on consumer preferences and production possibilities for each of the taxed goods. The complexity of the matter, however, suggests that we should generally prefer an income tax (with nearly neutral allocative effects) to a set of excises with uncertain impacts upon allocation.

National Emergency. The allocative distortions produced by excise taxation may be desirable if there is some reason to limit consumer and producer sovereignty. During wartime, consumers' demands must be subordinated to national security. Goods necessary for a war effort can be denied to consumers either through rationing (an inefficient and frequently inequitable procedure) or by levying very high excises on vital commodities.

International Trade. Economists generally are vehement advocates of unrestricted international trade, but a variety of political considerations work to limit trade for many goods. If the alternative to taxation is the imposition of a quota or rationing system, excises on imports are likely to be preferable from the viewpoint of resource allocation. The United States now imposes quotas on imports of many major goods, including textiles, sugar, and oil. High import duties are levied on many other goods, largely as a response to the political demands of domestic business and labor rather than as an attempt to correct a resource misallocation.

USER CHARGES

Many of the excises levied by governments are charges for the use of facilities or services that the public sector provides. The outstanding example at the federal level is the excise on gasoline. During the enactment of the interstate highway network in the late 1950's the gasoline excise was doubled (to 4 cents per gallon), and the receipts were added to the Highway Trust Fund. The revenues paid into this fund are statutorily required to be used for the extension of highway services, either by building more roads or by improving capacity on existing roadways. Thus, users of federal highways (and nonfederal ones, too) pay a tax whose base is related to road use. The excess of revenue over the cost of providing the service then is used to increase the level of service.

The popularity of user charges at the federal level has been increasing. In addition to highway users, visitors to national parks frequently must pay a user charge for admission; air travelers must pay a 5 percent excise on their fare, to pay for federal air control services; and aircraft using federal airports must pay landing fees calculated on the basis of airport cost and use. The federal Office of Management and Budget regulates charges for the use of facilities owned by the federal government or its contractors. Even within the bureaucracy, the Defense Department has instituted trust fund operations for some of its facilities and services. Budgetary charges thus are levied on users of military air and sea transport services, among others.

Similar charges are plentiful at state and local levels. States levy excises on gasoline (usually greater in amount than the federal tax) and often create trust funds for the revenue. Automobile licensing is another form of user charge. When local governments provide water or sewage treatment facilities, they customarily charge consumers for their use of water or their disposal of sewage by a metering system that constitutes a user charge.

In theory, user charges are an attractive example of excise taxation levied on the benefit principle. Since the only payers of these excises are the consumers who use the goods or services, willingness to pay the excise implies that the consumer values the good at least at its "market" price. If consumers' valuation is high and exceeds the cost of providing the service, then the level of service should be increased, just as in the case of any private sector good. When private goods are provided through the public sector, user charges always offer a theoretical method of determining the extent of demand.

Unfortunately, user charges and trust funds frequently fall short of their theoretical promise. One reason is the price formula used by governments to set charges; the other reason is the narrow definition of services provided. Most user charges are based on a simple average-cost calculation. Users of Defense Department air transport, for example, pay the average ton-mile cost, computed by dividing the total cost of all air cargo transportation by the total number of ton-miles of cargo (that is, the number of miles of each flight multiplied by the number of tons of cargo on that flight). If air traffic at a federal airport is heavy, the (average-cost) landing fee is low since the total cost of the airport is very nearly constant. If many travelers visit national parks, the admission fee may be reduced since the cost to the National Park Service rises very little. But as we saw in Chapter 5, average-cost prices are inimical to economic efficiency. The widespread use of average-cost pricing prevents the efficient use of publicly provided services and facilities. From the viewpoint of resource allocation, user charges are no better than any other revenue device that fails to equate MRS and MRT.

The other problem with user charges is that they usually fail to consider substitute means of providing the service that consumers demand. In New York City the Triborough Bridge Authority has operated at a surplus for many years while transportation in Manhattan and commuting in general has become ever more difficult and costly. By statute, however, the revenues of the Bridge Authority cannot be captured by the city government or any other regional authority for use in solving the area's more general transportation problems. The result is that drivers can cross into Manhattan easily but cannot either use their cars or dispose of them once they get there. Bottlenecks at the bridges are eliminated by increasing capacity rather than by diverting traffic to other modes of transportation.

The same problem characterizes trust funds in general. Federal highway funds, for example, cannot even be used to provide nonhighway facilities for automobile travelers, let alone alternative transportation modes such as mass transit (rail or bus). Statutory limitations on the use of trust fund revenues frequently cause user charges to distort resource allocation, rather than improve it by charging consumers for the benefits they receive from public programs.

GENERAL SALES TAXATION

There are many different types of general consumption taxes. In their broadest form, they all are basically neutral with respect to resource allocation among consumption goods and favor saving compared to current consumption. As with income taxation, the chief issue in the case of consumption taxes is not allocation. Instead, an evaluation of general consumption taxation rests on equity and the specific nature of the tax.

Sales Taxes. State governments commonly levy *ad valorem* taxes on retail sales of most commodities. Many states exempt food and drug purchases from the tax base; some states also exempt clothing and other goods. Personal services usually are excluded from taxation. Thus, sales taxes exclude the largest single category of expenditure for most families, housing, as well as repairs, professional fees, laundry, and other items.

An alternative to taxing retail sales is to levy the tax on either manufacturers or wholesalers. Although taxing earlier in the production process is administratively simpler, it offers the complication for a state government that goods retailed in the state frequently will not be produced in it and thus would not be subject to an early-stage tax. The chief advantage of taxing retail sales, however, is that the tax does not become part of the seller's markup. A 4 percent sales tax levied on manufacturers may become part of the cost base to which they apply a 20 percent markup, and thus a 4.8 percent tax is passed on to wholesalers. If they then mark up their costs by another 20 percent, retailers will include a 5.76 percent tax in the prices they charge. This process is called "pyramiding." When markups are high, pyramiding can cause final prices to consumers to rise substantially more than the amount of the tax.

Turnover Tax. Some countries, including Italy and the Soviet Union, levy an *ad valorem* tax on a good at each stage of production. The advantage of this tax is that the rate may be very low, since the tax is levied several times on every good. Its disadvantages are both allocational and distributional. Goods with lengthy production processes are taxed more often than others; for example, the tax on agricultural commodities is lower than the tax on processed food products. Thus, demand is distorted, and consumers with preferences for highly taxed goods pay a higher effective tax than other consumers. Turnover taxes combine the worst features of both excise and sales taxation.

Value-added Tax. "Value added" is the difference between the revenue that a firm receives from selling its output and the cost of its purchases from other firms. Conceptually, this difference is equal to the cost of factors of production plus the firm's profits. If producers are allowed to deduct the cost of capital equipment (purchased from other firms), then total value added in the economy is equal to the value of all consumer goods. If producers cannot deduct the price of capital goods (but may only deduct a depreciation allowance), then total value added is equal to national income. An *ad valorem* tax on value added, therefore, is a proportional tax on either total consumption or total income.

The consumption variant of the value-added tax is the one most often proposed. Such a tax is closely similar to a comprehensive retail sales tax, for it reduces the extent of pyramiding (since wholesalers and retailers can deduct taxes paid at prior stages of production) while maintaining the tax on all commodities. In practice, a value-added tax could be levied on personal service items more easily than a retail sales tax. Thus, the base of a value-added tax could be broader and its allocational distortions less significant than those of a retail sales tax. These advantages have led some states and countries to introduce value-added taxation. Since the federal government does not levy a general sales tax, there has been considerable opposition to adding a value-added tax to the other elements of the federal tax structure.

EQUITY

The argument most frequently leveled against both sales and excise taxes is that they are inequitable. Excises are claimed to be inequitable both because they discriminate against consumers who prefer taxed commodities (horizontal inequity) and because the commodities that are taxed are those comprising a larger portion of poor consumers' budgets than those of wealthy consumers (vertical inequity, since the tax is regressive). Many studies have indicated that the income-elasticity of commodities like beer and cigarettes is low, so that the percentage of income devoted to consuming these goods falls as income rises. Taxes on these commodities, therefore, are levied at higher effective rates on the poor than on the rich.

Much of the same argument applies to more general retail sales taxation. If food is not exempt, there is little question that the incidence of the tax is quite regressive, especially at low income levels. If food is exempt, the regressivity of the tax depends on its coverage of personal services. The income-elasticity of most personal service items seems to be quite high and thus excluding them from the tax base confers a greater benefit on wealthy consumers than on poor ones.

Empirical studies of the incidence of sales and excise taxation have suffered from poor data on consumption patterns at different income levels. In addition, the "income" that is reported by consumers in response to questionnaire inquiries may not conform well to either personal income (on the National Accounts basis) or the "gross income" measure developed in Chapter 7. Another problem is that short-run fluctuations in income may fail to influence spending habits, and families whose long-run income is high may spend a large percentage of their lower short-run income on taxed commodities. For these reasons, studies showing the incidence of sales taxes to be either regressive or basically proportional are equally suspect.

If a value-added or retail sales tax could be levied on all consumption expenditures, its incidence probably would be nearly proportional but slightly regressive. (No study has ever shown consumption to be an increasing function of income.) Since actual consumption taxes are far less than perfectly comprehensive, the exclusion of personal services probably introduces an element of regressivity that outweighs the progressivity stemming from the exemption of food and drugs.

Exempting food and drugs is not the only concession that states make to sales tax regressivity. Some states exempt clothing expenditures, although studies have indicated that the income-elasticity of clothing purchases is close to unity. A more promising approach is to offer an income tax credit for sales taxes paid, thus reducing each family's income tax liability. While this tax credit approach does benefit the poor more than the rich, it does not improve the equity of sales taxation for the many poor families who have zero income tax liability. Moreover, the revenue costs of such a plan are quite high, since the tax credit must be offered to all taxpayers. A further inequity arises because taxpayers' weekly disposable incomes fall under the tax credit plan, with a once yearly increment in disposable income stemming from the tax credit. Studies of low-income families' economic behavior have noted that income fluctuations of this kind are likely to be especially harmful to the poor. Overall, therefore, attempts to make sales taxation progressive (or at least proportional) must be judged unsuccessful.

OTHER ISSUES

State governments are not blind to the questionable equity of sales taxation; they have continued to levy retail sales taxes largely because of the stability of their yield. Unlike the federal government, states cannot afford to operate under deficit conditions for extended periods, and thus the cyclical fluctuations that occur in the revenue yield of income taxes have been a major drawback. Consumption, on the other hand, is very stable over the business cycle, and an *ad valorem* tax on total consumption can be expected to provide very stable revenues. The benefits of stability should not be downgraded: substantial costs can arise from unexpected interruptions caused by revenue shortages, and the demand for public services such as education and health (frequently provided at the state and local level) does not vary over the cycle.

Another advantage of sales taxes has been their flexibility in adjusting to changing revenue demands. It is politically easier to raise the sales tax rate from 3 to 4 percent than to increase the rates on income by 33 percent, although the net effect on taxpayers may be virtually identical in either case. Sales taxes are easy to administer and can fairly quickly be extended to new commodities without major changes in administrative procedures.

A shortcoming of sales taxes that has only recently become an acute problem is their rather slow revenue growth. Since personal services are usually excluded, increases in personal and disposable income are accompanied by an increasing fraction of consumption being diverted to untaxed uses. Thus, the tax base historically has grown less rapidly than income. Most studies of the income-elasticity of sales taxes conclude that an increase of 10 percent in income leads to an increase of about 9 percent (and almost certainly less than 10 percent) in tax revenue. When states had unused revenue sources and the demand for state services was not climbing rapidly, this slow growth was not a major problem. More recently, however, the rapid growth in demand (as evidenced by the rise in expenditures noted in Chapter 2) has forced many states to tax hitherto unused sources, primarily income, that offer a higher income-elasticity of revenue.

SUMMARY

There are two distinct types of consumption taxation: excises on specific goods or allocations of resources, and various forms of sales taxation levied on a broader consumption base. Excises are levied on many commodities at the federal and at state and local levels; the principal taxes are on tobacco, liquor, and gasoline. Most economists believe that excises are shifted extensively to consumers (although they are levied statutorily on sellers). The degree of shifting depends on the elasticities of demand and supply. If shifting is either complete or non-existent, excise taxation is equivalent to an income tax on consumers or producers of the taxed commodities or on factors of production. If shifting is partial, excise taxation probably will distort the allocation of resources more than an equal-yield income tax. This additional cost is called the "excess burden" of the tax. Despite the excess burden it imposes, there are many instances in which excise taxation may be justified: monopoly elements in production, external costs, the prior existence of other distorting taxes, national emergency, and demands for the restriction of international trade.

An increasingly popular type of excise is user charges for government services. In theory, user charges are fees for the benefits that consumers derive from publicly produced goods. In practice, however, two problems arise: user charges generally are levied on an average-cost basis, and the revenues derived from them frequently are not used efficiently.

There are several types of general consumption taxes: sales taxes at the retail, wholesale, or manufacturer's level; turnover taxes levied at each step of the production process; and value-added taxes assessed on the difference between a firm's revenues and purchases from other firms. Turnover taxes are both inefficient and inequitable, but the other forms of consumption taxation may be roughly equivalent to proportional taxes on income. In the forms in which they are used, however, retail sales taxes (the most popular consumption tax) often exempt food and other "necessities" and exclude personal services. Since the last-named are consumed primarily by high-income families, the effective incidence of most sales taxes probably is slightly regressive.

Sales taxation offers certain advantages: its yield is stable, relative to that of an income tax, and it can be adapted to changing revenue demands and shifting consumption patterns. Many states, however, have found that the growth in sales tax revenue is insufficient to keep pace with the demand for state services.

10 Other Taxes

In the economy as a whole, the largest single revenue source is the personal income tax, which accounts for close to $100 billion per year at all levels of government. Corporation income taxes and consumption taxes each yield about $40 billion per year, with the corporation tax being used chiefly by the federal government and consumption taxes primarily by states. The fourth largest source of revenue is taxes on earnings, sometimes called employment taxes and contributions, payroll taxes, or contributions for social insurance. These revenues have grown rapidly with the expansion of federal social security programs and benefits during the 1960's and will amount to $40 billion early in the 1970's. The fifth largest revenue producer, property taxation, yields close to $30 billion per year, primarily to local governments.

In this chapter we will examine taxes on earnings, property taxes, and the taxation of gifts and bequests. Estate and gift taxation is a minor revenue producer for the federal government (about $3.5 billion) and is still less important for states, but it raises some interesting economic questions and illustrates the difficulty of translating economics into tax statutes. Although governments collect more revenues from licenses and fees than from estate and gift taxation, licenses and fees are analytically equivalent to user charges, and we will not discuss them separately.

EMPLOYMENT TAXATION

The Social Security Act of 1935 marked the entry of the federal government into the provision of insurance services that previously had been in the domain of the private sector. Originally the act provided transfer payments to compensate for loss of income due to unemployment, old-age retirement, and death of the family earner (survivors' benefits). Later modifications extended coverage to workers' disability and to hospitalization expenses (medicare), broadening the title to Old-Age, Survivors, Disability, and Health Insurance (OASDHI). Social security is by far the largest federal social insurance program, but it is not the only one. A separate program applies to railroad workers' retirement and unemployment insurance, and still another covers federal civil servants.

The common feature of all these programs is that they apply to particular groups of workers who "contribute" (on a compulsory basis) in return for the promise of future benefits. The revenues received from these taxes are placed in several trust funds, from which benefits are paid when they become due. In the interim, the assets in the trust funds are invested in federal bonds, in effect making the assets available to the federal government for funding other programs.

The largest trust fund is Old-Age and Survivors Insurance. Like the disability, hospitalization, and railroad retirement funds, contributions are paid into it equally by employers and their employees. The schedule of rates has risen substantially in recent years, but the basic feature of equal contributions has been retained. On the other hand, only employers pay taxes into the unemployment insurance fund, the second largest trust fund, and the railroad unemployment compensation fund. Other trust funds cover veterans and civil servants.

The structure of these taxes is very simple. Membership in the various income transfer programs is extended to different industries and occupations by legislative enactment and now includes over 90 percent of all paid workers and self-employed persons with earnings over $400. Each employee's tax is a flat percentage of his "covered wages," the amount of his income subject to taxation. In recent years the coverage limit for OASDHI has risen rapidly and now is scheduled to reach $9600; it is safe to predict that the coverage limit will rise even higher as the average money wage approaches that level. The rate on covered earnings also has risen, partly because of the introduction of health insurance and partly to meet increases in the schedule of benefits. The combined rate for OASDHI (excluding unemployment insurance) will soon exceed 5 percent for both employees and employers. Self-employed persons pay at 1.5 times the rate levied on employers and employees. Railroad retirement rates are higher and lead to higher benefit payments. Unemployment insurance rates are statutorily about 3 percent of employers' payrolls, but employers can receive credits for payments into state funds, and the rate is usually reduced on the basis of past experience. Again, railroad unemployment compensation rates are somewhat higher.

In return for these tax payments, employees are entitled to collect future benefits. OASDI and railroad retirement pay cash benefits, the amount varying with the length of time during which contributions were made and the recipient's age and family status. The Tax Reform Act of 1969 raised the range of individual benefits from $64 (minimum) to $250.70 (maximum) per month. The minimum monthly family benefit now is $96; the maximum is $434.40. Medicare benefits, restricted to those over sixty-five years of age, provide hospitalization and some post-hospital services; in addition a voluntary supplemental program is available to cover 80 percent of doctors' fees. Unemployment compensation varies among states because federal involvement does not extend to specifying weekly benefits or their duration. Typically, both railroad and regular unemployment compensation are limited to twenty-six weeks and provide about half of the worker's previous wage.

The essence of the tax and benefit nature of social security is an intergenerational transfer of income from younger currently employed workers to older retired ones (and the disabled or unemployed). This transfer of income, like any other transfer payment, constitutes a response to the social consensus that a redistribution is desirable. In this case, the basis for the redistribution is that private individuals frequently are unable to insure against their own retirement, disability, hospitalization, or unemployment. These events may arise from causes the individual cannot guard against (such as cyclical recessions), or his perception of the future may not correspond to what he will actually experience (as if, for example, he refuses to consider the possibility of becoming disabled). When a person's income falls for these reasons, the distribution of current income will be inequitable, and costs may be imposed in a variety of ways on society at large (crime or delinquency) or on particular families.

Social security is frequently characterized as an insurance program (or a group of such programs), for the hazards from which participants are protected are usually insurable risks. Thus, private insurance policies are written for retirement income, survivors' benefits, medical care, and so on. Employment taxes, however, cannot be treated as user charges for the social provision of insurance because social security programs differ from private insurance in several ways.

Vesting. When an employee joins a private pension plan, his contributions usually are accompanied by his employer's, made in his behalf. The employee's payments remain legally his own, held in trust by the pension plan and managed in his behalf. The employer's share may not immediately pass to the employee but may instead be entered in an account that will become the property of the employee after some lapse of time. When the employee acquires a legal right to the employer's contributions, they are said to be vested in him. Typical vesting periods are one, two, or five years; immediate vesting is unusual, for employers use the vesting period to encourage employee retention.

All private pension plans must offer vesting after some period, or else employees would not subscribe to them. Social security tax payments are vested after the employee is "permanently insured" (usually after eighteen months of covered employment), but the vesting merely gives the employee a right to whatever future benefits are paid. Since benefit levels are set by the dictate of Congress, an employee has no guarantee that his eventual benefits will equal the sum of his tax payments, compounded at the prevailing interest rate. (In fact, all retirees to date have received real benefits worth more than the compounded value of their payments.) If employment taxes were true user charges, the dollar payments of both employees and employers would have to be vested in order to induce employees to join the social security program.

Actuarial Stability. Many critics of social security programs have pointed out that benefits paid exceed the compounded value of tax payments. Thus, current beneficiaries are being paid out of the current payments of other workers, rather than solely on the basis of their own past taxes. This practice is perfectly sound as long as we recognize that the payment of benefits rests on the federal government's general taxing power rather than on individuals' tax payments.

Compulsory Payments. Since individual workers would not contribute voluntarily to social security without actuarially sound vesting, payments must be compulsory (taxes rather than true contributions). As we saw in Chapter 6, however, there is no guarantee that individuals can equate their personal preferences for social security with their tax cost. (This is true especially if they would prefer not to buy insurance at all, since social security sets a minimum on the amount of insurance they must have.) A true user charge, of course, lets consumers express their preferences for public services by relating the amount of the charge to the level of consumption.

Income Redistribution. As well as redistributing income from younger generations to older ones, social security redistributes income from the rich to the poor. The ratio of a high-income worker's benefits to his taxes is smaller than that of a poor worker. Both rich and poor receive an intergenerational transfer, but the poor man's transfer is larger than the rich man's. Regardless of the social merits of this pattern of income distribution, it would not be part of a private pension plan unless the participants were very altruistic.

Shifting and Incidence. Statutorily, employment taxes constitute an excise tax upon labor income. The interesting issues are whether the different taxes are shifted and to whom and what the overall pattern of tax incidence is. As we saw in Chapter 7, there is little evidence that income taxation affects the supply of work effort. There is even less chance that employment taxes have any such effect, since the rates are so much lower (4 to 5 percent compared with income tax rates as high as 50 percent). The employee half of employment taxes, therefore, can be assumed with confidence to remain on employees.

The employer portion (including unemployment taxes) is a little harder to analyze. In the case of excise and sales taxes on output, we saw that the producer might shift the tax forward if consumers' elasticities of demand were low, or backward if factors of production were inelastically supplied. Our conclusion that the tax was shifted forward rested on studies that show demand for most taxed goods to be inelastic with respect to price. Employment taxes, however, are not levied on particular goods but are very nearly universal (since coverage is well over 90 percent of the labor force). Accordingly, the tax cannot be shifted forward because higher prices would simply reduce consumers' real incomes and cause them to decrease their demands for all goods (as with an income tax). Ultimately, this reduction in the quantity demanded would cause producers to cut back on their demands for factors of production, which is precisely the nature of backward shifting. Even if the OASDHI benefits financed with the employment tax receipts maintain aggregate demand at its pretax level, the tax will raise the relative price of labor and thus will lead to a substitution of capital for labor. Employers' ability to make the substitution they desire may depend on their economic power and that of the unions they face, but the inelastic supply of work effort probably will enable producers to shift their portion of employment taxes to labor in the long run.

Whether employer tax payments are shifted to employees or not, employment taxes are generally regressive. If coverage of all occupations were complete, the tax would be proportional up to the coverage limit and regressive with respect to earnings thereafter, since the ratio of tax liability to total earnings would fall. In fact, coverage is not complete, and uncovered occupations tend to be those entailing casual employment at low wages. As a result, employment taxes are mildly progressive at the lower end of the earnings scale, roughly proportional over the middle range, and regressive beyond the coverage limit.

When we examine the incidence of employment taxes with respect to total income, much the same pattern emerges. At the very bottom of the income scale, covered earnings are a fairly small percentage of total income because of both incomplete coverage and the importance of other sources of income. From about $4000 to $10,000, employment taxes are virtually proportional to total income, and as the coverage limit rises in the future the range of proportionality also will rise. Especially above $15,000, the importance of non-earned income causes the effective employment tax rate to fall and the tax becomes regressive.

Aside from the administrative simplicity of levying a flat-rate tax on payrolls, it is hard to justify employment taxes as a means of financing social security programs. The taxes cannot be considered as user charges (say, for insurance against unemployment), and even if they could, there is no valid reason to exclude low-income families and individuals who do not happen to work in covered occupations from social security benefits. On the contrary, such people are likely to be most in need of the benefits of these programs. Earnings are not an especially good measure of ability to pay for social security, and the coverage limit does not correspond to either the income level beyond which people no longer want social insurance or the tax base necessary to finance the programs. The goals of efficiency and equity would both be met more nearly if the present system of financing social security through employment taxation were modified, either by a general tax on all earnings or by a simple surcharge on each person's individual income tax liability.

PROPERTY TAXATION

Property taxes are one of the oldest forms of taxation and still provide the bulk of local government revenues. They are the largest revenue source for state and local governments (taken together), yielding perhaps $5 billion more than sales and excise taxes at the state and local levels. There are several kinds of property tax: the real property tax, levied on land and structures; the personal property tax, upon consumers' durables such as automobiles and furniture; and the intangible property tax, assessed upon financial assets (bank accounts, common stocks). Of these, the tax on real property is by far the most important. Personal property is extremely hard to assess for tax purposes, and intangible property is highly mobile and thus provides a poor tax base. As a consequence, these taxes are levied only rarely and then usually at the state level. The real property tax, however, is nearly universal among local governments.

The structure of the real property tax, like that of employment taxes, is quite simple. First the value of real property is determined, usually by some kind of assessment procedure, and then a flat-rate tax is levied on the assessed value. The property owner's tax liability is, therefore, the product of the assessed value of his property and the statutory tax rate. In practice, the statutory rate is usually fixed by a local government by dividing its needed revenue by the assessable property tax base. Thus, an evaluation of the real property tax is really an evaluation of assessment practices.

Methods of Assessment. Assessments usually are supposed to reflect 100 percent of "fair market value," the price that a particular parcel of land and structures would command on the open market. The best way to estimate fair market value, of course, is to adjust recent market prices of similar parcels for differences in size, accessibility, or scenic values. Even where prices of similar parcels are available, however, methods of adjustment may be crude or inaccurate. More generally, similar parcels may not be available in the market either because of the uniqueness of a plot of land or a structure or because of the absence of market transactions for parcels of that type. Even single-family housing in long-established residential neighborhoods can be difficult to assess because individual houses may be quite different and the frequency of transactions usually is too small to permit accurate adjustment.

When market prices are not available as a basis for assessment, assessors frequently use either replacement cost or original construction cost less depreciation. Aside from the difficulties in calculating depreciation, both of these bases require the assumption that the current use of a parcel is the use to which it would be put by a new owner. Suppose that the parcel in question contains a thirty-year-old factory. Changes in technology may have made its facilities obsolete, and its market value may be far below its initial or replacement cost. But if there are no recent transactions in similar property, an assessor will have no alternative to using one of these bases in making his assessment.

Uniformity. Effective property taxes, the ratio of tax liability to actual market value, usually lie between 1 and 4 percent. But property in any jurisdiction usually is not assessed evenly, and assessments and effective rates vary widely among jurisdictions. Using as his estimate of market value a sample of single-family home sales, Netzer has shown that actual assessments deviate greatly from market value.[1] Half of the areas in Netzer's sample show average deviations of more than 30 percent from the median assessment ratio. That is, if the median assessment ratio for single-family houses is 50 percent (half of all houses are assessed above this percentage of market value and half are assessed below), then in half of all Netzer's sample jurisdictions the typical homeowner could expect his assessment to vary between 35 and 65 percent of true market value.

A further problem is that particular jurisdictions may consciously try to assess different types of property at different fractions of true market value. Assessors in Washington, D.C., have tried to assess residential property at 50 percent of market value and commercial property at 65 percent. Similar practices in Massachusetts were ended by a court case in 1961. Unequal assessments may also result from methods of estimating market value that discriminate in favor of certain types of property. Netzer cites assessment ratios of 36 percent for residential property, 55 percent for commercial, and 43 percent for industrial property in Cuyahoga County, Ohio.[2]

Frequency. If assessment ratios are to be kept uniform, assessments must be updated constantly to take account of changes in market value. Annual reassessments are extremely rare. If reassessments are made, say, every five years, then someone whose property has appreciated in value during that time will gain at the expense of someone else whose property has not changed in value. In practice, new construction frequently is reassessed more often than older structures, so that there is a systematic bias in favor of owners of older property.

To some extent property taxes can be considered to be true benefit taxes. Many of the services provided by local governments affect property values, and thus it is appropriate for taxes to be levied on property owners. Some of the services are transportation (which increases accessibility), police and fire protection, and even education (since property values reflect, in part, the quality of local government services). But the equity aspects of the property tax and its impact on growth are less satisfactory than its benefit rationale.

[1] Dick Netzer, *Economics of the Property Tax* (Washington, D.C.: Brookings Institution, 1966), pp. 177–78 and Table 7–2.
[2] *Ibid.,* p. 80.

Taxes on residential and nonresidential property traditionally are treated separately in calculations of incidence. Nonresidential property taxes are considered to be an excise on a factor of production, but because they affect different products unequally, they usually are assumed to be shifted to consumers in the form of higher prices. Accordingly, the incidence of taxes on nonresidential property probably is mildly regressive, although the particular assumptions employed about shifting may introduce an element of progressivity in high income brackets.

Residential property taxes also are traditionally assumed to be regressive in incidence, for two reasons. One is the difficulty of assessing the market value of expensive residences and assessors' presumed unwillingness to encourage taxpayer suits by wealthy property owners. The more important reason is that economists have always posited an income-inelastic demand for housing, believing that expenditures on housing would rise less rapidly than income (both for the same person, as his income rose, and for different people at different income levels). If housing really is a larger percentage of the expenditures and income of poor people than of rich people, a flat-rate tax on housing obviously is regressive.

This widely held belief was challenged in a 1963 study by Reid, who argued that housing expenditures really were highly elastic with respect to long-term, or "permanent," income.[3] If Reid's findings are correct, the regressivity of the property tax with respect to current income is misleading, and the tax really is progressive in the sense that people with high incomes over their lifetimes will pay a higher percentage of their incomes in property taxes than will people with lower lifetime incomes. There are other errors of measurement that also might make the residential property tax less regressive than it initially appears to be. Another view of property tax incidence is suggested by Mieszkowski.[4] If factors of production are mobile and are paid their marginal products, then a tax on property merely reduces the rate of return of wealth holders. Property values will fall because people will prefer to hold assets other than real estate. Thus, the incidence of the real property tax will be progressive, similar to the long-run incidence of the corporation income tax. These arguments have served to soften but not silence the traditional criticism that property taxation is highly regressive.

---

[3] Margaret G. Reid, *Housing and Income* (Chicago: University of Chicago Press, 1962).

[4] P. M. Mieszkowski, "On the Theory of Tax Incidence," *Journal of Political Economy* 75 (June 1967): 250–62.

Regressivity is not the only basis on which property taxation may be inequitable. There is the stock-flow problem that also arises with capital gains taxation and any other tax on wealth. The property tax is levied on the taxpayer's *stock* of assets of a certain type, but the tax itself is one of the allocations he must make of his *flow* of income. Many fixed-income recipients, especially retired workers whose homes represent a large fraction of their life's savings, consume housing services far out of proportion to their current dollar incomes. Although one might argue that these people should have considered their property tax liability when they bought their homes, the fact remains that in a world of imperfect foresight and imperfectly rational consumers the incidence of the property tax may be very unfair.

Not only does the property tax violate the criterion of vertical equity (by its probable regressivity) and impose high costs on fixed-income recipients and the aged, but it also fails to meet the general criterion of horizontal equity. Like any excise, it discriminates against (levies a higher tax on) those consumers who place a high value on the taxed commodity, in this case residential property and other goods that make intensive use of real property as a factor of production. Defenders of property taxation have argued that it merely closes a large loophole in traditional sales taxation, since housing services are excluded from the base of sales and excise taxes. But in practice there is no attempt to align property tax rates with other excise or sales tax rates. Moreover, as was argued in Chapter 9, we cannot show that levying another excise on top of existing excises will increase the efficiency of resource allocation, so we cannot justify property taxation in this way.

A traditional argument in favor of the property tax has been its alleged neutrality with respect to allocation. Since property is fixed in supply and its total factor return is in the form of pure rent, a tax on the amount of rent will not affect the amount of the factor actually supplied. Unfortunately, this argument is valid only in the short run, and the long-run effects of the property tax may be much less acceptable. In the long run, no type of property is truly fixed in supply. (Even the supply of land can be varied if demand warrants. For example, land-fill operations or extensive regrading may create usable property where none formerly existed.) But the property tax base is not limited to land; in addition, it includes "improvements" such as structures and other changes in the raw land comprising a parcel of property. Thus, the property tax base can expand or contract, depending on whether the rate of return on "improvements" exceeds that on other investments (and, implicitly, on whether capital's productivity is greater than labor's).

In the long run, therefore, a tax on real property will make the net rate of return on certain types of capital lower than on others. Several allocational distortions will result. (1) If a company has an inelastic demand for structures, it will try to locate where its property tax is lowest (subject, of course, to other constraints such as labor availability). Land values and property taxes are highest in central cities and decline fairly regularly with distance from the city. Thus, plants will tend to migrate from central cities to the suburbs, imposing external costs in the forms of pollution, extra travel time, and the decline of central cities. (2) If the same tax rate is levied on land and improvements, land use will be less intensive than if land alone were taxed or if it were taxed at a higher rate than structures. Although it is difficult to separate the value of land from the value of improvements, the uniform rate levied by most property taxes makes land use less intensive than would differential rates. (3) Property taxation raises the prices of goods that use property-intensive production techniques. It also makes housing more expensive than other types of consumption, although the net effect depends on the relative magnitudes of excise and property tax rates. (4) Since property taxes are deductible from federal taxable income, a subsidy is offered to owner-occupied housing relative to rental housing. Owner-occupied (single-family) housing is a less intensive use of land than rental housing, and thus the deductibility of the property tax reinforces the tendency already noted for low-intensity land use.

The fact that real property is fairly mobile in the long run recently has indicated another shortcoming of the property tax. If property were truly fixed in supply, local governments could levy whatever taxes they felt were necessary to obtain desired amounts of revenue, and apart from possible inequities there would be no economic repercussions. But since real property can move in response to tax rates, local governments have often been placed in competition with each other and thus have tried to keep their tax rates as low as possible. Their problems have been compounded by the failure of property tax revenues to grow as fast as the demand for local services. Estimates of the income-elasticity of property tax revenues usually fall near or just below 1.0, indicating that revenue will grow slightly less rapidly than income. Since the demand for state and local public services typically has risen faster than income, the property tax has not provided an adequate revenue source for local governments.

Overall, the shortcomings of the property tax seem to outweigh its advantages. The drawbacks include too low a growth rate of revenue yield, the likelihood of a regressive incidence pattern, substantial horizontal inequity due to uneven assessments, unequal impact on different commodities, taxpayers' inadequate cash flow, and long-run distortions in resource allocation. The principal advantage of the tax is the stability of its revenue yield. Taxpayers' familiarity with the tax and the low cost of administering it are also favorable. The property tax is likely to become less important a source of revenue as local governments rely more and more on other taxes and grants-in-aid.

ESTATE AND GIFT TAXES

Bequests and gifts offer an attractive tax base for several reasons. From an equity standpoint, a tax on large estates and gifts is likely to be quite progressive in incidence. Taxes on large bequests can help reduce the concentration of wealth. Since recipients are likely to consider bequests and gifts as windfalls, unrelated to their own earning activities, an estate or gift tax should have minimal allocational effects. Similarly, donors or testators are unlikely to experience major disincentives from such a tax. In theory, therefore, estates and gifts offer a tax base that is neutral with respect to allocation and attractive from a distributional standpoint.

Most countries levy some form of estate or gift tax, and the United States is no exception. The federal government taxes both decedent estates and gifts *inter vivos* (between living persons), and almost all states levy taxes on inheritance (on the recipient rather than on the giver). The structure of the federal estate tax is progressive. The first $5000 of a taxable estate is taxed at 3 percent, the second $5000 at 7 percent, the second $10,000 at 11 percent, and so on up to a marginal rate of 77 percent levied on taxable estates larger than $10 million. Federal gift taxation is also progressive, with the rates that donors pay on taxable gifts being three-quarters those on taxable estates. Neither federal nor state taxes are major revenue producers. The federal estate and gift taxes regularly yield 1.5 to 2.5 percent of total federal tax receipts. State receipts from inheritance and gift taxes usually average about 2 percent of total state tax revenues.

Before discussing details of the tax law, we will examine the allocational effects that estate and gift taxation might be expected to have upon donors and donees. Since the tax is an excise upon gifts and bequests, the total amounts of gifts and bequests should fall due to its imposition and total consumption by wealthy people (who otherwise would leave large estates) should increase. Thus, these taxes may reduce total saving and the growth rate in the economy. This argument, however, assumes that the motives of the donor are entirely selfish. If a donor wishes to provide a certain amount of well-being for his heirs, the tax may have the opposite effect of increasing his saving so that his gross estate may be larger than, and his net after the tax the same as, his total estate before the tax was imposed. That is, the income effect may dominate the substitution effect; in any case, we may expect them to work in opposite directions. Donees will also experience an income effect to the extent that the tax reduces their expected income and wealth, and they may also increase their saving to compensate for the reduction in the gifts or legacies.

If total saving is relatively unaffected by estate and gift taxation, total investment probably will also be unaffected. Most investment is financed by corporate saving, and there is no reason to think that corporate decisions will be altered by a tax on personal gifts or estates. The composition of investment may be altered, however, if the estate tax law leads to an increase in the amount of wealth handled by professional executors or trustees. These professional managers are likely to prefer safe, low-yield investments to riskier ones, and as a result the social rate of return on investment may fall somewhat.

Another allocational impact of estate taxes may be felt by small businessmen whose estates consist largely of their companies. The assets of such firms typically are quite illiquid, and the tax liability under the estate tax may force the company out of business. This effect is minimized by clauses in the tax law that permit deferred payment of the tax liability in such cases. Nonetheless, the tax may cause testators to shift their assets into a more liquid form, with some effect upon the allocation of resources.

None of these impacts of estate and gift taxation is likely to cause major distortions of resource allocation. Other forms of the taxes, such as inheritance taxes upon the recipients of bequests, are no more likely to create misallocations. Thus, our chief interest in these taxes centers on how particular provisions of the statutes affect equity.

Exemptions. The federal gift tax grants a $30,000 lifetime exemption to each donor. In the case of a married couple, the joint lifetime exemption is $60,000. Thus, a married couple need not pay any gift taxes on the first $60,000 of donations over their lifetimes. Beyond that amount, they must pay each year on the additional gifts made in that year. The federal estate tax grants a decedent an exemption of $60,000 of his gross estate (all property, including insurance, owned at the time of death, plus revocable trusts and gifts made in anticipation of death), so that the taxable estate is zero unless the gross estate is at least $60,000 (for a single decedent with no deductions).

Exclusions. The federal gift tax excludes from taxable gifts the first $3000 transferred to each donee each year. Again, the exclusion applies also to the spouses' gifts. Thus, a married couple can exclude from gift taxation $6000 per year per donee. Despite the very favorable provisions of the gift tax, a remarkably small amount of income is transferred *inter vivos*. The picture that emerges is of wealthy individuals clinging to their assets as a hedge against uncertainty, fear of their inability to influence their heirs, and perhaps an irrational aversion to splitting up their property.

Deductions. The most important deduction from a gross estate is the marital deduction, which allows a decedent to deduct up to half the value of his gross estate if he transfers it to his spouse. Deductions are also allowed for the miscellaneous expenses of settling an estate, funeral expenses, and charitable contributions. The marital deduction combined with the $60,000 exemption lets estates of up to $120,000 (net of other deductions) escape the estate tax entirely. For larger estates, the value of the marital deduction is still substantial since it permits estates to be taxed at much lower marginal rates, in the same manner that income splitting benefits married couples under the personal income tax.

Trusts. One of the most popular devices for avoiding estate taxation is the establishment of trusts that pay income to one or two generations of heirs and then confer their property upon a succeeding generation. Most states limit the duration of a trust to the lives of those beneficiaries alive at the time of its creation, plus twenty-one years. To see how this device benefits the wealthy, suppose that N. A. Bob, a millionaire several times over, establishes a trust at the moment of his death at age eighty-four. In the trust, he creates his wife, children, and living grandchildren as successive *life tenants* (entitled to receive income from the trust) and eventually passes the property in his estate to his great-grandchildren (called the "remaindermen"). Bob must pay estate taxes on the amount of the trust, but his children and grandchildren pay no taxes as the estate passes through their generations. In effect, the trust enables Bob to skip two generations of estate taxation. The property that N. A. Bob, IV, receives (perhaps a century after his great-grandfather's death) is much greater than it would have been if N. A. Bob, II, and N. A. Bob, III, also had had to pay estate taxes in order to transfer the property to their sons.

Trusts are used primarily by very wealthy individuals (with total lifetime transfers over, say, $2 million). Over two-thirds of such decedents establish trusts, and over a third of all their bequests are made through the trust device. Since these are the people whose estates are taxed at high rates (the marginal tax rate at $2 million is 49 percent), the availability of trusts exempts from taxation a disproportionately large amount of wealth. About half of total transfers escape at least two generations of estate taxes through the use of trusts. Consequently, trusts cause a substantial reduction in the effective progressivity of the estate tax.

Charitable Foundations. An unlimited deduction from a decedent's gross estate is allowed for charitable bequests. Although only fairly small percentages of total bequests are given directly to charities, until recently this provision created a large loophole in the estate tax law. Individuals could incorporate their assets, establish private charitable foundations, endow them with a (nonvoting) majority of stock in their self-corporations, and then bequeath the voting minority to their heirs. The foundations could then carry on business as usual, paying salaries to the heirs as officers of the foundations. Under this device, property would escape estate taxation indefinitely, for there is no limitation on the duration of a charitable foundation.

Many of the abuses of this provision were eliminated under the 1969 Tax Reform Act. Instead of accumulating property, foundations now are required to distribute their income for the charitable purposes underlying their establishment. They may not hold large amounts of stock in unrelated businesses, nor may they make investments that conflict with their charitable purposes. Moreover, a 4 percent tax is imposed upon foundations' net investment income (including capital gains). The result of these restrictions should be to reduce the ability of foundations to exercise increasing amounts of economic power against the intent of estate taxation.

This outline of the principal features of federal estate and gift taxation has only hinted at the techniques available for tax avoidance. As a result of both the provisions of the tax law and the ingenuity of estate planners and tax accountants, estate taxation is more a nuisance tax upon wealth than a serious attempt to reduce the concentration of assets. The details of the tax law give rise to many instances of individual inequity, with the chief contributors being the marital deduction and the use of intergenerational trusts. Gifts *inter vivos* offer an avenue of avoidance that has not been very popular with the wealthy, but the operations of private foundations provided a major loophole until they were restricted by the Tax Reform Act of 1969. The net impact of estate and gift taxation is so minor that its allocational effects, unimportant in theory, are likely to be negligible in practice.

PART FOUR Techniques of Government Resource Allocation

There is a great deal of difference between the public sector resource allocation that we observe in the real world and that which was justified on the basis of economic analysis in Part Two. Actual allocation decisions are made through the budgeting process, described in Chapter 11. There is frequently a large gap between budgeting practice and the recommendations of economic theory, but current techniques of budgeting within the executive branch of the federal government constitute an attempt to bridge this gap. The methodology of systems analysis, used extensively in executive budgeting, is the subject of Chapter 12. One of the thorniest and most important issues in public resource allocation and systems analysis is the evaluation of government investments and the choice of an appropriate interest rate, as we discuss in Chapter 13.

BIBLIOGRAPHY

A good description of the federal budget and its significance is presented by David J. and Attiat F. Ott in *Federal Budget Policy,* revised edition (Washington, D.C.: Brookings Institution, 1969), chapters 2 and 3. Aaron Wildavsky's *The Politics of the Budgetary Process* (Boston: Little, Brown, 1964) is an incisive and entertaining discussion of federal budgeting. For an encyclopedic treatment of congressional appropriations, see Richard F. Fenno, Jr., *The Power of the Purse* (Boston: Little, Brown, 1966). Good discussions and illustrations of program budgeting are available in Arthur

Smithies' *The Budgetary Process in the United States* (New York: McGraw-Hill, 1955), and in *Program Budgeting,* edited by David Novick (Cambridge, Mass.: Harvard University Press, 1965).

Many of the aspects of systems analysis are discussed by Roland N. McKean in *Efficiency in Government Through Systems Analysis* (New York: Wiley, 1958). Some examples of military applications are available in Charles J. Hitch and Roland N. McKean's *The Economics of Defense in the Nuclear Age* (Cambridge, Mass.: Harvard University Press, 1961), and in *Analysis for Military Decisions* (Santa Monica, Calif.: Rand, 1964), edited by E. S. Quade. Many aspects of analysis relevant for government decisions are discussed by contributors to the U.S. Joint Economic Committee's *The Analysis and Evaluation of Public Expenditures: The PPB System* (1969).

The Joint Economic Committee Compendium contains two papers on the selection of a discount rate. See William J. Baumol's "On the Discount Rate for Public Projects" and J. Hirschleifer and David L. Shapiro's "The Treatment of Risk and Uncertainty." An overview of the controversy over discounting is presented by Peter Steiner in *Public Expenditure Budgeting* (Washington, D.C.: Brookings Institution, forthcoming).

11 Budgeting

THE FEDERAL BUDGET

Many purposes are served by the federal budget. It provides the most comprehensive picture of the federal government's total expenditures and receipts and thus offers some indication of the aggregate fiscal impact of federal programs. In orthodox Keynesian macroeconomic theory, the excess of government receipts over expenditures—the budgetary surplus—is one of the major tools for adjusting aggregate demand. The budget offers the President and his close advisers a vehicle for implementing their policies through the expenditures of the various executive agencies and departments. It also provides a chance for Congress to scrutinize total federal expenditures and the programs of each agency. Finally, the budgetary totals of both revenues and expenditures are the most popular simple indicators of the extent of economic activity in the public sector.

At other levels of government, the budgetary process usually is similar to the federal one. State and local budgets are not indicators of stabilization policy because a budget balance must be maintained if a state or local government wants to retain its fiscal stability. (The federal government faces no such immediate constraint because most of its debt is held internally, by U.S. citizens, and because it has ultimate power over the money supply.) But state and local executives face the same kinds of scrutiny from legislatures and the general public as does the federal executive branch.

Beginning with fiscal year 1969, the federal government adopted a unified budget designed to display all its activities in a manner permitting comparisons between programs and an assessment of the overall impact of the budget. The chief attribute of the unified budget is that it aggregates all the expenditure and revenue activities of the federal government and presents them in a single account. A summary of this budget (as originally proposed for fiscal 1971) is shown in Table 11.1.

TABLE 11.1   Unified Budget Summary, Fiscal 1971

Budget authority	
Proposed for current action by Congress	148.1
Becoming available without current action by Congress	86.7
Deductions for offsetting receipts	−16.8
TOTAL BUDGET AUTHORIZED	218.0
Receipts, expenditures, and net lending	
Expenditures account	
Receipts	202.1
Expenditures (excluding net lending)	200.1
EXPENDITURE ACCOUNT SURPLUS	2.0
Loan account	
Loan disbursements	8.6
Loan repayments	7.9
NET LENDING	0.7
Total budget	
Receipts	202.1
Outlays (expenditures and net lending)	200.8
BUDGET SURPLUS	1.3

SOURCE: Executive Office of the President, Bureau of the Budget, *The Budget in Brief, Fiscal Year 1971,* p. 7.

Budget Authority. The first item in the unified budget is an accounting of appropriations authority and the semicommercial activities of government agencies. The first line shows the request for new appropriations from the Congress. The second line shows the amount of expenditure authority available from previous congressional action. Most appropriations are for one-year periods, but trust fund operations

—OASDHI and the Highway Trust Fund, for example—carry continuing expenditure authority. In addition, from time to time Congress may grant multiyear appropriations to executive agencies for particular programs. The third line nets out both intragovernmental transactions (expenditures by one agency that appear as another agency's receipts), including those between the trust funds and other agencies, and marketed services such as those of the post office.

Receipts, Expenditures, and Net Lending. This section contains the heart of the unified budget. In the expenditures account, receipts are independently determined from forecasts of the federal tax structure's yield. Line 2, expenditures (excluding net lending), is derived from total budget authority by subtracting the balances and obligations carried over from the preceding fiscal year. Thus, the expenditure account surplus refers to the excess of current federal revenue over the expenditures that the government will newly commit itself to make during the current fiscal year.

The loan account includes federal lending to private individuals (for example, small businessmen and college students) and collectivities (such as loans from the Rural Electrification Administration (REA) to local cooperatives). In any year, some proportion of past loans is repaid, but the difference between current lending and current repayment is a net drain on the federal treasury.

Another drain arises over time if loan repayments are not large enough to amortize the original loans. Because many federal agencies lend at interest rates below the market rate, this net drain, or subsidy, can be substantial. Suppose that REA lends $27,355 to a local cooperative at 2 percent and schedules annual repayments of $1000 for forty years. If the market rate of interest at the time of the loan is 6 percent, then the repayments will only be sufficient to amortize a loan of $15,046. Thus, the initial loan is equivalent to a cash subsidy of $12,309 and a 6 percent loan of $15,046. Current practice is *not* to include this subsidy explicitly in the expenditure account, largely due to questions about the appropriate rate of interest to use with government loans. This question will be explored more deeply in Chapter 13.

Another interesting aspect of the loan account concerns private loans insured by the federal government. No outlay of federal money is involved, but the authority must be available to make such an outlay if the borrower should default. This difference between budget authority and outlays is shown in the detailed tables underlying the budget summary in Table 11.1. The difference is greatest for housing, as might be expected in view of the magnitude of federal mortgage insurance programs.

Total Budget. Net lending is added to expenditures (excluding net lending) to produce total outlays. When outlays are subtracted from receipts, the difference is the government's budget surplus. Of the planned surplus of $1.3 billion in fiscal 1971, the administration intended to use $1.2 billion to reduce public holdings of federal debt. The remaining $0.1 billion was to be applied to the government's cash account and miscellaneous minor items.

OTHER BUDGET CONCEPTS

In presenting a set of accounts that depict the many aspects of the federal government's finances, the unified budget is conceptually superior to the alternative budget concepts that were used before fiscal 1969: the administrative budget, the consolidated cash statement, and the National Income Accounts (NIA) budget.

The Administrative Budget. The administrative budget was popular with Presidents because it enabled them to understate the magnitude of their expenditure programs. Unlike other budget concepts, the administrative budget excluded trust fund operations for the reason that they lay outside the control of the administration. Whatever the political validity of this argument, it makes little economic sense, for trust fund receipts are available to fund other federal programs through intragovernmental transactions and loans. Moreover, the stabilizing (or destabilizing) impact of the federal budget works to a large extent through the income-maintenance programs of the social security trust funds. The other major difference between the administrative and unified budgets (ignoring several minor adjustments) is the treatment of the sale of participation certificates in loans owed to the federal government. The unified budget treats these certificates as a means of financing the net federal deficit, not as an offset to net federal lending.

The Consolidated Cash Budget. This is the closest of the three alternative budgets to the unified budget concept. It includes the federal trust funds, and its accounting is on a cash (rather than an accrual) basis. (The cash basis of the unified budget involves slightly different timing from that of the consolidated cash budget, but the difference will be minor until the unified budget is converted to accrual accounting at some future date.) The principal differences between the consolidated cash and unified budgets are that the consolidated cash statement does not treat "market-type" receipts as negative expenditures; it excludes the retirement contributions of federal employees;

and it includes transactions of the District of Columbia and two privately owned, federally sponsored institutions (federal land banks and federal home loan banks). Like the administrative budget, the consolidated cash statement treats sales of participation certificates as offsets to net lending (negative expenditures) rather than as a means of financing the federal deficit.

The NIA Budget. The National Income Accounts budget is not really a budget at all; instead, it is the representation of the federal government's activities in the National Income and Product Accounts. The accounts trace productive activity in the economy, emerging with GNP on the output side and factor incomes, indirect taxes, and capital consumption on the input side. The accounts are maintained on an accrual basis instead of the cash basis of the other budgets. Accrual accounting measures the flows of productive services as they occur, not necessarily as they are remunerated. Since the financial aspects of the federal budget are less important than its economic impact, accrual accounting is the proper conceptual basis for the budget. The other major differences between the NIA budget and the unified one are that the former excludes net lending—the reasoning being that assets are merely exchanged, not created—and includes government contributions to federal employees' retirement plans (excluded as intragovernmental transactions in the unified budget). The NIA budget also excludes some minor items, notably certain domestic and foreign loans.

Since different types of federal expenditures and revenues have different impacts on resource allocation and stabilization, no one budget figure provides a comprehensive indication of the fiscal impact of federal programs. Only the unified budget is both consistent in its treatment of the timing of all receipts and expenditures and comprehensive in its coverage. The strength of the unified budget is not that its totals of receipts and expenditures are more accurate indicators of the impact of federal programs than the other budgets' summary statistics. Instead, the unified budget presents a set of data that, taken together, convey an accurate picture of federal economic activity. Our concern in the rest of this chapter is with the individual decisions that determine what numbers appear in the federal budget.

THE BUDGETARY PROCESS

The President's budgetary submission to Congress, a summary of which is shown in Table 11.1, is only one of the middle steps in the long and complex chain of events comprising the budget cycle. Economic considerations are not always dominant in this process; instead, the budget is a political document that may be influenced by economic analysis. In making decisions, participants in the budgetary process rely on strategies, rules-of-thumb, and past experience with their "adversaries" at least as much as upon a comparison of economic costs and benefits.

Three principal groups participate in the budget cycle: agency officials, the President's central economic advisers, and the Congressmen who dominate the appropriations process. Agency officials are department-level and bureau-level planners and administrators whose responsibilities include formulating projects and long-run plans for fulfilling their agencies' objectives. The constraints upon their plans are the availability of funds and the political and economic acceptability of their programs. The central economic advisers of the President include the Secretary of the Treasury, the Chairman of the Federal Reserve Board of Governors, the three members of the Council of Economic Advisers, and especially the Director of the Office of Management and Budget (OMB) and the Chairman of the new Domestic Council.[1] The latter two agencies are responsible primarily for the planning and implementation of individual federal programs. The other advisers concern themselves largely with the aggregate economy: prices, employment, GNP, total revenue, and the balance of payments. The key Congressmen and Senators are those who sit on the appropriations committees, especially the committee and subcommittee chairmen. They usually view their role as restraining the extravagance of the executive branch participants in the budgetary process.

The budget cycle has three distinct parts. The first consists of the deliberations within the executive branch over the budget to be submitted to Congress. The second begins with the President's budget submission (in the January before the beginning of the fiscal year for which the budget is prepared) and ends with congressional action on the many individual budget requests. The third phase is implementation of the budget enacted by Congress, both over the current fiscal year and for as long after that as expenditure authority survives.

Executive Budgeting. Preparation of the budget for, say, fiscal 1972 began in the fall of 1969 in most agencies and led to the budget sub-

---

[1] The Domestic Council was established by the executive branch reorganization in 1970. Prior to the reorganization, the OMB was known as the Bureau of the Budget, and its director was called the Budget Director.

mission in January 1971. At the beginning of the budget cycle, OMB identified program issues and asked agencies to focus on them in the coming budget. These program issues were either politically sensitive topics, areas in which the economic effectiveness of agency programs was in question, or studies of how an agency's policy should develop in a specific direction. Under the 1970 reorganization, OMB and the Domestic Council are supposed to help the President make preliminary decisions about key program areas. In addition, the recommendations of the other central advisers about the state of the economy, the availability of revenue, and the urgency for particular kinds of programs became part of the President's decision process. In response to these early decisions about program priorities, agencies prepared budget requests for particular program areas.

These requests were submitted during the spring of 1970 in the form of draft program memoranda containing agency proposals and whatever justification the agencies were able to develop. Only 100 or 200 issues per year become the subject of program memoranda and special program issue studies, but even these strain the analytical resources of most agencies. In many cases, therefore, program memoranda do not contain adequate analytical support for agency requests. Instead, there may be appeals to political goals or hopeful predictions about the effects of the programs proposed. The draft memoranda and the studies underlying them were reviewed by OMB by late spring and were returned to the agencies for revision. Meanwhile, OMB revised its overall budget guidelines to be consistent with later forecasts of the state of the economy and political demands. On the basis of this revision and the draft program memoranda, OMB recommended tentative program decisions to the President. The President's decisions on expenditure and revenue policy were given to the Director of OMB during the summer, and the Director then formalized them in letters to agency heads late in the summer.

As the agencies revised their draft program memoranda to meet OMB's comments, they also prepared the other parts of their budget submissions, program and financial plans, and drafts of the legislation they will need to implement their new programs. Program memoranda explore only single program issues, but program and financial plans display in much less detail all the expenditures an agency plans to undertake and the programs on which resources will be spent during the coming fiscal year (and usually several years into the future). Only a few of the programs in a program and financial plan are analyzed in program memoranda. The other programs an agency may operate are budgeted from year to year by reliance on the concepts of base and fair share.

An agency's base consists, informally, of the programs it has operated over so long a period that they are no longer the subject of executive or congressional evaluation. For example, price supports are part of the base of the Department of Agriculture, and the operation of the FBI is part of the base of the Department of Justice. Over time, the base increases as the size of the clientele group grows or as the cost of serving the group rises. The base may also expand if new programs become accepted as parts of it. For most agencies, programs in the base amount to over 90 percent of their total budgets. (Exceptions are new agencies, such as the Office of Economic Opportunity, and those with single programs that are always in the public eye, such as the National Aeronautics and Space Administration.)

The fair share of an agency is the proportion of general increases in expenditures that it may expect on the basis of past experience. In the course of the normal growth of the economy, federal revenues rise substantially from year to year. The increase typically is not allocated to only one or two agencies but is spread through the entire executive branch. Even without strong program justification, an agency may expect to be able to fund a new program with its fair share of the increase in total federal expenditures.

Within the executive branch an effort has been made to replace political concepts like base and fair share with a reliance on analyses of alternative programs. We will examine this new approach more closely later in this chapter, but it can be noted here that the concepts of base and fair share still appear in the internal budgeting decisions made within agencies.

Agencies sent their revised program memoranda, program and financial plans, and draft legislation back to OMB by the end of September 1970. During the fall OMB evaluated the revised memoranda, held formal hearings with OMB examiners and agency officials, and then made final recommendations to the President about specific program issues. The President reached his final decisions in December, in the light of OMB recommendations and the latest information and forecasts about the state of the economy. If an agency disagreed with OMB's recommendations, it could appeal them to the President, and in unusual circumstances it might ask the President himself to reconsider. Once final decisions were made, however, the agencies had about a month to revise their memoranda and program and financial plans, and draft legislation for final submission to Congress as part of the President's budget message in the third week of January 1971. During the last few hectic weeks of the cycle, OMB put all the agency material together and prepared a draft of the budget message itself for the President's approval.

Congressional Appropriations.[2] Only at this point, with the budget cycle a year old, did Congress become involved. There are two stages in congressional approval: authorization, passing upon the objectives for which funds are to be spent, and appropriation, the decision to commit specific amounts of funds in a particular fiscal year. Expenditures occur when the appropriated money actually is disbursed by the executive agencies. Both authorizations and appropriations usually are annual, but expenditures can be made up to two years after the expiration of the spending authority as long as the contractual obligation to make the expenditure was undertaken during the fiscal year for which the funds were appropriated.

Authorization precedes appropriation in the congressional review process. Authorization for a program consists of enabling legislation, which must be passed by both House and Senate and signed into law by the President (or passed over his veto). As an example, suppose that the Defense Department budget includes a request for funds to design an advanced manned bomber. If this is a new program, it will be considered first by the House and Senate armed services committees. Only after both houses of Congress have approved the program in principle is a budget appropriation considered by the appropriations committees. Once a program is approved, however, it may not need to be reevaluated in each fiscal year. Consideration in later years usually is limited to determining the level of appropriations.

The House Appropriations Committee dominates the congressional budget review process. The committee consists of fifty members who are divided into thirteen subcommittees (plus a secret committee that appropriates funds for the Central Intelligence Agency), each consisting of from five to twelve members. Each committee member sits on an average of two subcommittees and rarely participates in the deliberations of any of the others. The appropriations process begins with open hearings at which each subcommittee gathers testimony from agency officials, the central economic advisers, and private citizens affected by the proposed budget. Following these hearings, the subcommittee holds a closed "markup" session at which its recommendations take shape. The marked-up appropriations bill is then reported to the full Appropriations Committee, which rarely alters the subcommittee bill in any major way, and then is passed on to the full House. Debate on appropriations legislation usually is limited strictly, and it is unusual for the committee (and thus the subcommittee) bill to be changed on the floor of the House.

---

[2] For an exhaustive treatment of this subject, see Richard F. Fenno, Jr., *The Power of the Purse* (Boston: Little, Brown, 1966).

The markup process consists chiefly of changing the line items in the budget, the specific resources that an agency is authorized to buy. (Typically, these are authorized manpower ceilings or items of capital equipment.) The basis for the markup is testimony in open hearings, but a subcommittee does not usually make explicit estimates of the effect on program outputs when it cuts or adds to line items. Instead, the agency commonly is assumed to be capable of doing essentially the same job with different resources. Changes in line items thus usually are interpreted as rewards or penalties for performances that Congressmen find admirable or deficient, based largely on the testimony of clientele groups and the Congressmen's own predisposition toward the agency's activities. In particular instances, of course, congressional interest may center on specific programs. Changes in line items then have the effect of curtailing or expanding these programs.

Because their subcommittees' recommendations almost always are accepted by the full House, the thirteen subcommittee chairmen are among the most powerful men in Congress. They exercise extensive control over the composition of their subcommittees (and, as senior members of the Appropriations Committee, over new appointments to the full Appropriations Committee), control the scheduling of hearings and markup sessions, write the formal reports of their subcommittees, and preside over the House delegation in conference with the Senate. The informal power derived from these formal prerogatives is so great that subcommittee chairmen can wield an effective veto power over programs they dislike and can frequently oppose the President successfully if they disagree with his budgetary requests.

The situation in the Senate is a little less rigid. The Senate Appropriations Committee has twenty-seven members, each of whom sits on an average of seven of the twelve subcommittees. The hearing and markup process is similar to that in the House, but the Senate is more willing' to open up floor debate on appropriations and frequently to alter subcommittee and committee recommendations quite substantially. An individual member of the House has virtually no chance of effecting a change in the Appropriations Committee's bill because of deference shown to seniority in the House and the limited time for debate on the House floor. Neither of these restrictions limits an individual Senator's ability to persuade his colleagues to alter the committee's recommendations.

House subcommittee chairmen usually view themselves as "guardians of the public purse" and thus almost always appropriate less than the President's request. Some of these cuts are restored in the Senate. Since the Senate considers appropriations after the House has finished, the appearances of agency officials and presidential advisers before the Senate subcommittees frequently have the aura of an "appeals court."[3]

On rare occasions, Congress may appropriate more than the President has asked for. When this happens, it is usually because the agency in question has a close relationship with powerful Congressmen, probably including the subcommittee chairman, who are strong advocates of the agency's programs. (Defense is the best example, but many other agencies also have found advocates among Congressmen.) Thus an agency can, in effect, appeal the President's budget request to Congress. In most cases, however, agencies and OMB prepare their budget submissions with the expectation of being cut by Congress, and they may well inflate their initial requests to provide some leeway for the expected deflation.

Consideration of the President's budget request is only one of the items of business facing Congress each year, and appropriations legislation often is used as a political weapon by factions in Congress. Consequently, action on appropriations always carries over into the fiscal year for which the appropriations are being made. Agencies that begin the fiscal year without enacted appropriations have no legal authority to continue operations. Typically, Congress gets around this hurdle by enacting "continuing resolutions" authorizing agencies to continue operations at their current level. But when the appropriations lag reaches into the second half of the fiscal year (that is, past January 1972 for the 1972 fiscal year), the costs of congressional inaction can become very high. Not only is an agency unable to introduce new programs in an orderly way, but in the rush to "catch up" once the appropriations legislation finally is enacted an agency usually will incur costs that could have been avoided if funds had been available earlier.

The full budget cycle thus may extend over two years and always lasts at least eighteen months. Especially during congressional review, all the participants exhibit strategic behavior of a complex kind. Deliberate overstatement of requests by agencies in the expectation of congressional reductions is only one of many devices used by agency officials and central economic advisers to pry desired appropriations out of the subcommittees. On the other side, Congressmen demand that agencies be very responsive to congressional prerogatives, whether these be requests for information, tailoring of projects to benefit particular areas, or (on occasion) using funds for purposes

---

[3] In recent years the Senate has begun hearings on some appropriations before final House action was completed.

that the agency does not really want but that a Congressman may believe in strongly. The political nature of this process concerns us only insofar as it provides a standard against which to compare alternative budgetary systems.

Executive Apportionment. When Congress has acted upon an agency's appropriations legislation and the President has signed the bill into law, the agency must translate the congressional appropriation into cash expenditures. The first step in this procedure is for the agency to restructure its budget in light of congressional revisions of the President's initial requests. The agency then sends OMB a request for apportionment of the appropriation over the fiscal year. Apportionments usually are quarterly and may vary in amount to reflect differences in the operation of individual programs over the fiscal year. OMB ordinarily acts as a cashier, passing on the agency's requests to the Treasury so that the agency may be given authority to draw upon federal bank accounts. On occasion, however, OMB may slow down or accelerate apportionment as a countercyclical device. On still rarer occasions OMB has refused to apportion appropriated funds, to block a program that Congress authorized against the wishes of the central executive branch.

Federal expenditures usually follow the incurring of obligations fairly closely, but obligations may carry over into a succeeding fiscal year if the good being purchased is an item of capital equipment or if the federal agency has contracted with a private company for either physical goods or professional services. When an expenditure actually occurs, it usually is drawn on the Treasury accounts at Federal Reserve Banks. The responsibility for maintaining expenditures within appropriation and apportionment limits rests with individual agencies, but OMB retains an overseeing capacity. Congress also retains a supervisory authority through the General Accounting Office, a congressional agency charged with auditing the activities of the executive agencies. The General Accounting Office may audit both public agencies and the private companies with which they do business. Recently, it has tried to standardize federal accounting procedures to prevent the misuse of federal funds.

PROGRAM BUDGETING

The system of budgeting just described is incremental, especially during the congressional phase. Once a program is approved as part of an agency's base, continued funding is nearly automatic. Congressional attention is focused at the budget margin, on new programs and on those that are being expanded greatly or that are changing in character. Congressional concern usually is with less than 10 percent of an agency's appropriations. The other 90 percent is included in the agency's base and thus escapes scrutiny.

The basic function of a budget and a budgeting system is to allocate resources among competing ends. Most economists and many political scientists who have studied the operation of incremental budgeting are dissatisfied with it, for they feel that it frequently ignores important program issues and treats others capriciously. Critics of incremental budgeting argue that not enough consideration is given to the availability of alternative programs and that congressional acceptance of programs too often reflects political advantage instead of economic benefits. Defenders of incremental budgeting point out that the system works tolerably well at fairly low cost and that it is compatible with decentralized decision-making. To evaluate these arguments, we must consider the alternative of program budgeting initiated in the executive branch in 1965.

Program budgeting was introduced because the President's central economic advisers (primarily the Budget Director) thought they did not have enough control over the allocation of resources among different agencies and projects. In incremental budgeting, the focus is on each agency's additional expenditures. Budgetary review implicitly assumes that on-going programs (those in the base) need not be re-examined and that new programs need be compared only to others operated by the same agency. Typically, each agency's budget is considered apart from that of any other agency; different subcommittees frequently are responsible for budgeting similar programs. The close liaisons established between agencies and Congressmen frustrated attempts by the Budget Director and even the President to impose a unified structure on total federal expenditures.

To facilitate the comparison of programs within each agency, the Budget Director wanted a budgeting system that would relate the resources used by each program to the program's outputs. To compare similar programs in different agencies, a common basis for measuring outputs had to be established. The most generally applicable way to compare outputs is by their economic value (when it can be measured). This measure of the value of programs offers the secondary benefit of permitting some programs to be compared to others of an entirely different nature, the only common element being that both programs use scarce resources and produce outputs having an economic value. Thus, the Budget Director's objectives could be met by a budgeting system that introduced elements of economic rationality into federal resource allocation.

The program budgeting system introduced in 1965 and named the Planning-Programming-Budgeting System (PPBS) requires agencies to align their activities into a program structure. The objective of the program structure is to identify the different programs that are devoted to the same end (for example, remedial education or highway safety) and to measure the resources used by each program. Even if no measure of the amount or value of output is available, the program structure permits agency officials and the central advisers to compare programs on a heuristic or intuitive basis. The program structure is formalized in the current executive budgetary process as the program and financial plan. As an example, Table 11.2 shows one of the sections of the urban transportation subprogram in the Department of Transportation program and financial plan for fiscal years 1968–1970. The complete plan shows outputs and the value of benefits in another table and provides similar breakdowns of other programs into program subcategories.

TABLE 11.2   Fiscal Year 1970 Program and Financial Plan: Highways (Thousands of Dollars)

	Fiscal year		
	1968	1969	1970
Interstate system	1,428,300	1,460,500	1,460,500
Other primary	56,900	58,500	58,500
Secondary system	57,300	60,400	60,400
Urban extension	182,000	194,200	194,200
TOPICS		180,000	180,000
Railway-highway grade crossings	25,900	19,800	19,800
Roadside hazard reduction and spot improvement	77,800	81,900	81,900
Roadside beautification, and billboard and junkyard regulation	400	9,500	25,900
Relocation assistance		35,900	35,900
Metropolitan area planning	21,900	18,800	18,800
Advance acquisition of rights-of-way		40,000	40,000
SUBTOTAL	1,850,500	2,159,500	2,175,900

SOURCE: Jack W. Carlson, "The Status and Next Steps for Planning, Programming, and Budgeting," in Joint Economic Committee, *The Analysis and Evaluation of Public Expenditures, The PPB System* (1969), Attachment 9, Table 2, p. 736.

The planning function of PPBS is introduced through another aspect of the program and financial plan or program structure. Although congressional appropriations are usually made annually, the PFP projects levels of program operation and resource costs, based on current decisions, for several years into the future.[4] This feature of PPBS is especially useful for decisions about capital-intensive projects with long lifetimes and benefit streams and for projects that are introduced as small "pilots" but quickly grow to entail large resource costs. (A good example of such a project was the supersonic air transport, the SST, that was first funded as a $90 million appropriation for research but might ultimately have required $3.5 billion of federal funds. The "foot-in-the-door" technique has been a favorite strategy of many agencies.)

Interagency budgeting and the link with the incremental, line-item system still used by Congress are facilitated through program memoranda, which generally require an agency to analyze all the activities in a particular program category, discussing the relationships among different programs and stating the agency's objectives in a broad program area. More detailed evaluations of particular subcategories and program elements in a "program package" are carried out in special analytic studies. These analyses require at the least that program outputs be stated in quantifiable terms and preferably that an agency develop a technique for measuring the value of its programs. Thus, a special analytic study is intended to be a systematic evaluation of the programs that an agency operates toward a particular purpose (such as retraining high school dropouts). We will discuss the techniques of systematic analysis in the next chapter and analyze some examples in Part Five.

To recapitulate, the elements of PPBS are simple: (1) a program structure that relates resource inputs to program objectives and outputs, (2) a multiyear projection of program operations to assist in planning and developing new programs, and (3) analyses (program memoranda and special analytic studies) of individual program areas, typically requiring quantification and, ideally, evaluation of program outputs. Nonetheless, PPBS has caused considerable uneasiness among Congressmen and agency officials and has been extremely difficult to implement in many agencies that have adopted it wholeheartedly. The difficulties of implementation largely result from an imperfect understanding of what federal programs are intended to

---

[4] The complete program and financial plan for the program elements in Table 11.2 projects costs, outputs, and benefits through fiscal 1974.

achieve and how to measure their success. We will discuss this problem more fully in the next chapter.

Congressional and agency displeasure with PPBS stems from some of its departures from traditional incremental budgeting. The requirement that agencies merely identify their outputs (not measure or evaluate them) has proved troublesome for some agencies and provides a source of embarrassment for Congressmen whose favorite programs have general or vague impacts. In other words, PPBS threatens to interfere with the political aspects of budgeting. Another problem is that the information requirements for PPBS are much greater than for incremental budgeting. Agencies must maintain a running account of *all* programs, not only those whose levels of funding are changing rapidly, and Congressmen must busy themselves with detailed examinations of many more programs than the few that they scrutinize during the traditional review process. Still another incursion on congressional prerogatives is the interagency comparison of programs, often cutting across lines of appropriations authority well established in both House and Senate.

But the major fear of both Congressmen and agency officials is that PPBS is the instrument of centralizing budget power in the hands of a few advisers close to the President. Under incremental budgeting, before 1965, each agency's allocations and appropriations were determined principally by a two-sided game in which the players were agency officials and Congressmen. OMB staff members participated in a relatively minor way on the agency side, affecting the requests that an agency presented to Congress. PPBS changed the sides, substituting the Director of OMB for the agency officials, and also changed the game by placing much more information and expertise at the disposal of the executive branch. Some Congressmen have welcomed the opportunities that PPBS offers for more rational (that is, more nearly efficient) resource allocation and have tried to acquire the technical expertise and larger staffs necessary to use PPBS. But most Congressmen (including appropriations chairmen) have resisted it, partly for reasons of economy and partly as an infringement upon their political prerogatives. Consequently, PPBS is widely used only in the executive budgeting process. Although the PPBS background materials are available to support the President's budget submission, congressional appropriations still are made primarily on a line-item basis.

OTHER BUDGETING SYSTEMS

Program budgeting is only one of the reforms and modifications of traditional budgeting practices that have been proposed for government use. Three other budgeting systems are performance budgeting, zero-base budgeting, and the separation of capital items into a capital, or divided, budget.

Performance Budgeting. Program budgeting is a device for allocating resources among programs. Performance budgeting is a similar technique for allocating resources *within* a program. Program budgeting links resource inputs to the eventual outputs of the program and chooses those programs that yield the maximum value of output per dollar of input. Performance budgeting takes as given the requirement that a certain amount of output be obtained (although neither the amount of output nor its nature may be well specified) and concentrates on producing that output in the least-cost way. Performance budgeting establishes "performance measures" to evaluate the productivity of resources. These measures usually are indicators of workload, such as the number of pages typed or tax audits processed. They are intermediate measures of output, related to the attainment of some objective that cannot easily be quantified.

The value of performance budgeting is as a management tool. It does not help to plan new programs or determine levels of funding based on the value of outputs, but it does indicate whether economies can be realized by reallocating resource inputs within and between operational programs. Compared to program budgeting, performance budgeting is a vehicle for optimization or efficiency at a lower level.[5]

Zero-Base Budgeting. As its name implies, this is a budgeting technique that begins with the position that the agency's base contains no programs and no funding at all. In the limit, zero-base budgeting implies that an agency would have to justify all its programs compared to all alternative uses of the funds. Since many agencies cannot describe their program's outputs in a way that permits comparisons with the programs of other agencies, zero-base budgeting usually is restricted to making an agency compare each of its own programs to all its other programs.

Zero-base budgeting is costly in terms of time and its information requirements. Even program budgeting, which necessitates the definition, measurement, and evaluation of output, is usually restricted to analyses of changes at the margin. Zero-base budgeting involves comparisons *in toto* of each dollar spent on each program with each dollar

[5] For some examples of the use of performance budgeting at the state and federal levels, see Jesse Burkhead, *Government Budgeting* (New York: Wiley, 1965), pp. 133–38.

spent on every other program. Although the idea behind zero-base budgeting is appealing, an actual zero-base budget would require either a long budgetary cycle or a large staff of budget analysts. Moreover, all the problems of measuring and evaluating outputs arise in zero-base as well as in program budgeting.

Capital Budgeting. Government expenditures include the purchase of capital equipment such as buildings, vehicles, computers, and typewriters. When these goods are purchased by private firms, only their depreciation is treated as a current expense in recognition of their multiyear productive lifetimes. When the government buys the same goods, they are entered as "capital purchases on current account" and are treated as current expenses in full. The result is that expenditures in the federal budget are not closely related to benefits. Agencies are given an incentive to economize on capital items that bulk large in current budgets, even though the capital goods might be much more productive in the long run than the other resources that the agency will use in their place.

A solution often proposed to this problem is to separate capital expenditures from other government purchases and to enter only the flow of depreciation in the government's current account. A separate capital budget would offer several advantages. The time pattern of current expenditures would correspond more closely to that of current benefits, as long as depreciation charges really reflected the use of capital equipment. Much of the political onus attached to high capital expenditures would be eliminated since it would generally be understood that the current, not the capital, account was the best measure of government expenditures and the true federal deficit or surplus. And use of a capital budget would let government investment be compared explicitly with private capital formation. This procedure would help to eliminate one of the biases against public expenditures, their "nonproductivity."

The principal argument against a separate capital budget is that it would give a misleading impression of the impact of current federal expenditures upon the rest of the economy. If the level of aggregate demand is one of the considerations underlying formation of the budget, then total capital purchases, not their depreciation flow, are the relevant magnitude. State and local governments and private firms need not worry about aggregate demand when they compile their budgets, but the special responsibility of the federal government carries with it the necessity for special treatment of its purchases. Some less important problems with a capital budget include the classification of expenditures resulting in capital formation outside the federal government (say, by rural electric cooperatives and small businessmen) and the decision about whether some receipts should be entered in the capital budget on the grounds that they would have been used for private investment in the absence of the tax.

On balance, the idea of separating capital expenditures from current ones probably has more drawbacks than advantages. But the main favorable argument, that society's allocation of resources is distorted by current budgetary practices that overemphasize capital expenditures, is a strong one. One of the advantages of PPBS is that it displays capital and operating costs over the duration of a project, thus permitting a more rational comparison of alternative programs with different resource compositions. Capital budgeting is not a desirable reform for the federal budget document, but the concept underlying it should be implemented in the federal budget process.

SUMMARY

The unified budget adopted in fiscal 1969 is a significant improvement over the administrative, consolidated cash, and National Income Accounts budgets that had been in use earlier. Although differences among most of the four budgets are not great, the unified budget presents a set of summary accounts that give a consistent picture of the varied impacts the federal budget has on the rest of the economy.

The budgetary process underlying the budget document has three main sections: the preparation of the executive budget, congressional review of the President's budget submission, and implementation of actual appropriations legislation by OMB and the executive agencies. The budgetary process within the executive branch begins about a year before the budget submission in the January preceding the beginning of the fiscal year. The President's budget is the result of consultations between agency planners and administrators, on one side, and the central economic advisers, chiefly the Director of OMB and the Chairman of the Domestic Council, on the other. Congressional review is dominated by the subcommittee chairmen of the House Appropriations Committee, who produce appropriations legislation for individual agencies after a complicated process in which consideration of the economic aspects of programs usually is secondary to political considerations. After enactment of appropriations, the budget returns to the executive branch where OMB apportions it among agencies and monitors the operation of individual programs.

The congressional budgeting process is incremental and focuses on the line items, or resource inputs, in the budget. Dissatisfaction with this process led in 1965 to the implementation within the executive branch of program budgeting (PPBS). Under PPBS, an agency is called upon to review all its activities in particular areas in the form of program memoranda and to justify its requests for new programs (or for retaining existing ones) through special analytic studies. All its activities, not only those summarized in program memoranda, are presented in the program and financial plan, the basic document of the program budget.

The advantages of program budgeting are its multiyear outlook, identification and comparison of alternative programs, and evaluation of the economic aspects of particular programs. Its disadvantages are the high cost of analysis and the often-unsolved problems of defining, measuring, and evaluating the output of many public programs. Critics also fear that PPBS will become the vehicle for increasing domination of the budget process by the President's central advisers.

The principal alternatives to program and incremental budgeting are performance, zero-base, and capital budgeting. Performance budgeting is useful for low-level management decisions. Zero-base budgeting is conceptually appealing but would be costly and inefficient to introduce on a large scale. Capital budgeting is intended to offset the bias against capital-intensive public projects that arises because capital expenditures are treated as current ones. Although a capital budget document is probably not desirable, a more general implementation of PPBS would help achieve the objectives underlying the capital budgeting proposal.

12 Systems Analysis

Systems analysis is the name given to a group of techniques for analyzing alternative allocations of resources. The decisions in question need not be public ones; in fact, most practitioners of the art of systems analysis are employed by the private sector to study the allocation alternatives open to private firms. There are many different types of systems analysis, but we will limit our discussion to two: benefit-cost studies and cost-effectiveness analyses. These techniques, most commonly used in PPBS studies, are the most important for public sector resource allocation.

BENEFIT-COST ANALYSIS

For our purposes, a system can be thought of as any way of transforming inputs into outputs. Inputs are the factors of production that governments use to produce public sector goods and services. The outputs of public programs are much more difficult to specify without referring to specific systems. This difficulty is recognized in the generality of the guidance that OMB offers to agencies in implementing PPBS. OMB defines outputs only as quantifiable "end products or services" produced by the government. As "end products," outputs are the means by which government programs affect the private sector; that is, they are not supposed to include goods or services that one government agency produces for another's use. Outputs, therefore, "do not measure the benefits of the program," the value that private producers and consumers place upon the government's outputs.

Table 12.1 shows the output measures for the part of the Department of Transportation's program and financial plan reproduced in Table 11.2. The outputs listed are for the most part the products physically produced by each program element. Thus, the output of highway systems is the number of miles of roadway, and a measure of output of the roadside beautification project is the number of billboards removed. These outputs are the goods and services that the Department of Transportation bestows on the private sector.

TABLE 12.1   Fiscal Year 1970 Program and Financial Plan:
            Highways—Outputs

	Fiscal year		
	1968	1969	1970
Interstate system outputs: lane miles	1,550	1,550	1,550
Other primary outputs: lane miles	360	365	370
Secondary system outputs: lane miles	350	375	375
Urban extensions outputs: lane miles	1,085	1,225	1,225
TOPICS	—	—	—
Railway-highway grade-crossing elimination outputs: crossings improved	237	214	292
Roadside hazard reduction; spot improvement outputs			
Miles of highway reconstruction to acceptable standards	995	1,037	1,037
Projects completed	45	104	104
Roadside beautification; billboard and junkyard removal outputs			
Number of billboards removed	70	—	920
Number of junkyards screened or removed	195	—	300
Relocation assistance outputs: number of displacements	—	43,045	43,045
Metropolitan area planning outputs: number of studies	205	210	215
Advance acquisition of right-of-way outputs: number of states using advanced funds	—	17	32

SOURCE: Same as for Table 11.2, p. 734 (modified).

We can construct similar output measures for the activities of other agencies. Thus, the output of federal power facilities is the amount of electricity generated, some of the outputs of the post office are the amounts of mail of different classes actually delivered, the output of the Upward Bound Program of the Office of Economic Opportunity is the number of participating high school students who actually enter college, and so on.

To get an idea of what the systems that produce these outputs are worth to us (that is, how much we might be willing to spend on them), we must convert the output measures into benefits. Benefits signify the value of outputs, measured in dollar terms whenever possible. The conversion of outputs into benefits can be extremely difficult. For example, what is the dollar value of the miles of roadway constructed for the interstate highway system? What is the value of the removal of billboards for the sake of highway beautification? What is the value to society of an additional participant in Upward Bound? And what is the value to the participant?

In some instances the valuation of outputs is straightforward. Many of the outputs produced by public agencies, such as postal services and electric power, are marketed and thus are evaluated by producers and consumers. If the market prices adequately reflect the marginal cost of production and the marginal evaluations that consumers place on the output, then benefits at the margin are simply equal to the market price. Even if the prices of government outputs are not perfectly efficient (in the sense of equating MRS and MRT), they may correspond closely enough to the prices set in private sector markets to yield usable estimates of benefits. For example, publicly produced electricity can be valued at its market price even though the market price is the regulated one that sets consumers' marginal valuation equal to average cost. As long as the average cost is not decreasing rapidly, marginal cost will be close to average cost, and the inefficiency in allocation will be small. Thus, the market price is an acceptable measure of the marginal value of the government's output.

In the case of postal services, however, the use of "market" prices probably does not correspond closely enough to the private sector alternatives. The size of the postal deficit hints that the true marginal cost of postal services is substantially greater than the prices charged for them. Although we can estimate the true marginal cost by studying the operation of private firms offering similar services, conversion of this marginal cost into an estimate of total benefits requires us to adjust the output of postal services to reflect the reduction in demand that would occur if prices were set equal to marginal cost.

In measuring the benefits of government programs, the case of postal services occurs more frequently than that of electric power. We usually cannot rely on market prices to give us immediate estimates of the benefit that consumers derive from government outputs; instead, we have to impute benefits on the basis of shadow prices. Shadow prices can be thought of as the prices that would have cleared the market for government outputs if the outputs had been made available under the same conditions as private sector goods. The most common way of estimating shadow prices is to use the market prices of private sector goods that are similar to the public outputs. Thus, in the case of the post office, the market prices of messenger services and commercial package delivery may be adequate shadow prices for some postal outputs.

Where markets are not available to provide shadow prices, we must make our own estimates on the basis of assumptions about consumer behavior and the level of supply. If we want to evaluate the benefits of the interstate highway system, for example, we must calculate the dollar savings that users derive from it. The dollar savings then become our estimate of the value of the highway system, on the assumption that users would be willing to pay up to that amount to obtain the benefits that they actually receive. Similarly, a college graduate who owes his diploma to Upward Bound derives benefits from the program equal to the increase in his earnings.[1] This dollar value may be very difficult to calculate, but conceptually it is the measure of the benefit that the participant derives from the program.

In using shadow prices, the analyst must be careful that his estimates really are based on the preferences that consumers have expressed somewhere in the market. If the public output is flood control produced by a hydroelectric dam, for example, consumers' preferences may be estimated from the prices that they have paid for private insurance policies or from the expected value of the dollar savings that they will realize from the lower incidence of floods. The latter measure is a difficult one to use since the analyst must make some assumption about the pattern of land use (and the cost of restoration after the flood). But the former measure, the price of insurance policies, may also pose problems, as shown in Figure 12.1.

Before construction of a public flood-control dam, suppose that private insurance companies offered flood-damage coverage according to the supply curve S_p. The supply curve shows the cost of covering additional (more damage-prone) residents of the floodplain. The demand curve of the residents might look like D, assuming that each person must decide whether or not to buy a fixed amount of coverage. The market price, therefore, would be p_0, and N_0 residents would take out policies. The total value of these policies to consumers then would be $p_0 N_0$, the total market price, plus total consumers' surplus for the N_0 policy holders. Although we cannot discover the magnitude of consumers' surplus, we know that the value of flood protection is at least

---

[1] Plus, perhaps, some intangibles. See Chapter 16.

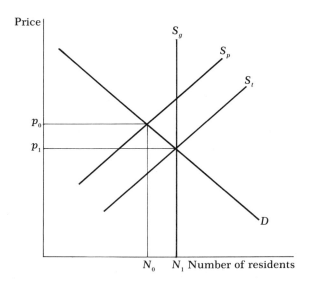

FIGURE 12.1 Evaluating Public Outputs

$p_0 N_0$ and that the N_0 policy holders place a marginal value of p_0 on their policies.

Suppose now that the government builds a dam supplying protection to N_1 residents. The supply curve of protection is S_g, since protection is a public good once the dam has been built. Accordingly, the government cannot recover the cost of the dam through charges levied on residents. In the absence of any information about the true value of the dam, the government may take p_0 as the shadow price of protection and thus estimate the value of the dam as $p_0 N_1$. This estimate, however, is incorrect for two reasons: it neglects consumers' surplus, which the government can never measure, and it overstates the marginal value of protection (which is only p_1 to the N_1 residents). Compared to other projects for which shadow prices can be estimated accurately, therefore, the dam will be overvalued. In this case, the use of incorrect shadow prices will lead to a misallocation between the dam and alternative public and private projects.

This overevaluation of the dam arises because the government extends the output of its program to some consumers who value it at less than its market price (in this case, the price of insurance). A similar overevaluation may occur if the government's production violates the constraints of marginal analysis. In Figure 12.1, now let S_p be the supply of electricity available in the floodplain from private sources, and let S_t be the total supply that will be available once the government's dam is operational. If the government bases its calculations of the benefits of its power production on the (predam) market price p_0, then it will overstate the marginal valuation (p_1) that consumers actually place on the equilibrium supply after the dam has been built (N_1). In this case, the government's production is not merely a small increment to total supply, and we cannot assume that the market equilibrium is substantially unaffected by the government output.

Another difficulty in evaluating public outputs is the impossibility of separating allocation and distribution. When the outputs of government programs are public or semipublic, the tax costs to individual taxpayers are not usually equal to the benefits they receive. Thus, the outputs of public programs generally cause a redistribution of income as well as a reallocation of resources. As long as the beneficiaries of public programs are not the same as the taxpayers (and all individual taxpayers are not in equilibrium), a simple summation of benefits must fail to describe accurately the true impact of the government programs. Unless public outputs are financed through an efficient set of user charges, a calculation of total costs and benefits must always be accompanied by a breakdown of the program's effect on the distribution of income.

This requirement is especially important when one of the objectives of the public program is the redistribution of income. Upward Bound, for example, is designed to increase the real incomes of certain underprivileged teenagers. The cost of this program is borne by taxpayers at large. The benefits that Upward Bound participants derive from the program may far exceed the costs to the rest of society, but the social decision to undertake Upward Bound must reflect a distributional judgment as well as an allocational one. The distributional judgment can be made only if the incidence of costs and benefits, as well as their magnitude, is part of the information on which the decision is based.

Once we have defined the outputs we want to produce and have decided how to evaluate them (that is, estimate the benefits they confer), the next step in benefit-cost analysis is to examine the alternative methods of production. Each distinct way of producing outputs is called a system. Some outputs may be produced with any of a number of systems; for others, there may be only a single technique of production. In either case, the task of the analyst is to identify the different systems that produce outputs from inputs and then to calculate the cost of producing outputs in different ways.

The identification of systems usually is not an economic problem. Instead, it depends on technological factors and perhaps on the state of knowledge about how to produce certain outputs. For example, one of the outputs of manpower-retraining programs (including those, such as the Job Corps, directed at minority group members) is supposed to be a lower delinquency rate among the participants. However, since social scientists do not really know whether these programs can achieve this objective, the systems they design may not include any really effective ways of reducing delinquency rates. Unfortunately, the design of systems is not a task in which economics can help very much, but good evaluations of systems can reveal whether they are producing the outputs they are designed to produce and whether they are doing so efficiently.

The systems analyst must be careful that his evaluation of a system includes an accurate description of its costs. The right measure of costs is always opportunity cost, the value of foregone alternatives. As an example, let us trace the use of this criterion through the design and construction of a high-speed intercity rail transit system for use in the "Northeast Corridor," the megalopolis stretching from Boston to Richmond.

The first step in the development of the system is to plan it, a task that requires the services of central administrators and engineers in the Department of Transportation. Since an opportunity cost is imposed by the use of office space and secretarial help within the Department of Transportation, it is correct to charge these costs to the system. No opportunity cost is imposed in the form of the services of the Secretary of Transportation or other "overhead" elements, however, so it is incorrect to "spread the overhead" over the marginal project (the rail system). Overhead costs are best treated as a non-allocable, long-run element of cost. In practice, most agencies display a separate program category called "general support" or "administration," which includes those costs of running the agency that cannot be attributed to particular programs.

When planning is complete, the system must be constructed. Both the construction and the acquisition of equipment impose capital costs that will be amortized over a long period of time. The lifetime of capital equipment usually is considered to be the "system life," unless there is some reason to expect the system to become economically obsolete before the capital goods have been depreciated. If capital goods have different lifetimes or if the system life is different from the amortization periods for the capital equipment, then the question of salvage value arises. Salvage value is what capital equipment is worth at the end of the system life. For most systems, salvage value is small, and it may even be negative if there are costs of disposing of worthless capital items.

The capital and operating costs of a system are best defined over the system life. For the rail transit system, capital items include construction and equipment, goods with one-time costs over the life of the system. Of course, short-lived capital items may have to be replaced during a system's life. Operating costs are the variable costs that must be incurred in each year as a function of the level of operation. Total system cost is the sum of the three components: planning, capital, and operating costs. (Planning costs are really a form of capital costs, since they are incurred only once in the lifetime of a system.) All these costs are the opportunity costs of the resources used. We always assume full employment, so opportunity costs are never zero if resources really are consumed. Total system cost, however, is not an adequate description of total cost because it neglects the time-phasing of the different costs. This will be discussed in depth in Chapter 13; for now, we may note that both capital and operating costs must be discounted to yield the present values of the time-streams of total cost. Present values are the amounts that must be sacrificed today to provide enough resources (if compounded at the market interest rate) for the specified time-stream of costs. Thus, if we reduce the time-streams that make up total system cost to their present-value equivalents, we can compare systems whose time-phasing of costs is different.

One further problem of costing arises with our example, the intercity rail transit system. Some of the resources employed in the intercity system are also used by another system, intracity commuter rail transit. Tracks, signals, equipment, and personnel are all joint costs of both systems. While it may be possible to separate the variable (operating) costs of the two systems, it generally is not possible to allocate construction costs for roadbeds, or land acquisition costs for intracity rights-of-way, between the systems. The way out of this difficulty is to rely on opportunity cost. If an operational commuter system already exists, the cost of the intercity system is simply the opportunity cost of the additional resources it uses. The resources available — at zero opportunity cost — from the intracity system do *not* represent a cost of the system that we are studying. On the other hand, if we build an intercity system and then wish to examine the feasibility of adding a commuter network, we should not charge the commuter system with the resource costs that have already been incurred by the intercity system.

Once we have charged a system with all the opportunity costs that it incurs, we must decide whether the system represents an efficient use of resources. That is, we must have a criterion for choosing particular allocations of resources among all the alternative public programs that exist. The criterion used by private producers to solve their allocation problems is profit maximization (at least within the competitive model and in the long run also in the real world). The analogue of this criterion within the public sector is maximization of net benefits.

Net benefits are defined as the difference between the present value of the dollar benefits that a system produces and the present value of the dollar costs that it incurs, both measured over the system life. The criterion of maximizing net benefits thus is equivalent to choosing those public programs that offer the largest increments of benefits over the costs of producing them. If our choice is between two mutually exclusive systems that produce the same output, the net benefits criterion tells us to choose the one that offers the greater excess of benefits over costs. If the choice is among many systems producing altogether different outputs, the net benefits criterion tells us to pick those whose outputs we value the most over their cost of production.

The net benefits criterion can be written as $B - C$, where B and C denote the present values of the benefit and cost-streams associated with a system. To use this criterion in selecting the efficient set of projects, the first step is to design systems that are efficient at the margin—that is, those for which marginal benefits equal marginal costs. (For all such systems, the marginal benefit-cost ratio— $\Delta B/\Delta C$ — is unity.) The criterion of maximizing $B - C$ then tells us to choose those systems for which $B - C$ is the largest. Obviously, we should never produce any system for which $B - C$ is negative, even if it is efficient at the margin.

For many systems, an analysis of marginal benefits and marginal costs is difficult because of indivisibilities that preclude marginal changes or uncertainty about either B or C. The $B - C$ criterion tells us not to build systems for which the marginal benefit-cost ratio is less than unity. In cases where marginal benefits or costs are hard to determine, however, the $B - C$ criterion is commonly replaced by the benefit-cost ratio, B/C. Unfortunately, the use of this ratio may lead to inefficiencies which would not occur under the $B - C$ test.

An example of the failure of the B/C criterion is shown in Table 12.2. Suppose that the government is interested in building a bridge at a particular river crossing. It may build either a highway bridge (system H), a pedestrian bridge (system P), or a railroad bridge (system R). It can build any of the three separately or it can build P and R together. The highway bridge, however, can only be built alone. Table 12.2 shows all combinations of costs and benefits when the systems are designed so that each is efficient at the margin. Under the $B - C$ criterion, the highway bridge is preferred, for its net benefits exceed those of either of the other bridges separately or of both together. The B/C test, however, leads to the least desirable bridge (P) first and the most desirable one (H) last.

This situation arises because the high B/C projects may not be capable of infinite replication. If we could build eight pedestrian bridges, each duplicating bridge P, they would yield net benefits of 400, double

TABLE 12.2   Benefit-Cost Criteria: I

	System			
	H	P	R	P + R
B	1000	100	300	400
C	800	50	200	250
B – C	200	50	100	150
B/C	1.25	2.0	1.5	1.6

the net benefits of bridge H. But if projects are unique, then the B/C ratio may lead us to choose systems with high average benefits but low aggregate ones.

Another case in which the $B - C$ criterion is preferred arises when capital is not available in unlimited amounts. An example is shown in Table 12.3, again with the three types of bridges and efficiency at the margin. Suppose now that any combination of bridges may be built at the particular river crossing, but the total cost must not exceed $100 million (set by Congress, perhaps, in the appropriations legislation). The $B - C$ test shows that bridge H again is preferred, with net benefits of 20. But if the projects are ranked by B/C ratio, bridge P will be built, and we will then look around for some other project on which to spend the rest of the $100 million. The only available one will be bridge R. Thus, if we use the B/C ratio, we will again buy a combination of systems that does not yield maximum net benefits.

TABLE 12.3   Benefit-Cost Criteria: II

	System			
	H	P	R	P + R
B	120	15	100	115
C	100	10	90	100
B – C	20	5	10	15
B/C	1.2	1.5	1.11	1.15

These examples may seem to be special cases. They show, however, that in some instances the B/C ratio does not help us choose the most efficient allocations of public resources. The net benefit test, $B - C$, is always as good as the B/C ratio, and in many cases the $B - C$ criterion is the only one that leads to the selection of the most desirable public programs.

Summary. We may use benefit-cost analysis when the outputs of government programs can be quantified and evaluated (as benefits) in dollar terms, usually through shadow prices or the market prices of close substitutes. Costs are the complete opportunity costs of the system that produces the benefits. We must measure costs over the lifetime of the system and then calculate the present values of the cost and benefit streams. We should choose those projects that offer the largest net benefits, $B - C$. This criterion is equivalent to the marginal benefit-cost ratio, $\Delta B / \Delta C$, but it is not the same as the total benefit-cost ratio (B/C) that is often used to compare public programs. B/C leads to improper program selection in many instances and never is preferable to the net benefits criterion, $B - C$.

COST-EFFECTIVENESS ANALYSIS

Benefit-cost analysis was first applied to projects in water resources (dams, river basin development, irrigation). It has also been used with some success in the areas of education, urban renewal, transportation, pollution, and recreation. But there are many important areas of government in which benefit-cost studies simply are not feasible, usually because of difficulties in the measurement or evaluation of outputs. These difficulties are greatest for projects in defense, regulatory activities, crime prevention, and areas where society's concern is largely with income distribution. To the extent that analysis is possible in these program areas, the methodology is that of cost-effectiveness analysis.

Even if we cannot measure the benefits we derive from particular public expenditures, we may still be able to make rational choices among alternatives in the same way that a consumer allocates his income without knowing precisely how much utility he will derive from each item he consumes. Cost-effectiveness analyses make the assumption that the outputs of public programs are useful and valuable, although we may not be able to say how useful or valuable (as we can, for example, measure the value of benefits). The choice among programs frequently must be made on the basis of the values that some public official imputes to different outputs. These imputations are much more crucial in cost-effectiveness than in benefit-cost studies, since in the latter case some guidance about the value of outputs is provided by either market or shadow prices. In benefit-cost studies, the public official is like a private producer who wants to maximize his profits. In cost-effectiveness studies, however, a better analogy is between the public official and the private consumer who is confronted with certain costs (prices) and an income constraint and who then tries to obtain the goods that will yield him the greatest utility.

Many government programs produce outputs that can be measured but not evaluated. For example, the Department of Commerce helps businessmen develop export markets by participating in trade fairs and conducting information programs. The outputs of these programs are the numbers of products promoted through trade fairs and publicity. To measure the value of these outputs, however, is extremely difficult. We do not know what the marginal impact of these activities is upon total exports, nor can we assess the benefits the economy derives from, say, an improvement in its balance of payments. Another Commerce Department activity is the conduct of basic research at the National Bureau of Standards. Outputs can be measured, either as instances of assistance rendered to businesses (calibration, development of standards) or as completed basic research (patents applied for or received). But again, we have no way of estimating the value that the economy places on these outputs.

Cost-effectiveness methodologies were first developed to aid decision-making in the Defense Department in the early 1960's. The benefit derived from Defense presumably is best thought of as deterrence, although the term "deterrence" is usually applied only to strategic (nuclear) capabilities. But even if we adopt an imperialistic position and ascribe the benefits of Defense to the protection of American commercial and industrial interests, it is virtually impossible to measure the value of any single Defense activity. Instead of trying to estimate the value of outputs, Defense systems analysts use rather low-level output measures such as firepower or weapon delivery capability. These measures of combat strength are not far removed, in many cases, from the inputs that generate them, but it has proved impossible to define higher-level output measures for most Defense systems.

The basic requirement for cost-effectiveness analysis is that the output be *specifiable*. This is a weak requirement, since it demands only that the public decision-maker understand what a system does and not necessarily how much of its output it produces. But even this requirement cannot be met by some programs. For example, what is the output of (any of) the activities of the State Department? Of the Antitrust Division of the Justice Department? In the latter case, we might specify the output as the number of cases brought or firms investigated, but such a definition of output would ignore the broad repercussions that some policies have throughout major sectors of the economy. In the former example, no objective description of output (except for certain foreign aid activities) has ever been developed.

If we can specify an output, then we probably have some idea of the different ways of producing it. (A counter-example is an output such as world peace or racial harmony, but even in these cases there is no lack of suggested policies.) Cost-effectiveness analysis consists of estimating the costs of different ways of producing similar outputs. The cost problems are the same as with benefit-cost studies: systems must be defined and the opportunity costs of the resources they use must be calculated. For example, we may want to compare trade fairs and informational activities as different ways of increasing exports. The systems involved incur resource costs for planning, capital equipment, personnel, displays, and so forth. Trade fairs may be labor-intensive, and disseminating information may be capital-intensive, so we must discount costs for purposes of comparability. In short, the cost side of cost-effectiveness analysis is precisely the same as in benefit-cost studies.

When we have defined an output and estimated the costs of different ways of producing it, we are left with the problem of choosing a criterion to guide our selection among alternative systems. We can find a criterion in the decision-making techniques of the individual consumer. If given a choice between apples and oranges, one way that he may decide is to see how many apples and how many oranges he can buy for the same amount of money. If the question is, rather, at which store to buy oranges, the usual criterion is the prices charged at different stores. When applied to the choice among public programs, these simple criteria are glorified as constant-cost and least-cost analysis.

Constant-Cost Studies. The constant-cost criterion is designed to provide a decision-maker (a public official) with information about the consequences of alternative policies. There is no attempt to judge the relative merits of the alternatives or to suggest to the decision-maker that any (or none) of the policies may be socially desirable. The objective of a constant-cost study is to determine the outputs that can be produced with different systems, all of which require the same commitment of resources. Thus, constant-cost studies tell the decision-maker what he can buy for his money.

This information may seem to be trivial; after all, any expenditure is made in anticipation of some result. But in many ways, constant-cost studies are the most difficult of all systems analyses. The inability of the analyst to specify outputs makes it hard to design systems. The systems that are analyzed in constant-cost studies often have complex impacts, so the analyst may have trouble merely discovering what the different outputs are and then communicating this information to the decision-maker. Or different systems may produce qualitatively the same outputs, but one system may yield more measurable outputs while another offers more intangibles. Some examples may help clarify these points.

One of the objectives of government policy has been to promote faster economic growth. During the early 1960's, in fact, economic policy was concerned with little else. One way to increase the growth rate is to increase labor productivity with more efficient capital equipment, but the development of new capital goods, technological change, rests on a foundation of basic and applied research. In allocating the funds that Congress has made available for research (and in seeking new appropriations), policy-makers would like to have some idea of what the likely payoffs are from various research activities. Unfortunately, economists have been unable to devise an empirically useful measure of technological change. We may discuss the impacts of particular research projects (usually after the fact), or we may estimate the overall productivity of capital and labor, but we have found it impossible to describe the impact that a research project is expected to have on a particular industry. Without any description of the process of technological change, however, we cannot evaluate systems (research activities) whose output is their effect on technology.

An example of complex outputs is provided by urban commuter roads. The immediate output, shorter commuting times, is fairly easy to identify and measure, and some analysts have even tried to impute a value to it. Another immediate output, however, is damage done to the property through which the road passes (through noise, pollution, and the destruction of neighborhoods). This output, too, can be quantified and included in the evaluation of the system. But commuter roads lead to changes in land use by altering residential patterns and encouraging the dispersion of employment. They also affect the urban tax base and commercial activity in the inner city. These impacts are much harder to measure because our understanding of interdependences within a metropolitan area is fragmentary. And even if an analyst can identify all these effects of a particular transit system, the methodology of his analysis is likely to be so complex that it will be hard to describe it to policy-makers, for he will need to incorporate economic, social, and political variables in a sophisticated simulation of the entire urban area.

When systems provide different mixes of outputs, the analyst's task is to present information about them to the policy-maker. For example, the control of crime may spur either stricter law enforcement by police or more extensive rehabilitative programs for prisoners. Suppose that the former system reduces street crime by 20 percent and causes an increase in community tensions. The latter program may reduce street crime by only 5 percent (for the same resource outlay) but may also improve community attitudes toward law enforcement. Even if the analyst can trace through these effects, he can only convey them to the decision-maker, for no objective weights (such as market or shadow prices) are available to construct an indicator of either program's desirability.

Constant-cost analyses are the only hope for comparing systems in any of these cases, when outputs are hard to specify, complex in their impacts, or multidimensional. Perhaps the most common use of constant-cost methodology is the last, when systems produce many outputs that cannot be aggregated but can only be presented explicitly to the policy-making official for his decision. Military weapons systems may be of different applicability in different "scenarios," and the decision-maker will have to choose among them on the basis of his subjective appraisal of the likelihood of different contingencies and the payoffs of each system in each case. Urban renewal policies may provide different mixes of residential, commercial, and industrial reconstruction, and the policy-maker may decide to ignore the market's weights (the relative profitability of different types of land use) in favor of some "master plan" for the redevelopment of a city. The beneficiaries of different income redistribution policies may differ, and someone must decide whether to increase the social security benefits that flow primarily to the aged or the manpower retraining programs that benefit chiefly younger workers. In all these case, constant-cost studies offer the only basis for comparing systems whose outputs are, after all, essentially incommensurate except in the minds of the public officials charged with making policy decisions.

Least-Cost Studies. Unlike constant-cost studies, which focus on the different outputs that can be produced for a given resource outlay, least-cost analyses concentrate on identifying the least expensive way of producing a given quantity of a particular output. The nature of the output is such that it cannot be evaluated (or else benefit-cost techniques could be used), but least-cost studies nonetheless suggest that certain systems should be preferred to others. In addition, least-cost studies provide some information on the overall desirability of programs, for they encourage a policy-maker to compare particular outputs that can be identified and measured.

A typical least-cost analysis begins with the statement of an objective, such as providing 1,000 new units of low-cost housing, and then estimates the cost of achieving this objective with different systems.

Some of the alternatives that might be examined in this case would include the following: public construction and operation, public construction and sale to private operators of rental housing, public subsidies for private construction, public provision of facilities (transportation, schools, stores) designed to encourage private construction, and a requirement that developers commit themselves to build a certain proportion of low-cost housing in order to obtain building permits for higher-profit buildings. The analyst's task is to determine the effectiveness of each of these systems and then to calculate the cost of the level of system operation needed to reach the objective.

Along the way, the analyst may discover that the least-cost method of producing 1,000 new units of low-cost housing requires the expenditure of $20,000 per unit in public funds. This information is likely to be very useful to the decision-maker, who had set the original target expecting the unit cost to be closer to $5000. The public official may then want to compare the cost of providing low-cost housing with the cost of increasing the productivity and income of low-income workers (and the unemployed). What has happened, in this example, is that the low-level suboptimization of the original least-cost study has led to a slightly higher-level comparison of alternative policies. The objective of the policy-maker has changed from providing housing to increasing the real income of particular families. As long as the objective remains quantifiable and single-dimensioned, least-cost studies of increasingly different systems may continue to be valuable inputs to the public official's decision.

In both constant-cost and least-cost methodologies, outputs are stated in physical terms (or are described as intangibles) while inputs, factors of production, are measured in dollars. A variant on these techniques of public decision-making is operations research, another group of methods for allocating given resources (stated in physical terms) to produce given outputs (also in physical terms). A typical operations research problem is to allocate a given fleet of garbage trucks to collect refuse from a particular set of locations. The resource inputs, trucks and men, are considered to be fixed for the purposes of the analysis. If the output is also fixed, the operations research problem is a study of the feasibility of doing the assigned job with the available resources. The objective may not be fixed—for example, it may be to collect as much refuse as possible within a certain time—in which case the problem is a sort of maximization. Operations research techniques frequently are highly mathematical, but they are not interesting from an economic point of view because they do not permit factor substitution or require the evaluation of outputs.

The differences among the various types of systems analysis can be seen by comparing the operations research problem, to collect refuse with a given fleet of trucks, to studies that would be made under the other methodologies. A least-cost study would determine the collection system of minimum cost for the given pickup locations; that is, the capital and labor inputs would be permitted to vary. A constant-cost study would examine the various outputs that could be produced for the cost of the garbage truck fleet: commuter transit if the money were spent on buses, highway safety if the money were spent on road-grading equipment, education if the funds were spent on schools, and so forth. Finally, a benefit-cost study would estimate the value that consumers place on the garbage pickup and would then recommend whether or not to undertake the program.

THE LIMITATIONS OF SYSTEMS ANALYSIS

Throughout our discussion of the different types of systems analysis we have pretended that analysts were infallible and that their recommendations always were accepted by public officials whose sole concerns were efficiency and equity. Neither of these assumptions, of course, applies to the real-world analysis of public programs. Instead, systems analyses are constrained by both economic and political considerations.

Economic Limitations. In surveying benefit-cost analysis, we dismissed the problem of valuing outputs by saying that we could use either the market prices of close substitutes or shadow prices that equal the value of government programs to rational consumers. Some of the difficulties in using shadow prices were illustrated in Figure 12.1, but the chief problem with both market and shadow pricing is the lack of information about the demand and supply curves. Econometric studies have made estimates of the demand and supply curves of many private goods, but there is usually a range of uncertainty resulting from inadequacies in the data underlying the estimates. We have even less information about the demand and supply elasticities for public sector outputs, for we cannot estimate them from observations of consumers' demand and producers' supply. Thus, the evaluation of public outputs is an inexact art, given both to conceptual errors of the kind described earlier in this chapter and to measurement errors resulting from a lack of information about demand and supply.

Another economic problem arises from the long lifetimes that characterize many systems. Hydroelectric power dams, for example, are productive over periods longer than fifty years; highways, airports, schools, hospitals, and other capital goods yield flows of services for twenty or more years. A systems analyst who estimates in 1975 the benefits that will accrue to consumers in 2015 must recognize that a great deal of uncertainty attaches to his projections. Even for shorter-lived systems (such as military weapons, usually assumed to have ten-year lives) the analyst's prediction of what the future will bring must be very unsure. For example, the deterrent value of a second-strike missile capability would vanish if an enemy were to devise an effective antimissile weapon. The fact that no such weapon exists today, at the time of the analysis, is no guarantee that it may not be developed soon enough to change greatly the offensive missile's deterrent value over its lifetime.

In addition to being uncertain about benefits, the analyst cannot be sure that his cost projections will be accurate. We have assumed full employment throughout our analysis of public expenditure decisions, but if substantial unemployment should occur, the resource costs of labor-intensive programs would fall. Some public projects would then become efficient, and the design of others would have to change to reflect the altered factor prices. Even without a drastic depression, moreover, technological change may cause shifts in factor productivities and prices, leading to incorrect estimates of costs. In the United States, production techniques have steadily become more capital-intensive. Over the lifetime of a capital good such as a hospital building, the development of capital-intensive medical techniques might create major shifts in the cost of providing medical services, causing the analyst's forecast of costs to be very wide of the mark.

One way the analyst may guard against these uncertainties and chances of error is to perform a sensitivity analysis, testing how well his rankings of alternative systems stand up to changes in the assumptions and estimates that he builds into the analysis. For example, a missile system may be preferred to a manned bomber system (on a constant-cost basis) over a ten-year lifetime. But is the ranking still the same if an enemy develops an effective missile defense in the sixth year of the system's life? Nuclear power generation may be less efficient than "fossil fuels" (coal and oil), given the current state of technology, but what happens to the ranking if the development of a "fast breeder reactor" halves the cost of the nuclear system? And do we want to produce more power at all if the growth rate of demand is 6 percent instead of the 12 percent that was used to forecast benefits?

These examples highlight the assumptions that may be parameters of any systems analysis. Another parameter that we have not mentioned so far is the interest rate, or rate of discount, that measures the opportunity cost of the funds that the government invests. Many capital-intensive public programs, especially water resources projects, are very sensitive to the discount rate used in evaluating costs and benefits. A complete sensitivity analysis succeeds in identifying all the "critical" parameters, the ones for which minor changes affect the original rankings of the alternative programs. The discount rate probably is the parameter that is most often critical, but uncertainty about costs and benefits and errors in estimation, especially for imputing shadow prices to outputs, also are major sources of "sensitivity."

Once the analyst has completed his study and performed a sensitivity analysis to indicate which assumptions are critical to his results, he then must present the entire package to the public official charged with making the decision. At this point, the economic evaluations underlying the systems analysis become inputs to an equally complex political evaluation.

Political Limitations. Some of the inputs that the public official receives from the systems analyst are the parameter values that are critical to the results. For instance, a missile system may be preferred to a bomber system if the useful lifetime of the deterrent threat is over seven years, but if the deterrent becomes useless after five years the bomber system may be clearly preferred. The five- to seven-year range is one of indifference or no clear preference between the systems. The policy-maker then must choose the parameter value that he considers to be the appropriate basis for selection. In the missile-bomber example, suppose that agreement is imminent on a disarmament treaty that may obviate the need for deterrent capability within three years. We might still expect a Secretary of Defense to argue in favor of a missile system because his political commitment is to erring on the side of more elaborate security measures. In other words, the political decision-maker's utility function may differ from the analyst's, so the policy recommendations emerging from systems analysis may be reversed (or ignored) by political considerations.

The policy-maker also must be sensitive to factors that an analyst may not be able to include in his study. In the example used earlier in this chapter, a highway bridge costing $800 million was preferred to a combination of pedestrian and railroad bridges costing $250 million. One of the political constraints, however, may be a limitation on debt financing that makes the $800 million bridge politically infeasible (even though it is economically preferred). Or the chairman of the appropriations subcommittee may have had lunch recently with a railroad lobbyist, and the highway bridge may be a political impossibility. Political factors such as these frequently are a determining influence on public expenditures. Systems analysis cannot eliminate them, but it can show the public policy-maker and the public the costs of the politically motivated decisions compared to the economic ones.

A third political constraint is the necessity to weigh the distributional aspects of different policies. Although systems analysis can identify distributional consequences, it cannot rank policies with different distributions of benefits without imposing the ethical judgments of the analyst. As we saw in Chapter 7, the process of making distributional judgments is a political one, and the responsibility and prerogative of the systems analyst is limited to making clear to the policy-maker just what the distributional alternatives are.

The political limitations imposed on systems analysis have dismayed some economists who have tried to improve the efficiency of public resource allocation.[2] Others have cautioned that both systems analysis and PPBS can merely increase the information available to political decision-makers, not supplant the primacy of political factors in public expenditure decisions.[3] In defense of efficiency analysis, many issues (such as the choice of the correct discount rate) have been clarified as the result of systems analyses, and program budgeting has pointed out areas of overlapping agency jurisdiction and contradictory policies. As the experience of systems analysts with different program areas increases and studies become less open to criticism, we may expect the role of efficiency analysis to increase in guiding public expenditure policies.

SUMMARY

Of many techniques for performing systems analyses, the two most common in the public sector are benefit-cost and cost-effectiveness analyses. Benefit-cost studies can be used when dollar values can be assigned to the outputs of different systems, and alternative projects can then be evaluated on the basis of their overall economic efficiency. In many cases, public programs confer distributional as well as allocational benefits. Although allocational benefits are adequately measured by the net benefits criterion, the distributional effects of public programs must be shown explicitly even if all benefits can be evaluated.

Cost-effectiveness analyses are used when outputs can be specified and perhaps measured but not evaluated. When outputs are multi-

---

[2] For example, see R. N. McKean, *Public Spending* (New York: McGraw-Hill, 1968).
[3] C. L. Schultze, *The Politics and Economics of Public Spending* (Washington, D.C.: Brookings Institution, 1969).

dimensional or unquantifiable, the appropriate technique is constant-cost methodology in which the outputs of different equal-cost systems are compared. If the nature and quantity of an output can be specified, then least-cost methodology may be used to find the least expensive system capable of meeting the output "target." Unlike constant-cost studies, least-cost analyses encourage the decision-maker to evaluate particular outputs against other uses of the same resources. As is true with benefit-cost studies, cost-effectiveness analyses also must display explicitly the distributional consequences of policy decisions.

Among the economic limitations on systems analysis are inaccuracies in the evaluation of benefits and uncertainty about both benefits and costs caused by the long lifetimes of many public programs. Political constraints include the different parameter values that a public official may choose as the basis for decision, the inability of the analyst to include political "realities" in his study, and the values that may be placed on distributional effects compared to allocational ones. These limitations of systems analysis have not prevented studies from making contributions in many program areas. As study methodologies improve, their role in public policy decisions probably will become more important.

13 Government Investment

A recurring theme throughout this book has been the impact of governmental policy on the decisions of savers and investors and on the composition of new investment, both public and private. In Chapter 5 we saw that allocation problems might result from capital-intensive methods of production, leading to public production of some private goods. In Chapters 7, 8, and 10 we examined the extent to which different taxes, especially the corporation income tax, distort individuals' preferences for future versus current consumption. Chapter 11 introduced public investment and the notion of a capital budget for the government and noted that some of the differences among the various budget documents are due to their treatments of government lending. In Chapter 12, the fact that many government programs involve costs and benefits over time had to be introduced into our criteria for choosing among different public programs. The interest rate was identified as a parameter that frequently is a key factor in ranking alternative programs.

As these references to capital and interest illustrate, government policy often involves the allocation of investible funds. The task of this chapter is to evaluate the resource cost of public investment, as an aid to making efficient investment decisions. We begin with a recapitulation of the theory of private investment and then continue with the determination of the public discount rate and a discussion of public investments that are not comparable to private ones.

230

THE INVESTMENT DECISION

Investments are made because capital is productive. This statement is simple, but it does not begin to answer the more basic question of why capital is productive. Economists generally have not had much success in answering this question. The productivity of capital is merely a technological fact of life: if we defer our consumption of $10 worth of resources today in order to invest until next year, then we can be confident (on the average) that more than $10 worth of resources will be available for our later consumption.

The reason we do not defer all our consumption (aside from some minimum necessary to sustain life) is another fact of life: other things being equal, most people prefer today's consumption to the same amount of consumption tomorrow.[1] Another way of describing this behavior pattern is to say that consumers have a positive rate of time-preference. If a person were truly indifferent between $10 of consumption today and the same amount next year, then we would say that his rate of time-preference was zero. Such an individual would always defer as much of his consumption as possible, as long as capital was productive and he could expect more goods next year than today.

The productivity of capital induces people to forgo current consumption in order to increase their future consumption possibilities. On the other hand, consumers' positive rate of time-preference deters them from buying capital goods that do not offer substantial increases in future income. When equilibrium exists in the market for capital goods, consumers are supplying funds for all the investments that offer to increase future income by more than consumers' marginal rate of time-preference. Investments that are less productive than the marginal rate of time-preference are not undertaken, for the promised future consumption is insufficient to induce consumers to defer their current consumption.

The price that investors are willing to pay to convince consumers to defer current consumption usually is stated as a percentage return on the amount of consumption deferred, and called the "rate of return." For simplicity, consider the following one-year example. N. A. Bob, owner of Fly-by-Night Enterprises, has developed a new widget production process that will enable him to produce $130 worth of widgets next year if he invests $100 now. Bob has no funds of his own but can

---

[1] The other things that must be equal include the total amount of consumption (so that we are not trading the last $10 of today's goods for the first $10 of next year's) and the relative prices of the goods involved.

borrow from I. N. Vestor if he can convince Vestor to reduce his current consumption. Bob does not know what Vestor's rate of time-preference is, but it will be profitable for him to offer Vestor up to $130 in order to borrow $100 today. Thus, the rate of return on the widget process is 30 percent.

Vestor will be glad to lend Bob the funds he needs as long as Vestor's rate of time-preference is less than the rate of return that he expects. As Vestor saves more and his current consumption falls, however, his rate of time-preference probably will rise since he will place a greater value on his current consumption. In Figure 13.1, the *MTP* curve expresses this aspect of Vestor's preferences. Bob will have to offer higher rates of return to induce Vestor to lend additional capital. Bob's ability to offer these higher rates of return probably will fall, reflecting the likelihood that the marginal productivity of additional capital will be decreasing, as along the *MEI* curve in Figure 13.1. Eventually, equilibrium will be established at r_0 and I_0, when the marginal rate of return on additional investment equals the marginal rate of time-preference of lenders. The price that equates the marginal rate of return and the marginal rate of time preference is called the "market rate of interest."

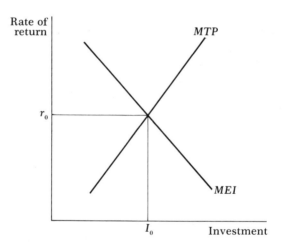

FIGURE 13.1   Investment Equilibrium

The significance of the market interest rate is that it tells consumers what the opportunity cost is of their current consumption. In our example, Vestor knows that as long as he can earn 30 percent on the money he lends to Bob, every dollar's worth of current consumption makes him forgo $1.30 of income next year. More generally, the interest rate in a capital market that allocates resources efficiently measures the highest rate of return on any investment currently available to society. Bob's widgets may be the most productive investment open to Vestor, but if another, more productive, investment should become available, the market rate would rise (as the new borrower tried to bid funds away from Bob), and Vestor's opportunity costs of current consumption also would rise.

We can use the market interest rate to compare present and future income. If the market rate is i, we could invest R_0 today and receive $(1 + i)R_0$ next year. Writing R_1 for next year's income, we have

$$R_1 = (1 + i)R_0.$$

In two years, we could receive

$$R_2 = (1 + i)R_1 = (1 + i)^2 R_0,$$

assuming that the market interest rate is constant over the entire period. In general, the income that we could earn n years from now is

$$R_n = (1 + i)^n R_0.$$

Another way of looking at these relationships is to note that R_1 next year is equivalent to a certain amount of income this year, the amount we would have to lend (at i percent) in order to get R_1 next year. Today's equivalent of R_1 next year, called the "present value" of the future income, is

$$R_0 = R_1/(1 + i),$$

as we can see by dividing the first equation in the preceding paragraph by $(1 + i)$. In general, the present value of receiving R_n n years from now is

$$R_0 = R_n/(1 + i)^n.$$

This result can easily be extended to a stream of future receipts. Bob's widgets may pay a stream of future returns, given by R_1 in year 1, R_2 in year 2, and so forth, out to R_n in year n (after which no returns are paid). The present value to Vestor of this stream of returns is the sum of the present values of each of the annual returns. Thus, the present value of the stream R is:

$$PV(R) = \frac{R_1}{1 + i} + \frac{R_2}{(1 + i)^2} + \cdots + \frac{R_n}{(1 + i)^n} = \sum_{j=1}^{n} \frac{R_j}{(1 + i)^j}.$$

The significance of the present value is that it tells Vestor how large an amount of money he would have to invest at the market interest rate i in order to obtain the stream of returns R. If Bob offers Vestor the stream R, Bob should not expect Vestor to be willing to lend any more than $PV(R)$. $PV(R)$, therefore, will become the market price of the stream R. Given the rates of return and rates of time-preference that determine the market interest rate, lenders will offer to pay up to $PV(R)$ for the stream of returns, and borrowers will be unable to offer any larger stream.

Before going into a more sophisticated analysis of private investment, let us apply the methodology developed thus far to an earlier example. In Chapter 11, we discussed the budget problem that arises when the government lends money at less than the market interest rate. Suppose that the Rural Electrification Administration lends funds to a rural cooperative and schedules repayments of $1000 per year for forty years. For this loan,

$$R_1 = R_2 = \cdots = R_{40} = \$1000.$$

If the market interest rate is 6 percent, then

$$PV(R) = \frac{1,000}{(1.06)} + \frac{1,000}{(1.06)^2} + \cdots + \frac{1,000}{(1.06)^{40}} = \sum_{j=1}^{40} \frac{1,000}{(1.06)^j}$$

$$= 1,000 \left(\sum_{j=1}^{40} \frac{1}{(1.06)^j} \right).$$

If we look up the value of this sum in a table of compound interest rates, we find that $PV(R)$ is $15,046. That is, no private investor would be willing to pay more than $15,046 for the REA's stream of repayments, for if an investor lent more than $15,046 he could expect to receive a larger repayment-stream from some other investment.

If the REA discounts the repayment-stream at 2 percent, however, it will value the repayment-stream at $27,355. Since no private lender would pay more than $15,046 for this repayment-stream, if the REA lends the cooperative $27,355, its loan actually includes an outright transfer of $12,309 in addition to the true amount of the loan, $15,046. (If the market rate were 2 percent, the transfer from the REA to the co-op would be zero.) Later in this chapter, we will discuss whether there is any reason for the government to use an interest rate lower than the market rate.

All investments are not alike, of course. They differ in the date of maturity, the pattern of returns over their lifetimes, and the confidence the borrower and lender have that the promised repayment-stream will be the actual one. Our formula for calculating present values incorporates the first two factors but assumes that the stream of returns is paid with certainty. As we saw in Chapter 7, however, the riskiness of different investments may provide a basis for investors to choose among them.

We may interpret the riskiness of an investment as the variability that the investor foresees in R, the stream of returns. Under this definition, two investments with the same expected returns may not be equivalent if one of the streams offers a larger range of possible outcomes than the other. This was the case in Chapter 7, when the Fly-by-Night bonds offered the same expected return as the government bonds, but the chance of bankruptcy was higher for Fly-by-Night than for the government. Economists usually postulate that lenders respond to the different riskiness of various investments by demanding a higher expected return on the risky investments than on the safe ones, thus compensating for the greater chance of loss with the riskier investments. On the basis of this kind of lender response, we should expect the market interest rate on risky investments to be higher than the rate on safe ones.

As long as capital markets function well, allocating investible funds among alternative investment opportunities, the market rate of interest on comparable investments should tend toward uniformity. Comparable investments are all those to which investors (lenders) are indifferent; according to the preceding argument, therefore, comparable investments are those of equal riskiness. Because the distant future is harder to predict than tomorrow, we should expect investors to demand a larger risk premium for lengthy investments than for short-term ones. Because small firms are statistically more likely to fail than large ones, we should expect lenders to demand a higher interest rate on loans to small firms than on those to large corporations. Because new industries have more questionable futures than established ones, we should expect interest rates on new firms' issues to be higher than on those of older companies. Differing degrees of riskiness may account for most of the dispersion in interest rates that we observe in the market.

The presence of differing rates of return, however, is evidence of a subtle form of market imperfection. As well as demanding higher rates of return on risky investments, investors can compensate for risk by diversifying their investments, either by buying shares in mutual funds or by investing in businesses with many different degrees of risk. If all investors could diversify completely, then it can be shown that they could reduce the riskiness of their portfolios to zero, in effect assuring that they would receive their expected rates of return with certainty.[2] The notion behind this proposition is that if an investor owns shares of, say, a thousand different businesses, then the probability that he will become bankrupt is virtually zero even if the probability of any one firm's bankruptcy is very high. Under perfect diversification, no single firm comprises more than an infinitesimal part of any investor's portfolio, and thus the investor's probability of sizable loss becomes very small.

If investors could diversify completely, there would be only one rate of return in the market, that equal to lenders' marginal rate of time-preference. (Since all investments would be effectively riskless, simple market behavior would bring this result about.) But we can observe that there is not a single rate of return in the market, and thus we can infer that the opportunity for perfect diversification does not exist for all investors. Capital markets, therefore, cannot be allocating investible funds with perfect efficiency, and investors must be including a risk premium in their calculations.

As long as investors include a risk premium, however, the gross rate of return to society (including the risk premium) must always be greater than investors' marginal rate of time-preference. In addition, the level of investment must be lower than the socially optimal level. This argument is directly parallel to that in Chapter 8, where we showed that the corporation income tax would reduce lenders' net rate of return and increase society's gross rate of return while decreasing the level of investment. The market imperfection caused by risk and incomplete diversification has extremely important implications for the choice of a public discount rate, as we shall see in the next section.

As was shown in Chapters 11 and 12, the public sector is responsible for capital formation no less than the private sector. The government borrows money from investors who otherwise might have lent to private firms and uses its revenue to demand capital goods that otherwise might have become the investment goods of the private sector. Efficiency in resource allocation requires that the government undertake efficient investments. If we ignore the fact that public investments (highways, communications, water resources, education) are productive, then as a society we will allocate too few resources to capital formation as well as too few resources to the public sector.

---

[2] Technically, this conclusion holds only if the risk of failure of one investment is independent of the risk attached to any other investment. The assumption of independence may be violated in some cases, particularly when the economy as a whole experiences a boom or slump, but it is generally an acceptable simplification of investors' options.

On the other hand, it is important that we treat public investments comparably to private ones. If we fail to discount the future benefits that we will receive from government investments, then we will undertake too many such investments and allocate too many resources to the public sector. The remainder of this chapter is devoted to a discussion of how to determine the efficient level of government investments.

DISCOUNTING PUBLIC INVESTMENTS

Determining the correct rate for discounting public investments has been one of the most controversial topics in the theory of public finance. It is also one of the most important in terms of its impact on the level and composition of government expenditures. Until recently, most economists and almost all government analysts believed that the appropriate rate of discount (interest rate) to apply to public expenditures was the cost of borrowing money. This cost has been very low for the Treasury, usually 2 to 4 percent, although the "tight money" episode in 1968–1969 drove the rate on long-term Treasury borrowing up to around 5.5 percent.

During the 1960's, some economists began to argue that the government should recognize that its investments withdrew resources from the private sector and that the correct discount rate for the government to use was the opportunity cost of capital, the rate of return in the private sector. Other economists disagreed, claiming that the government used resources that would not otherwise have been made available for investment and that the private opportunity cost therefore was irrelevant. According to this view, the sources of government funds determined the appropriate discount rate. Still others felt that public investment decisions were qualitatively different from private ones and that the private motivations leading to a determination of the market interest rate should not be allowed to influence more altruistic government investments. We will discuss each of these arguments in turn. In the course of our discussion, we will discover the special assumptions under which the government borrowing rate is the correct discount rate.

The Private Opportunity Cost. If N. A. Bob wants to borrow investible funds to increase the output of widgets, he must bid the funds away from other investors. The return that Bob expects on his investment depends on demand conditions, the cost of capital goods, and his own efficiency as a manager. If Bob's investment opportunities are not favorable enough to enable him to outbid other borrowers, the funds he might have used will go to other investors who will use them to produce other goods and services. If he does succeed in obtaining the funds he needs, then the resource cost to society of Bob's investment is the goods and services that otherwise could have been produced with the funds Bob uses. For Bob's investment to be an efficient use of society's scarce investible funds, therefore, the value of the goods and services that he produces must be greater than the opportunity cost of the resources he uses. In percentage terms, the prospective rate of return on his investment must exceed the market rate of interest, since in a properly functioning capital market the rate of interest measures the marginal productivity of investments that actually are undertaken.

When we consider the government's use of investible funds instead of N. A. Bob's, the same principle applies: for public investments to be efficient, they should yield a rate of return greater than their opportunity cost. Thus, if capital markets allocate funds properly, the government should use the market rate of interest as its discount rate in evaluating the desirability of public programs. Although this is a very simple rule with a great deal of analytical validity, it has been criticized for its unrealistic assumption that capital markets function efficiently. There are several sources of inefficiency in the allocation of investible funds: the corporation income tax, lenders' risk aversion, and nonmaximizing behavior on the part of borrowers. But advocates of the private opportunity cost rule claim that none of these imperfections alters the validity of their approach.

As we saw in Chapter 8, the corporation income tax creates a divergence between the gross rate of return that a corporation earns on its investments and the net rate of return, after taxes, that eventually accrues to its stockholders. To recapitulate the argument, the pretax rate of return to a typical corporation is shown in Figure 13.2 as MEI. The imposition of a tax reduces the corporation's ability to repay its investors, so the after-tax rate of return falls to MEI'. For simplicity, we assume that stockholders' willingness to lend to corporations is not affected by the tax, so the supply of funds to the corporation remains stable, as shown by S. The corporation's equilibrium level of investment falls, however, from I to I', and the rate of return to investors also falls from r to r'.

At the new level of investment, society as a whole is receiving a higher rate of return, r'', on corporate investment. This higher rate of return arises because the corporation has been forced to forgo some investments whose after-tax rate of return is less than r' (but whose pretax return is greater than r). Although investors in the corporation

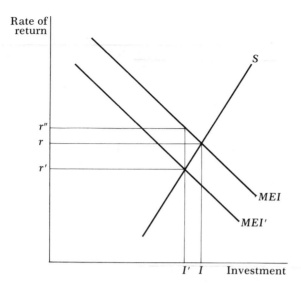

FIGURE 13.2   Corporate Investment

receive a rate of return of only r', the goods and services produced with the investible funds that the corporation borrows are valued by society at a rate of return of r''.[3] Thus, the true opportunity cost to society of the corporation's investment is r'', not r'. If the government cares about efficiency in its investment policy, it should undertake only those projects that yield a rate of return greater than r'', the pre-tax rate of return on corporate investment.

The policy impact of this argument is enormous. The traditional approach toward government investments has been to discount future costs and benefits either at zero or at the coupon rate on Treasury bonds. (A more recent approach recommended using the actual yield of Treasury bonds, about 5 percent.) The after-tax private rate of return on capital, r', is roughly 8 percent for low-risk assets. If we accept the proposition that in the long run the corporation income tax is shifted completely to capital income, the pretax rate of return in the corporate sector, r'', must be about 15 percent. At this high a discount rate, many of the investments that governments historically have undertaken would be extremely inefficient.

Opponents of the private opportunity cost doctrine argue that government investments cannot be compared to private ones because of

[3] The difference between r'' and r' is the amount of revenue received by the government. This revenue is used to produce goods and services conferring benefits upon consumers other than the corporation's investors.

the difference in riskiness. Large corporations offer less risky investment opportunities than small firms *not* because the corporations' investments are inherently more conservative but rather because larger
firms diversify more effectively. Opponents of the private opportunity
cost approach argue that government investments are even less risky
than those of large corporations because the government undertakes
more investments than even the largest private firm and spreads the
risk among 200 million "stockholders." Thus, they argue, the r'' rate
of return on corporate investment is simply irrelevant for the evaluation of public investments, which should be discounted at a completely risk-free rate.

The trouble with this criticism is that it ignores the heart of the
private opportunity cost doctrine. Society's rate of return on private investment is r''. If resources are taken from an investment yielding r''
and allocated to an investment that yields a lower rate of return, then
the allocation of investible funds will be inefficient, by definition. If
private lenders are unwilling to make loans because they think that
investments are too risky, there may be an argument for the government to insure private borrowers or to borrow directly from private
lenders and then lend its funds to private borrowers. In either case,
aggregate investment will rise, and the rate of return will fall, but the
government will not undertake projects that offer a rate of return
lower than that which society receives from private investments.

Thus, the relative riskiness of public and private investment opportunities is irrelevant for the choice of a public discount rate. If risk is
high for private investments, private lenders will apply a discount
factor to private returns. Capital will not be allocated efficiently, for
the real rate of return that society receives on some risky investments
will be greater than on other (safer) investments. There is a justification in this market imperfection for government policy, but not for the
government's use of a discount rate less than the opportunity cost of
the funds that it borrows. The appropriate policy is to increase total
(private and public) investment, while maintaining efficiency in the
allocation of investment funds between public and private projects.
It is important to keep these two policy objectives separate, for a high
discount rate for public investments may be completely consistent
with a policy of lowering the overall rate of return on investment.

The third objection to using the private opportunity cost as the discount rate for public projects is that producers are not profit maximizers. A firm may use less than the optimal amount of capital
because of its management's aversion to extensive borrowing or because the producer does not know what the efficient factor combinations are. Forecasts of future demand may be incorrect, so unprofitable

investment opportunities may be undertaken and profitable ones forgone. Or lenders may ration capital to borrowers, so that the market interest rate gives no indication of the process of allocating investible funds among projects.

Whatever the merits of these arguments, they clearly are not germane to the private opportunity cost doctrine. The fact that producers stop short of the efficient level of investment does not mean that society should undertake investments offering much lower rates of return. Inaccurate forecasts plague public investment projects as much as private ones and really are only aspects of the riskiness of investment decisions. If capital is rationed, the supply curve of funds may be discontinuous instead of smooth (as in Figure 13.2), but the market imperfection still does not invalidate the concept of using the private opportunity cost to discount public investments.

Most economists now agree that the private opportunity cost is conceptually the correct measure of the discount rate to use for government investments. Our discussion of this rule has simplified some complex issues, such as the role of risk and the shifting of the corporation income tax. The presence of market imperfections in the allocation of capital may create serious measurement problems, to which we shall turn next. But the goal of efficiency requires that public investments be undertaken only if they offer a rate of return greater than their opportunity cost.

Sources of Funds. Under the private opportunity cost rule, the discount rate to be used is the rate of return on the private investment projects that would have been carried out if the government had not preempted the investible funds. But if private investments are of differing riskiness and yield, then we cannot use a single figure such as the pretax rate of return on corporate investment as the private opportunity cost. Instead, we have to discover where the government's investible funds come from and what the opportunity cost is in each of these alternative uses. In other words, we must construct an average of the private opportunity costs, weighted by the proportions of total government investment financed from each source of funds.

The justification for this procedure is that markets are imperfect and that the same real rate of return will not characterize investments of differing risk. If the government borrows funds for a public investment, it will reduce the supply of funds for all private investments. The opportunity cost will be the average rate of return in forgone private investments, some of which are risky and some of which are not. In addition, however, the government probably will finance its investment at least partially with tax revenues that may cause a reduction in saving (the supply of investible funds) but that also will reduce consumption by some amount. Thus, we need to estimate the opportunity cost of forgone consumption as well as that of the private investments that will not be undertaken because of the government's expenditures.

Several authors have tried to make estimates of the discount rate resulting from the sources of funds approach. Krutilla and Eckstein estimated the rate at 5 to 6 percent in a period of rather low interest rates (1958, when the government borrowing rate was about 3 to 4 percent).[4] More recently, Eckstein has claimed that the weighted average of opportunity costs is about 8 to 9 percent.[5] In general, the sources of funds rule yields a lower discount rate for public investments than the private opportunity cost rule.

The difference arises because of the market imperfections postulated in the sources of funds approach. If capital markets functioned efficiently, funds would flow to those projects that offered the highest rates of return (including a risk premium). Since actual rates of return differ widely among projects, we can infer that lenders are not perfect income maximizers and that capital submarkets are segmented. When the supply of funds in, say, the safest investment class falls, more funds do not flow in from other submarkets. Instead, the interest rate in that submarket rises and the level of investment falls, with only small secondary effects on other risk classes of investment.

If capital markets were not segmented, the sources of funds rule would always yield the same discount rate regardless of the method of funding of government investments. For example, if the government drew its funds entirely from one source, submarkets would adjust and restore the same balance of funds and the same pattern of rates of return that had existed before the government's funding operation. But if capital markets are segmented, the method of government funding can alter the relative rates of return in the different submarkets and thus can affect the opportunity cost of public investment.

Efficiency requires that government investments be undertaken only if they offer a return greater than their opportunity cost. If capital markets are completely segmented, however, the opportunity cost of public investment may be equal to the government's borrowing rate. This low opportunity cost would arise only if none of the funds used by the government otherwise would have been used for private invest-

[4] John V. Krutilla and Otto Eckstein, *Multiple Purpose River Development* (Baltimore: Johns Hopkins Press, 1958).

[5] Statement of Otto Eckstein before the Subcommittee on Economy in Government, Joint Economic Committee, *Economic Analysis of Public Investment Decisions: Interest Rate Policy and Discounting Analysis* (1968).

ments offering a rate of return higher than the government's borrowing rate. Even then, all public investments would have to be financed by borrowing. If the government taxed away income otherwise used for consumption, the opportunity cost of the funds to the taxpayer would be the rate of return that he could have earned if he had saved instead of consuming. Thus, the government borrowing rate is the appropriate discount rate to use in evaluating public investments only under very restrictive assumptions: complete segmentation of capital markets, so that no government funds are withdrawn from private investment projects offering a higher rate of return; and total debt funding, so that no investment is financed by taxing people who otherwise might have saved their income.

The Social Rate of Time-Preference. The private opportunity cost rule approaches the question of discounting and efficient allocation of investible funds from the standpoint of the preferences that individual consumers and taxpayers express for private and public goods. If private capital markets function efficiently, the opportunity cost of government investment is also the rate of time-preference that individuals express in their willingness to lend. If capital markets are not perfectly efficient, there may be a divergence between the private opportunity cost and individuals' rate of time-preference. In this case, the government should undertake policies designed to eliminate this divergence by increasing the level of total investment until the rate of return to society is equal to the rate of time-preference. Whether or not capital markets are efficient, the basis for efficient allocation is that the return on all investments should equal consumers' rate of time-preference.

Most economists have claimed that this criterion of efficiency is inappropriate for public investments, although it is correct for private ones. They argue that the government must have a longer time-horizon than individual consumers, since the government must be concerned with the distant future and with providing capital goods for unborn generations. According to this view, individual consumers and producers cannot be relied upon to express society's preferences for future capital goods because individuals' horizons are so much shorter than those of the entire society. Thus, the government must make an independent decision about the rate of time-preference that applies to society, as distinct from that determined in the market where individuals express their time-preferences. Once the government determines such a rate of social time-preference, it should use that rate to discount the investments it makes.

The argument for a social rate of time-preference can be based on considerations other than the proposition that the government must take a "long view" compared to the "short view" of individual borrowers and lenders. One argument may be that public investments are not accurately evaluated, for they provide benefits that usually accrue either externally or publicly. In such cases, there is a prevalent underestimation of the value of public outputs (for example, using the reasoning of the Downs model), and too small a fraction of total investment is public. We can compensate for this undervaluation of public benefits by discounting future outputs at a lower rate, in effect inflating future public benefits relative to private ones.

This basis for a social discount rate lower than the private opportunity cost is unsatisfactory because it leads to inefficiency in the composition of public expenditures even in the unlikely case that it restores the proper balance between public and private investment. In particular, low discount rates tend to favor projects with distant benefits over those with current benefits. This point is illustrated in Table 13.1, which compares two hypothetical public investments. Project D is a hydroelectric power dam with a lifetime of fifty years. For simplicity, we assume that it yields zero benefits for twenty years and $1 million per year for the next thirty years, after which its output falls to zero. Project R is a manpower-retraining program whose benefits are increased earnings of $100,000 per year for forty years (the productive lifetime of the trainees). We ignore distributional considerations and assume that both programs require outlays whose present values are equal.

TABLE 13.1   Alternative Public Investments (Millions of Dollars)

	D			R		
		PRESENT VALUE			PRESENT VALUE	
Year	Benefits	At 4%	At 12%	Benefits	At 4%	At 12%
1	0	0	0	0.1	0.0962	0.0893
5	0	0	0	0.1	0.0822	0.0567
10	0	0	0	0.1	0.0676	0.0322
20	0	0	0	0.1	0.0456	0.0104
30	1	0.308	0.033	0.1	0.0308	0.0033
40	1	0.208	0.011	0.1	0.0208	0.0011
50	1	0.141	0.003	0.0	0.0	0.0
TOTAL, 1–50	30	7.892	0.835	4.0	1.979	0.824

Both projects may yield externalities, but the social benefits from the retraining program are likely to be greater than those from the dam. The use of a low discount rate, however, introduces a substantial bias in favor of the longer-lived project. At a discount rate of 4 percent, the dollar benefits from the dam have a present value about four times as great as those from the retraining project. If we evaluate the projects at a "market rate" of 12 percent, however, the two investments are virtually equivalent. A strong case could be made for the retraining program on the grounds that the direct benefits are nearly as great as those of the dam, and its external benefits (not shown in Table 13.1) probably are large enough to tip the balance in its favor. But the use of an artificially low discount rate overcompensates for the externalities and drives the government's investible funds into an inferior project.

Another argument for using a social rate of time-preference lower than the private rate is that over time increasing levels of real income and the satiation of current wants will reduce the urgency of current consumption. This claim may be viewed with considerable skepticism, since there has been no observed tendency for market interest rates to fall over time. Even if there were such a trend, rational public policy would not require reducing today's consumption to increase the capital stock with which to produce income for future generations. Instead, we should try to tax the (presumably) wealthier future generations to provide for our own consumption, in the name of intergenerational equity. Finally, this argument for a low social discount rate cannot be used to justify public investment. Even if the argument were valid, it would justify increased *total* investment, not a greater share of public investment.

Thus, the basis for a social rate of time-preference lower than the private rate comes back to the notion of a "long view" appropriate for the government but not for individuals. Even if we concede that the interests of the government are not the same as the sum of the interests of individual citizens, there are difficulties with the social time-preference rule. One problem is that it offers no prescription for choosing a particular discount rate. If we cannot rely on markets to indicate the degree of time-preference, what kind of behavior can we rely on? Proponents of the social time-preference rule suggest the use of a low rate such as the government borrowing rate, but there does not seem to be any analytical basis for selecting one low rate over any other.

The other problem is that we still have no assurance that we will undertake socially efficient investments if we base our choice on social rather than private benefits. We cannot impute values to the nonmarketed benefits that government investments may produce for future generations any more than we can evaluate current nonmarketed benefits. Using an artificially low discount rate only understates the costs of government investments without giving us confidence that we are receiving large enough benefits to justify the outlay. It seems to make more sense to confront the issue directly, recognizing that an efficient allocation of investible funds between public and private sectors, and within the public sector, can only be made if the benefits of public investments are accurately estimated. If we can estimate benefits accurately, then we should undertake government investments only if these benefits exceed their resource cost, the opportunity cost of the funds in the private sector.

Summary. We have concluded that the conceptually correct discount rate to use in evaluating public investments is the opportunity cost of the investible funds. In general, these funds otherwise would be used for private investment projects. If capital markets function efficiently, the opportunity cost of government investment is the social rate of return to private investment, which can be measured most easily as the pretax rate of return in the corporate sector (about 15 percent). If capital markets do not function efficiently, the opportunity cost of public investment can be calculated only by tracing through the sources of government funds. This procedure requires estimates of the effect of government investment on different risk classes of private investment and estimates of tax incidence and the opportunity cost of funds to taxpayers. Sources of funds calculations usually estimate the appropriate discount rate for public projects as something less than 10 percent.

The alternative to an opportunity cost calculation is to use a rate such as the government borrowing rate. This rate can be justified as the social rate of time-preference, but the arguments for using such a rate of time-preference are not convincing. The government borrowing rate is the opportunity cost of public investment only under the restrictive assumptions that all public investments are financed by borrowing and that displaced private investments have a lower rate of return than the government borrowing rate.

When the opportunity cost of public investments is the basis for the discount rate, it is crucial for efficient allocation that the benefits of government projects be estimated accurately. If there are systematic biases toward underestimating government benefits (as was claimed in Chapter 2), the use of the correct discount rate will not lead to the efficient selection of investment projects. If market imperfections create a divergence between the opportunity cost of capital and consumers' rate of time-preference, the correct government policy is to try to eliminate the imperfection by increasing the level of total investment. The existence of such a difference in rates of return should not be made the excuse for the government's use of an artificially low discount rate.

NONMARKETABLE BENEFITS

Our discussion of the proper interest rate to use in discounting the future benefits of public investments has assumed implicitly that the opportunities for exchanging public benefits for private ones are described by the market rate of interest. In the case of the hydroelectric dam or the retraining project, for example, the benefits were dollar flows that could be matched by the benefits produced by entirely different kinds of investments. We turn now to the analysis of government investments whose benefits cannot be made commensurate with those of private investments and therefore cannot be exchanged over time.

As an example, suppose that the Department of Transportation wants to choose between two alternative programs for reducing the frequency of automobile accidents. The damages involved are both property damage and personal injuries including fatalities. Table 13.2 presents hypothetical information about the cost-streams and benefit-streams of the two projects. These questions confront us: Which of the two programs is preferable? Should we try to obtain funds for either of them?

Program U (for "urban") is a relatively small-scale plan for improving safety at urban bottlenecks. Due to the concentration of property in urban areas, program U promises to save nearly as much in undamaged property as it costs in public funds. Since traffic densities in urban areas are high, program U will also save many lives and prevent many injuries. Program R (for "rural") is much more ambitious, for it entails replacing long stretches of dangerous highway. Property savings are small relative to the program's cost, but program R will prevent many more injuries and fatalities than program U.

The first step in our analysis is to calculate the present values of the cost-streams. At a 10 percent discount rate, program U's present cost is $228,100 and program R's is $2,196,100. We can also reduce the property savings to present values, for they represent benefits valued by the market. There is no question that the value of $1 of savings three years from now is less than the value of $1 today. The present value of property saved by program U is $144,900, and program R offers present savings of $269,100. Thus, the net present cost of program U is $83,200 ($228,100 − $144,900), and that of program R is $1,927,000 ($2,196,100 − $269,100).

TABLE 13.2   Accident Prevention Programs

	Year					
	1	2	3	4	5	TOTAL
Program U						
Cost ($000)	100	100	50	25	0	275
Property saved ($000)	20	30	40	50	60	200
Injuries prevented	300	250	200	150	100	1,000
Fatalities prevented	45	40	35	25	15	160
Program R						
Cost ($000)	500	600	700	600	500	2,900
Property saved ($000)	20	40	80	150	250	540
Injuries prevented	500	500	550	600	700	2,850
Fatalities prevented	50	55	60	65	75	305
R − U						
Injuries	200	250	350	450	600	1,850
Fatalities	5	15	25	40	60	145

Program R's net costs obviously are considerably higher, but it offers somewhat larger benefits in terms of fewer personal injuries and fatalities. Nearly three times as many injuries will be prevented by program R as by program U and nearly twice as many fatalities. The question of whether the additional injuries prevented and lives saved are worth the expenditure of additional funds whose net present value is $1,843,800 ($1,927,000 − $83,200) depends on how highly we value the injuries and fatalities prevented.

In making his decisions about the relative and absolute merits of the two programs, however, the policy-maker cannot simply look at the total injuries and fatalities prevented or at the overall difference between R and U. Program U's time pattern of nonmarketable benefits is very different from program R's. Most of the benefits from U accrue early in its lifetime: the benefits in year 1 (in both injuries and fatalities prevented) are three times as great as those in year 5. With program R, however, both injuries and fatalities prevented rise about 50 percent over the life of the system. To ignore this difference and simply concentrate on the total benefits over the system lifetimes would be equivalent to assuming that an injury or fatality prevented today is worth the same as one prevented five years from now. Each of us will place his own subjective evaluation on injuries and fatalities, but it is safe to assume that most people would prefer the system offering the earlier profile of benefits, other things being equal.

In our example, of course, other things are not equal. Program R costs more and offers larger absolute benefits. Only the decision-maker can choose between R and U, for only he can place an evaluation on these nonmarketed benefits. But he must also consider their distribution over time. Whatever preference the policy-maker might have for R over U on the basis of the two programs' total costs and benefits, we should expect his preference to be weaker than it would be if the time pattern of benefits were the same in both cases. There is no way to reduce this time pattern to a single number, as we could do if all benefits were marketable and subject to discounting. In the case of nonmarketable benefits, therefore, the time distribution of benefits is an explicit datum in the choice between investment projects.

The problem of nonmarketable benefits arises frequently in the analysis of government investments. For example, defense expenditures that yield time-streams of deterrence provide such benefits. Investments in space exploration are another example. When externalities occur, as in education, and it is difficult to measure their value, then we can only show their time distribution explicitly as a guide toward making the public investment decision. Such cases are analogous, in a way, to the distributional considerations that arise in benefit-cost studies. We cannot aggregate income redistribution into a single indicator of the "goodness" of a program since we cannot compare the utility that different people gain and lose. We can aggregate other aspects of benefits and costs, since markets exist to aid us in evaluating them. But if we cannot compare benefits over time instead of over different people, then we cannot use market data to construct simple indices of these benefits.

SUMMARY

Capital productivity, expressed as the rate of return on investment, and consumers' positive rates of time-preference interact in the market for investible funds. The equilibrium price for investible funds is the market rate of interest, which tells consumers the opportunity cost of current consumption. The market interest rate also tells borrowers what rate of return they must expect on their investments in order to make the investments profitable. The interest rates that we observe in the market vary in response to the riskiness of different investments, since lenders prefer investments with a high degree of certainty to others that promise the same average return but a larger variation.

Since government investments are productive in the same way as private investments, we must apply a discount rate when we evaluate the future benefits that public investments offer. After a great deal of controversy and discussion, most economists have accepted the principle that the correct discount rate is the opportunity cost of investible funds in the private sector. If capital markets do not allocate funds efficiently, however, this opportunity cost cannot be observed directly, but must be calculated as the average rate of return on those investments that are forgone because of the government's preemption of funds.

If the benefits from government investments cannot be evaluated, then it is incorrect to apply a discount factor at all. In such cases, where the benefits are (for example) lives saved or enemy threats deterred, the time pattern of benefits is an explicit part of the investment decision. These benefits are comparable to the redistributional effects of other government expenditures: we cannot aggregate either the distributional aspects of marketed benefits or the time distribution of nonmarketed benefits into a single index, so the entire distribution of benefits must be taken into account by the public policy-maker.

PART FIVE Cases in Public Resource Allocation

In this part, we will examine four examples of how public policy has responded to market imperfections. Our discussion of benefit-cost analyses of water resources systems in Chapter 14 includes the methods of evaluating benefits and the problems that arise in designing systems, determining their costs, and ultimately choosing among alternative ways of developing water resources. Just as water resources development was the seedbed of benefit-cost methodology, the Defense Department offered the arena for the development of program budgeting. In Chapter 15, PPBS in Defense is compared with pre-PPBS budgeting, and some possible improvements are discussed. Education is predominantly a public responsibility, although many of its benefits are private. The implications of these multiple outputs for both efficiency and equity are studied in Chapter 16. Finally, in Chapter 17 we examine two aggravating urban problems, low-income housing and transportation, to assess the effects of alternative governmental policies.

BIBLIOGRAPHY

Some of the earliest studies of water resources are still the best: Roland N. McKean, *Efficiency in Government Through Systems Analysis* (New York: Wiley, 1958); John V. Krutilla and Otto Eckstein, *Multiple Purpose River Development* (Baltimore: Johns Hopkins Press, 1958); and Jack Hirschleifer, James C. DeHaven, and Jerome W. Milliman, *Water Supply* (Chicago: University of

Chicago Press, 1960). A recent collection of papers edited by Allen
V. Kneese and Stephen C. Smith is *Water Research* (Baltimore:
Johns Hopkins Press, 1966).

One of the first treatments of the application of systems analysis
to defense was Charles J. Hitch and Roland N. McKean's *The
Economics of Defense in the Nuclear Age* (Cambridge, Mass.:
Harvard University Press, 1961). Other useful references are
Charles J. Hitch's *Decision Making for Defense* (Berkeley: University of California Press, 1965); and Stephen Enke (ed.), *Defense
Management* (Englewood Cliffs, N.J.: Prentice-Hall, 1967). For a
thorough description and evaluation of current Defense Department practice, see John P. Crecine's *Defense Budgeting: Organi-
zational Adaptation to External Constraints,* RM-6121-PR (Santa
Monica, Calif.: Rand, March 1970).

A good discussion of the public interest in higher education is
presented by Roger E. Bolton in "The Economics and Public Financing of Higher Education: An Overview" in the U.S. Joint Economic Committee's *The Economics and Financing of Higher Education in the United States* (1969). Most of the seminal economic
analyses of education are collected in M. Blaug (ed.), *Economics of
Education 1* (Baltimore: Penguin Books, 1968). For a presentation
that is more hostile to the "human capital" approach, see John
Vaizey's *The Economics of Education* (London: Faber and Faber,
1962).

The federal urban renewal program is examined exhaustively
from a benefit-cost standpoint by Jerome Rothenberg in *Economic
Evaluation of Urban Renewal* (Washington, D.C.: Brookings
Institution, 1967). He is less critical than the author of an earlier
study of the first years of the program's operation; see Martin
Anderson's *The Federal Bulldozer: A Critical Analysis of Urban
Renewal, 1949–1962* (Cambridge, Mass.: M.I.T. Press, 1964). Externalities as a basis for urban renewal were initially discussed by
Otto A. Davis and Andrew B. Whinston in their article "The Economics of Urban Renewal" in *Law and Contemporary Problems* 26
(Winter 1961): 105–17. An excellent collection of essays on a range
of contemporary urban concerns is *Urban Problems and Prospects,*
by Anthony Downs (Chicago: Markham, 1970). For a thorough exposition of the costs of metropolitan transportation inefficiencies
and some hopeful predictions about the effects of public policy, see
William S. Vickrey's article "Pricing in Urban and Suburban Transport" in *American Economic Review (Papers and Proceedings)* 53
(May 1963): 452–65.

14 Water Resources

Most of the development of benefit-cost methodology has been made by the engineers and economists studying the design of water resources systems. One reason is that the economic impact of water resources development—harbors, rivers, and canals—has been known and studied since colonial days. Another reason is that most benefits and costs have been susceptible to economic evaluation. During the 1930's the notion that benefits should be measured in dollars and compared with costs became popular and eventually led to the formulation of a set of guidelines and recommendations for water resources research in the "Green Book."[1] The Green Book's proposals included the use of the B/C ratio as the criterion for project selection and the choice of a discount rate of 2.5 to 4 percent. Even these recommendations, however, constituted advances in benefit-cost analysis, for they permitted economists to identify key issues and concentrate on resolving ambiguities and misunderstandings. The improvement of benefit-cost methodology has proceeded sequentially, analyzing one issue (such as the correct criterion) and then moving on to another (such as the measurement of benefits). In this chapter we shall study the current state of benefit-cost methodology applied to water resources.

[1] *Proposed Practices for Economic Analysis of River Basin Projects,* Report to the Federal Interagency River Basin Committee Prepared by the Subcommittee on Benefits and Costs (May 1950).

MEASURING OUTPUTS AND BENEFITS

The benefits of water resources development depend on the physical characteristics of the system and the economic demands of consumers. The most interesting analyses are made of multiple-purpose systems, those providing a variety of outputs benefiting different groups of consumers. The principal outputs of most multiple-purpose systems are hydroelectric power, flood control, recreation, and irrigation. While any system (incorporating dams, canals, generators, and storage lakes) can produce all these outputs, the choice among alternative projects must reflect the values that consumers place on different outputs. For example, irrigation in the Pacific Northwest is of negligible benefit, and flood control in the Southwest is likely to be of low value.

In estimating the values of these outputs, we must be careful to include only the benefits directly related to the system we are analyzing. Suppose that as a consequence of a flood control project entailing the construction of a large storage lake there is a tourist boom, and new hotels, motels, and restaurants spring up, increasing aggregate income and employment. The question that the analyst must answer is how the flood control system affected overall resource allocation. Unless the resources employed in the tourist industry were formerly unemployed (or underemployed), we should expect that their productivity before the flood control system was built was roughly equal to their productivity in tourism after the system is in operation. In that case, there is no income gain attributable to the flood control system, for the increased income in tourism is matched by a decrease in the output of some other industry. The impact of the flood control system on tourism is called a secondary impact, and the "benefits" are secondary (or "pecuniary") benefits. In an efficient market economy with full employment of resources, the opportunity cost of secondary benefits is likely to be nearly as great as the amount of the benefits. Accordingly, these secondary benefits should not be included in the total benefits attributed to the water resources system, since the net benefit (secondary benefits minus their opportunity cost) is virtually zero.

Hydroelectric Power. As the demand for electricity has grown, both public agencies and private companies have become more interested in exploiting the hydroelectric potential of many river basins. The outstanding example of public hydroelectric development is the Tennessee Valley Authority, many of whose dams were begun during the 1930's to provide electricity to underdeveloped areas in Appalachia and the South. Most other hydroelectric facilities are located in the Pacific Northwest, where high annual rainfall and mountainous terrain create rivers with large energy potentials.

The power output of a dam (or a system) is simple enough to measure, in kilowatts, and to evaluate, at the dollar price that prevails in the market. (We will ignore the short-run allocation problem resulting from the decreasing-cost nature of production. Instead, we will assume that the long-run cost of production is just equal to the market price, so that production is efficient in the long run.) The problems that arise in evaluating this output are caused by the long life of hydroelectric systems and their scale of production.

The demand for electric power has grown rapidly throughout the United States, doubling every five or ten years in many places. Some of this growth has been due to population increases, but most has been caused by rising levels of average income and the high income-elasticity of demand for electricity. Systems analysts usually consider the life of a hydroelectric power system to be fifty years. In order to estimate future levels of production and benefits, demand must be projected over this lifetime. This projection introduces a great deal of uncertainty, however, since the demand for hydroelectric power depends on both income (which cannot be projected accurately for fifty years) and the prices of other power sources. These other prices depend, in turn, on technology (such as the development of nuclear power), which is difficult to project even five or ten years into the future. Estimates of the benefits of hydroelectric power have usually been understated in the past due to the rapid growth of demand, but future technological advances may bring down market prices, causing estimates made on the basis of current prices to be overstated.

Estimating benefits is also complicated by the scale of output of many hydroelectric dams and generating stations. These facilities are, to an extent, either/or propositions: either a dam is built or it is not; either generating capacity is installed or it is not. Output can be phased in as market demand grows by installing additional generators or perhaps even building additional dams, but the indivisibilities present in these adjustments suggest that supply will grow in jumps while demand rises at a constant or an increasing rate. Just before a new generator is installed, demand will be high, supply low, and the market price will have to rise to clear the market. Immediately afterward, the new generator will make supply much larger relative to demand, and the market price will have to fall. These discrete changes in supply may be large relative to total supply, leading to large fluctuations in price. Thus, indivisibilities in production make it difficult to estimate the benefits of hydroelectric power.

Despite these problems, the usual procedure is to estimate total benefits from generating electricity by projecting the growth of demand at some rate and assuming that the current market price will prevail over the life of the system. If the constancy of the market price is due to constant average total costs in the long run (as suggested in Chapter 12), supply is perfectly elastic in the long run, and the rate of growth of demand merely affects the frequency with which the system's output is increased. The benefits calculated in this way then can be tested for their sensitivity to particular assumptions, such as the growth rate or the price level. Sometimes the supply of power from other sources is included in the analysis, usually without assuming that any change in market price occurs.

Flood Control. The magnitude of flood damage depends on the amount of water a river discharges over its banks. The ability of a water resources system to control floods, therefore, depends on how much storage capacity it has for water that otherwise would be discharged by a flooding river. Storage is provided by the lakes that are created by dams, and their flood control capability is measured by the acre-feet of water that they can contain. Other means of providing flood control are dredging or channeling a river and constructing levees along its banks.

Conceptually, the benefits of flood control are equal to the sums that residents and property owners in the floodplain would pay to avoid flooding. Since these sums include the value attached to reduced loss of life and frequency of injury, they cannot be estimated by benefit-cost analysis. Instead, a good benefit-cost study will include an estimate of the reduction in property damage and, as a separate benefit, savings in injuries and fatalities. The estimated property benefits usually are calculated on the basis of the property damage caused by floods of differing degrees of severity and the probabilities of these different floods. As well as property benefits, flood control also reduces the loss of income due to unemployment and illness, and it thus confers a dollar benefit on those who are not property owners. These benefits can be included in the total dollar benefits of flood control.[2]

A more difficult benefit to include is the change in land use that comes about as the result of a reduced probability of flood damage.

[2] There is some evidence that residents of floodplains place rather low values on reducing flood damage. Instead, their adaptation to the risk of floods makes them value flood protection at less than the reduction in property damage. See Robert W. Kates, "Geography: The Case for the Specialized Generalist in a Science of Environment," in Morris E. Garnsey and James R. Hibbs (eds.), *Social Sciences and the Environment* (Boulder: University of Colorado Press, 1967), pp. 53–76.

This is not a secondary benefit, for the lower flood probability increases the productivity of the existing resource. If flooding has deterred the exploitation of valuable natural resources or if a floodplain is large and the benefits of more intensive land use are very general, these benefits may be great. Studies have tried to include this benefit (called "enhancement of land value"), but estimates obviously must be uncertain because they can be based only on land-use patterns in other areas and subjective evaluations by the analyst or beneficiaries.

Recreation. Recreational benefits from water resources development are universally recognized but hard to evaluate. The unit of measurement of recreational output is most often taken to be "user days," an indicator of the total number of consumers of the recreational facility. But this output cannot be evaluated unless we can develop some measure of the utility that different consumers derive from their recreational consumption. Recently there have been some attempts to estimate the dollar value of recreation through interview techniques, consumers' "willingness to pay" for goods closely related to recreation, and demand projections to which dollar values can be appended.

An interviewing study reported by Knetsch and Davis estimated the demand curve for a Maine forest area by quizzing the users of the area about the prices that they would be willing to pay for the services they were consuming.[3] The resulting demand curve was elastic over the range $60–$6 and inelastic up to $6. Based on an estimated user population of about 10,300, Knetsch and Davis calculated total benefit (the area under the demand curve) as about $71,000. This demand estimate could be used to price the recreation area or, if the government supplying the area were committed to a zero price for distributional reasons, could provide an indication of the amount that the government should be willing to spend in order to supply the facility.

This demand curve, based on direct questions about willingness to pay, was roughly consistent with another estimated by the same authors on the basis of expressed willingness to incur travel costs in order to use the recreational facility. The advantage of the latter method is that it does not rely upon what consumers say they would be willing to pay but estimates instead the value of recreation from the preferences underlying their actual allocation of resources. Knetsch and Davis estimated total benefits of $69,000 for the same forest area using this surrogate benefit measure.

[3] Jack L. Knetsch and Robert K. Davis, "Comparisons of Methods for Recreation Evaluation," in Allen V. Kneese and Stephen C. Smith (eds.), *Water Research* (Baltimore: Johns Hopkins Press, 1966), pp. 125–42.

According to our discussion in Chapter 6, however, the public nature of recreation facilities will lead consumers to understate their willingness to pay for them. Even though Knetsch and Davis trust their interview results, we should question their estimates of benefits. An alternative approach has been used by Davidson, Adams, and Seneca, to estimate the preferences that consumers would have to have in order to make recreational development economically efficient.[4] These authors projected demand (for the recreational facilities of the Delaware River estuary) as a function of socioeconomic population characteristics such as age, sex, race, educational attainment, income, occupation, and place of residence. They also estimated the extent to which the demand for recreation would be affected by the availability of facilities. Given population characteristics, they then calculated the amount of recreation that would be demanded if the Delaware were clean and if it remained polluted, and they concluded that boating and fishing use would rise by about 9.5 million user-days (between 1965 and 1990) if water quality were improved. The cost of improving water quality is such that, for example, a day of boating would have to be valued at about $2.50 in order to make the improvement of quality economically efficient. No attempt was made to discover whether $2.50 is a reasonable estimate of the value of a day of boating.

These summaries of recent research efforts do not fully convey the difficulty of estimating the value of recreational facilities. Perhaps the most significant aspect of these studies is that they try to relate the benefits of recreation to the other dollar benefits of water resources systems. Without such a comparison, recreational development probably will be underfinanced compared to projects that yield dollar benefits. Thus, these research projects offer some hope of improving the balance of outputs from water resources systems, especially in a society that seems to be placing ever increasing value on leisure time.

Irrigation. Arid land in southern California and the Southwest has experienced enormous productivity increases from irrigation. These productivity increases usually accrue to farmers and landowners since in many cases the prices of the agricultural commodities they produce are supported by the federal government. Moreover, irrigation water usually is provided at a price well below the long-run cost of production and often below the short-run marginal cost. Thus, farmers

---

[4] Paul Davidson, F. Gerard Adams, and Joseph Seneca, "The Social Value of Water Recreational Facilities Resulting from an Improvement in Water Quality: The Delaware Estuary," in Kneese and Smith, pp. 175–211.

receive a double transfer payment: one from the federal government in the form of artificially high commodity prices and one from the agency that supplies water in the form of artificially low irrigation costs.

Nonetheless, the benefits from irrigation projects usually are taken to be the increases in farmers' incomes. Higher incomes arise both because of increased yields per acre and because water-using crops such as green vegetables and sugar beets can be planted on irrigated land. More intensive cultivation, however, entails higher resource costs of production that must be netted out of the analysis. Thus, the usual measure of benefits is the increase in the net income of farmers in the irrigated area.

We should recognize that this measure is likely to overstate the economic value of the benefits of irrigation. Two reasons have already been mentioned: the inflated prices of agricultural produce and the artificially low price of irrigation water. In addition, the low price of water encourages farmers to use water and other factors inefficiently. Particular irrigation projects may have high benefits, depending on the geology and topography of the irrigated areas. But so many irrigation projects have already been completed that future irrigation sites are likely to be only marginally efficient. Bain and Caves, for example, have concluded that the benefits of additional irrigation projects in California are unlikely to be as great as the costs.[5] This conclusion applies especially strongly if the transfer element in federal price supports is eliminated from the measurement of benefits.

SYSTEMS DESIGN

In this section we will consider some of the problems in designing water resources systems to be evaluated with benefit-cost methodology. Under the general definition of Chapter 12, a system is any way of producing the outputs that we associate with water resources development (hydroelectric power, flood control, recreation, and irrigation). Usually water resources systems have common elements for producing these outputs: dams, canals or aqueducts, storage lakes, and generating stations. These elements pose common problems of externalities in production, joint products, mutual exclusiveness of projects, indirect costs, and distribution of net benefits.

[5] Joe S. Bain, "Water Resource Development in California: The Comparative Efficiency of Local, State, and Federal Agencies," in Kneese and Smith, pp. 51–67.

Externalities in Production. The best example of a production externality arises with multiple dams in a single river basin. Power is generated by the river's flow past the generators at each dam and varies with both the amount of flow and the height of the water's fall at the generating station. An upstream dam can increase the amount of power generated at downstream dams by regulating its own release of water to correspond to the downstream dams' low periods. In effect, the job of an upstream dam is thus to maintain the level of streamflow at downstream locations.

The additional power produced at downstream dams is an external benefit of the upstream dam's release policy, for the effect of releasing water is to increase the rate of flow at all downstream locations without any action by the downstream dams. The magnitude of this externality can be substantial, as is shown in Table 14.1. The example in the table, the Hungry Horse dam and downstream dams on the Columbia River and its tributaries, offers unusually high external benefits, but the nature of the externality is the same in other river basins.

TABLE 14.1   Externalities at Hungry Horse Dam

Dams	KW (000)	Owner
Hungry Horse (at site)	212	U.S. government
Downstream		
Kerr	78	Private
Thompson Falls	12	Private
Cabinet Gorge	50	Private
Albeni Falls	7	U.S. government
Box Canyon	14	Local government
Waneta	70	Private
Grand Coulee	163	U.S. government
Chief Joseph	83	U.S. government
Rock Island	16	Local government
McNary	49	U.S. government
The Dalles	52	U.S. government
Bonneville	34	U.S. government
TOTAL	628	
Total Hungry Horse power	840	

SOURCE: Roland M. McKean, *Efficiency in Government Through Systems Analysis with Emphasis on Water Resource* (New York: Wiley, 1958).

Unless all the dams in a basin are owned and operated efficiently by the same producer, the presence of this externality may lead to inefficient design and operation of water resources systems. Upstream dams may not be able to charge downstream dams for the additional power they produce, especially if there are many downstream dams with competing demands for water release. If upstream dams are privately built and operated, they probably will have less than the optimal amount of storage capacity since the owner will not incur the higher cost of a dam that provides greater storage to increase downstream generation. And once the dams are built, the owner of an upstream dam will not alter the release policy that maximizes his own power output, even if doing so would yield greater increases downstream.

The question that confronts the analyst designing water resources systems is what is the optimal policy for the federal government (since we are studying public resource allocation) if either upstream or downstream dams are privately owned. Should the government build the socially efficient dam, recognizing that to do so will confer a distributional benefit on owners of the private dams (if they are downstream)? Should the federal dam compensate a private dam in order to obtain the socially efficient allocation of resources (if the private dam is upstream)?

Interestingly, federal policy treats part of the problem adequately while ignoring the other part. If a federal dam confers an external benefit on a downstream private producer, the federal government forces the downstream producer to compensate it in the amount of his benefits from the federal dam's water release. The rationale for this (economically correct) procedure is that the federal government owns streambeds and grants licenses, in return for which it may demand compensation. If the federal dam is downstream, however, it does not have to compensate an upstream private producer, and consequently the private dam has no incentive to follow efficient storage and release policies. Thus, in the Hungry Horse example in Table 14.1, we may expect some of the interdependencies (between, say, Waneta and Albeni Falls) to be recognized, while others (between, say, Albeni Falls and Cabinet Gorge) are ignored.

Joint Outputs. As we noted at the beginning of this chapter, the interesting analyses of water resources systems are those in which several outputs are produced. If the objective of our analysis is to design a system that maximizes the net value of hydroelectric power (or flood control or irrigation), then our benefit-cost study will be rather straightforward (at least economically). But when we consider multiple objectives, we must make trade-offs among them.

For example, the scenic and recreational values of a river gorge with wild rapids must be lost if the hydroelectric potential of the site is exploited by a large dam that turns the rapids into a placid lake. (Of course, the lake may offer its own recreational values. Then there is a distributional problem because the people who use the lake probably are not the same ones who would hike and canoe in the gorge.) As another example, flood control requires storage capacity, but power generation and irrigation require streamflow. It may not be possible to meet both sets of objectives, and the policy-maker will have to decide which group of consumers he wants to serve. A small change in the valuation of benefits (or in the decision-maker's objectives) may lead to a reranking of system designs.

Mutual Exclusiveness. Another aspect of this problem is that the choice of one system frequently forecloses other options. Suppose that we can design three systems for producing multiple outputs in different proportions in a particular river basin. Perhaps the present values of net benefits are positive for all three systems. If we choose system P (the producer of the most electric power), then we have prevented ourselves from switching later to either F (providing flood control) or R (the one that is recreation-intensive).

There is no way to get around this problem, for water resources development frequently is irreversible, especially with regard to its ecological impacts. But the systems analyst may include in his calculation of benefits something called an "option demand." If system P forecloses our later use of the river basin's recreational potential, then it imposes costs not only on current users of the recreational facilities but also on potential users to whom the option for future use is worth some sum. If an irrigation dam in Arizona turns the Grand Canyon into a lake, then the option demands of potential future tourists are given up for the sake of the irrigation project. Option demands are not relevant to decisions about private goods that do not foreclose future alternatives. But for irreversible natural resources developments that affect large numbers of potential users, option demands may be very large.

As an example of the use of option demands, suppose that a Grand Canyon dam offers net benefits from hydroelectric power and irrigation valued at $100 million (at a 10 percent discount rate). The project also forecloses all future use of the canyon as a tourist attraction. If the value of the option demands were $10 million per year, the present value of all future option demands would be equal to the present value of the dam. It is not unreasonable to suppose that each potential visitor would pay 5 cents per year for the option to visit the Grand Canyon at some point in his lifetime. But the population of potential visitors is at least 200 million, even if we exclude all foreign tourists, so the value of option demands probably would be more than great enough to make the dam economically inefficient.

As an incidental point, we may note that the mutual exclusiveness of water resources systems makes the use of the benefit-cost ratio an incorrect criterion for choosing among alternative systems. As in the example in Chapter 12, we can build only one of the three systems (P, F, or R). If we choose the one with the highest B/C ratio, we will automatically be prevented from investing in either of the others, even though the others' B/C ratios may be positive and their net benefits may be greater. Thus, if we can rely upon our estimates of benefits and costs, we should always rank alternative water resources developments on the basis of their net benefits $(B - C)$.

Indirect Costs. Comparatively little is known about the ecological impact of water resources development, but it has become apparent that large dams may impose a variety of indirect costs on the economy. One effect that was noted early was that dams prevented certain fish, notably salmon, from carrying out their reproduction cycle by returning upstream to their spawning locations. Naturalists have constructed "fish ladders" to enable these fish to bypass the dams, but a reduction in spawning has been observed nonetheless.

Another problem is that the silt that a river carries in suspension while it is flowing drops out of suspension when the river enters the quiet lake formed by a dam. Siltation in any one year is small compared to the volume of any large lake, but over the lifetime of a dam siltation may cause a significant reduction in storage capacity and thus in both power generation and flood control. Eventually, the lifetime of the dam may be shortened, and the dam's actual benefits may not reach the projected ones.

Lakes created by storage dams frequently are valued for the recreational opportunities they provide. When a dam is operated for hydroelectric power or irrigation, however, the release of stored water sometimes causes a significant drop in the water level behind the dam. This "draw down" can create shoreline mud flats, reducing or eliminating the recreational values of the lake. This cost is just another example of the jointness of outputs already mentioned.

Finally, some geologists have suggested that large lakes may create seismic effects through the additional pressure they place upon the earth's crust. So little is known about seismology that we cannot eval-

uate this argument, but it is worth noting that dire predictions of ecological impacts also were ignored until they began to come true. The
earth's crust is a closed system, and pressure exerted at one spot must
be vented somewhere else. At the least, developers should be careful
about planning water resources systems in earthquake-prone areas.

Distribution of Costs and Benefits. When projects are compared on
the basis of their benefits and costs, it is idle to pretend that the net
benefits criterion incorporates all the data relevant to the government's investment decision. As an example, suppose that all the benefits and costs of projects P, F, and R can be calculated with perfect
accuracy and that all three systems offer exactly the same present
value of net benefits. The government, however, can only build one of
the systems since they are all mutually exclusive. Its choice, therefore, can only be made by comparing the distribution of net benefits.
(We assume either that there will be some financing of the project out
of general revenues or else that some of the beneficiaries will pay less
than they benefit while others pay more.)

If the government is able to choose among equally efficient projects
on the basis of the distribution of their benefits, however, there must
be some public preference for one distribution of benefits compared to
others. But if such a preference exists, it will also exist when projects
are not identically efficient. It is perfectly reasonable to expect society
to express its distributional preferences in return for some loss in
efficiency. For example, we may choose a recreation-intensive project
over one that offers hydroelectric power with a higher net present
value, simply because of the distributional judgment that we should
subsidize users of recreational facilities instead of consumers of
electricity.

Haveman has shown that just such a trade-off of distributional
gains for allocational ones does occur in congressional appropriations
for water resources development.[6] The distribution, however, is ex-
clusively geographical, rather than by income, race, occupation, or
other socioeconomic characteristics. The choice of location as the distributional criterion reflects the disproportionate weighting of western
influences on congressional appropriations committees. Other economists have attempted to introduce tabular descriptions of the distribution of benefits into analyses of water resources systems.[7] These

[6] Robert H. Haveman, *Water Resource Investment and the Public Interest*
(Nashville, Tenn.: Vanderbilt University Press, 1965), p. 49 and tables 2 and 4
(pp. 44, 48).
[7] A. M. Freeman, III, "Six Federal Reclamation Projects and the Distribution
of Income," *Water Resources Research* (1967).

attempts, however, have been hampered by the absence of adequate data on the distribution of benefits. Thus, Weisbrod cites studies of the distribution of recreation benefits in which the rationale for a particular incidence of benefits is the *assumption* that the users of the park are residents of certain counties or of an entire state.[8] Data on the place of residence and other socioeconomic characteristics of beneficiaries might be easy to obtain, but only in a few cases have they actually been collected.

More ambitious attempts to integrate distributional considerations into benefit-cost analysis have been made on occasion. One method is to infer a public distributional preference from the projects that actually are undertaken (including some that are inefficient) and to evaluate projects on the basis of this distributional criterion as well as the net benefits rule.[9] Another technique is to estimate the net benefits of redistributional projects by assuming that both gainers and losers have particular utility functions, an approach similar to that of the "sacrifice" theories of taxation discussed in Chapter 7.[10] These approaches yield conclusions about the extent to which society departs from the efficient allocation of resources in its search for distributional equity. But they have not yet been accepted by most economists as legitimate modifications of the simple net benefits criterion.

THE SELECTION OF PROJECTS

If the sole basis for choosing among alternative systems were the present value of the net benefits that they offer, public investments in water resources development could be completely efficient, and the task of the systems analyst would merely be to improve his data collection methods and the accuracy of his forecasts of demand. In reality, there are both economic and non-economic sources of inefficiency in the selection of projects: the choice of a discount rate, the question of public versus private development, and political factors such as constraints on the use of prices.

Importance of the Discount Rate. Because of the capital-intensity of water resources systems and the long system lives, the discount rate is frequently a key parameter in the ranking of projects. For example,

[8] Burton A. Weisbrod, "Income Redistribution Effects and Benefit-Cost Analysis," in Samuel B. Chase, Jr. (ed.), *Problems in Public Expenditure Analysis* (Washington, D.C.: Brookings Institution, 1968), pp. 187–88.

[9] *Ibid.*, pp. 190–209. See also the comment by Haveman following Weisbrod's paper.

[10] A. Myrick Freeman, III, "Income Distribution and Planning for Public Investment," *American Economic Review* 57 (June 1967): 495–508.

in their discussion of the Hell's Canyon case, in which the choice was between a single federal dam or three smaller, private ones, Krutilla and Eckstein concluded that, at the prevailing rate of 2.5 percent used to discount water resources systems, the federal high dam was to be preferred to the private dams.[11] At the modest rate of 5.5 percent, however, the advantage of the public dam disappeared: the *marginal* benefit-cost ratio (the additional benefits of the single dam divided by its additional costs, compared to the three-dam scheme) was only 0.9. The rates of interest that were recommended in Chapter 13, of course, are considerably above 5.5 percent, and we may conclude that if the private opportunity cost of capital were the discount rate, the three-dam plan clearly would have been more advantageous.

Critics of federal water resources projects (especially those of the Army Corps of Engineers and the Bureau of Reclamation) have argued that the use of a low discount rate has made many projects appear efficient that would be very inefficient if discounted at the private opportunity cost of capital. Some support for this view can be found in Budget Bureau Circular A-94 (of June 26, 1969), which discusses the use of discount rates for public investments. The Budget Bureau specified the minimum rate to be used as that set by the Water Resources Council,[12] related to the current yield on government bonds. (At the time of publication of the Circular, this rate was 4.875 percent.) In addition, the Bureau announced its intention to require higher rates to be used in certain cases, indicating its view that the Water Resources Council rate was too low to reflect the true opportunity cost of public investment. This clear preference of the Water Resources Council for a discount rate below the private opportunity cost suggests that many federal water resources projects would be unattractive if evaluated at the correct discount rate.

Public Versus Private Development. During the 1950's, a popular subject for debate was "public power," the development of hydroelectric sites by the federal government instead of by private utilities. Proponents of federal projects cited the undeniable successes achieved by TVA in supplying power and stimulating economic development over a large region. Opponents claimed that public systems received unfair advantages in the form of tax exemption and access to public funds at lower interest rates.

[11] John V. Krutilla and Otto Eckstein, *Multiple Purpose River Development* (Baltimore: Johns Hopkins Press, 1958), ch. 5.

[12] An *ad hoc* group established in 1965 and composed of the Secretaries of Agriculture, Interior, HEW, Transportation, and the Army, and the Chairman of the Federal Power Commission.

This issue arose largely because of its political overtones, but some substantial economic questions also are involved. As we have seen, private development of river basins is likely to be inefficient because the externalities of power production will be ignored unless entire basins are developed by single utility companies. Even then, utilities are likely to ignore nonmarketable benefits (flood control, recreation) in designing their systems. The same arguments apply to the development of irrigation systems by local governments, which may not take into account their impact on downstream water users and beneficiaries other than the farmers who demand irrigation.

On the other hand, public multipurpose development of river basins has not been universally successful. It is now becoming clear that in many cases the ecological impact of water resources systems has been ignored by public as well as by private developers. The use of low discount rates probably has encouraged investments that were economically inefficient. Even when there is a market imperfection (such as externalities in the production of electric power) and thus a basis for public action, federal policy has not always been able to compensate for the imperfection and secure the efficient allocation of resources. For example, consider the asymmetric policy toward externalities discussed earlier.

Because of nonmarketable outputs like flood control and recreation, there is a strong case for public development of many river basins. When development is mixed (as is usually the case since most utilities are privately owned), there is a compelling argument for coordinated operation of the overall water resources system. Jointness in production, as in the case of the power externalities, and jointness of outputs, such as recreation and irrigation, cause the private equilibrium to be socially inefficient. But our discussion of water resources systems has shown that there are many cases of inefficient public design and operation. Repetition of these mistakes can be avoided only by improved benefit-cost analyses of alternative patterns of development and use.

Efficiency and Pricing. Political demands for income redistribution sometimes are implemented through the selection of water resources projects. An excellent example is presented by Hirschleifer, DeHaven, and Milliman in their discussion of California's Feather River Project.[13] This project is intended to transport water from its source in northern California to both residential and commercial users in south-

---

[13] Jack Hirschleifer, James C. DeHaven, and Jerome W. Milliman, *Water Supply* (Chicago: University of Chicago Press, 1960), ch. 11, pp. 335–47.

ern California. Hirschleifer, DeHaven, and Milliman suggest that the efficiency of such an investment could be determined by instituting a market for water through metering devices. The strength of demand, whether estimated from other preferences or revealed by consumers' demand for water at various prices, would then provide a basis for choice among the alternative water supply systems. The authors go on to conclude that the Feather River Project now under construction offers *negative* net benefits. Their conclusion agrees with Bain's, cited earlier, and shows the consequences of failing to perform an adequate analysis of benefits and costs.

The reason markets are not created with water meters seems to be that the political costs of metering are high. To some politicians, water should not be supplied according to the test of the market; instead, it is a "necessity of life" that must be made abundantly available to all at a zero cost. Of course, the cost of supply is never zero. If water is not metered, the cost of providing it must be found in general tax revenues. But as we saw in Chapter 5, determining the efficient level of supply entails efficiency at the margin. Thus, political prohibitions on the use of pricing are merely a device for transferring income to those with high demands for water relative to their tax liabilities. This conclusion applies whether the water is used for residential or commercial purposes. And it carries the corollary that these redistributional devices impose an efficiency cost in terms of the misallocation that results from the difference between the marginal cost of supply and the (zero) price charged for the marginal unit of consumption.

SUMMARY

Many of the advances in benefit-cost methodology have come in the development of water resources, principally because the major categories of benefits—hydroelectric power, flood control, recreation, and irrigation—can be measured and evaluated with some success. All the types of benefits pose some problems for the systems analyst, but estimates of dollar values usually can be made. In the case of electric power, the uncertainty of the future makes benefit estimation difficult. Flood control is hard to evaluate because of the importance of physical factors and the possibility of "enhancement of land value." Recreational facilities are rarely priced at all, and the public-good problem described in Chapter 6 arises in attempts to estimate benefits. Irrigation usually is overvalued due to subsidies to farmers from both federal and lower levels of government.

One problem in designing water resources systems is that different elements of a system may confer externalities. This is especially true when there are several hydroelectric dams, since upstream dams influence downstream dams' generating ability. Another problem is that competing outputs may be produced by a system, and the choice among alternative designs may depend on the relative weights attached to different outputs. Alternative water resources systems are mutually exclusive: if we develop a river basin one way, then we cannot develop it in any other way. This characteristic makes the use of the benefit-cost ratio an incorrect criterion for choosing among systems. Because the ecological consequences of water resources systems are often irreversible, an analyst may try to include option demands in his evaluation of benefits. He should also recognize that a system can impose several types of indirect costs.

The distribution of net benefits from water resources development is of both theoretical and practical interest. Appropriations decisions often are made on the basis of the geographical incidence of benefits. We should expect society to be willing to forgo some gain in efficiency for the sake of its distributional preferences, but attempts to integrate distributional judgments into benefit-cost analyses have not yet been satisfactory. All we can ask is that the distribution of benefits, as well as the magnitude of overall net benefits, be estimated explicitly and made a basis for the choice among projects.

One of the most important parameters in benefit-cost studies of water resources systems is the discount rate. There is some evidence that if the opportunity cost of capital were used to discount the costs and benefits of federal projects, many fewer projects would be economically efficient. Numerous inefficiencies can be found in the actual design and operation of both public and private systems. Even though some of the outputs (power and water) of such systems are private goods, there is a strong case at least for public coordination of the different facilities in a given river basin. Efficiency is difficult to achieve, however, as long as political considerations preclude the use of pricing methods under the misleading guise of distributional equity.

15 Defense Budgeting

National defense represents by far the largest category of government expenditures both at the federal level and for all levels of government taken together. In fact, the "defense business" is the largest enterprise in the world, much greater in size than any domestic corporation, with expenditures larger than those of any state and most foreign governments. None of this gigantism would be economically interesting if defense were not the archetypal public good, one for which resource allocation decisions are extraordinarily difficult because of our uncertainty about how inputs produce outputs. In this chapter we will examine the way that budgetary decisions are made within the Defense Department and some of the allocation problems that arise.

BUDGETING BEFORE PPBS

The Department of Defense and the four Services (Army, Navy, Air Force, and Marines) were created after World War II out of the Departments of the Army and Navy, which previously had been administratively independent. During the early years of the Defense Department, budgetary appropriations were made for each decentralized bureau within the Services. In the 1950's a recommendation of the Hoover Commission (1947–1949) led to the creation of five appropriations categories uniform to all the Services. These line items (research, procurement, personnel, construction, and operations) are still retained in the line-item budget that is submitted by OMB and the Defense Department to Congress.

When the Defense Department was first created, officials envisioned a budgetary process that would begin with a specification by the President and his National Security Council of the desired objectives of military actions, subject to the availability of resources. The President would then outline his military budget to the Secretary of Defense and thereby to the Joint Chiefs of Staff. The Joint Chiefs would prepare strategic plans for attaining the President's objectives and would allocate the responsibility for these objectives among the Services. When the Services responded with proposals for force levels, the Joint Chiefs would aid in translating the Service proposals into dollar and manpower terms for referral to the President. If the proposed Defense budget exceeded the President's desired expenditures, he would refer the budget back to the Joint Chiefs and, if necessary, to the Services for revision.

This system might have worked well if specific missions had remained the responsibilities of individual Services. During World War II, for example, the Army had the responsibility for waging sustained land campaigns, the Navy for escorting supplies and troop ships and fighting sea battles, the Marines for making sea assaults, and the Air Force for strategic and tactical air warfare. Following World War II, and especially during the 1950's, all the Services succeeded in diversifying their missions. The Navy developed its own carrier-based air arm for tactical combat and Polaris-equipped submarines for strategic deterrence. The Air Force expanded its logistical activities and added unmanned missiles for the strategic mission. The Marines developed the capability to fight sustained land battles, while the Army added an extensive air support wing with both helicopters and traditional fixed-wing aircraft. Thus, even if the Joint Chiefs had been able to link presidential objectives to particular weapons systems and force levels, it would have been difficult for them to assign individual missions to the different Services.

Although the adoption of uniform line-item categories made possible some comparison of the activities of the four Services, force-level decisions throughout the 1950's were not often made by systematic evaluation of the alternatives proposed by different Services. The Joint Chiefs tended to view their role as the making of broad decisions about desirable force levels, usually unrelated to the budget constraints facing the President. Decisions about funding different programs were made by the Services and coordinated by the Budget Bureau and the Comptroller of the Defense Department. When the Services offered competing alternatives, the choice frequently was based upon comparisons of costs and low-level outputs such as man-power demands and production feasibility. Symbiotic relationships between the Services and various Congressmen, together with the political climate of the decade, led to large budgets, extensive re-search programs, and frequent duplication of effort and weapons systems by different Services.

Some attempts were made both to limit military appropriations and to improve the economic rationality of resource allocation. On one occasion, when the annual budget submission was due and the Joint Chiefs' budget requests greatly exceeded the President's willingness to commit resources, a single line item for aggregate Defense spend-ing was included in the budget and Services were forced to revamp their requests to fit within this total. Another technique was for the Secretary of Defense to ask the Services to rank their force-level re-quests according to the priority attached to each. Unfortunately, the Services were able to subvert this device by attaching high priorities to programs that the Secretary did not favor and low ones to programs that he was committed to, thus forcing him to accept large budgets to obtain the programs he wanted. Still another approach was for the Secretary first to understate the size of the overall Defense budget and then to offer a supplement in order to see what programs the Services considered to be marginal.

Despite these devices, the pre-1961 budgeting system did not offer a vehicle for efficient resource allocation. Its chief deficiency was that it encouraged the comparison of all programs within a Service (de-spite their diversity of missions) and discouraged the analysis of sim-ilar programs operated by different Services. In this respect, the pre-PPBS budgeting system in Defense exhibited the same short-comings that were mentioned in Chapter 11 as reasons for the Budget Director's introduction of program budgeting throughout the federal government in 1965: lack of control by central administrators, no basis for comparing alternatives, and no guide to the value of pro-grams or to the efficiency of resource use.

PPBS IN THE DEFENSE DEPARTMENT

During the 1950's, a group of economists and analysts at the Rand Corporation, an Air Force contractor, had developed a proposal for a program budgeting system to be used in Defense. When Robert McNamara became Secretary of Defense in 1961, he named one of these economists, Charles Hitch, as his Comptroller. Hitch, in turn, added to his staff a number of the other Rand analysts and instituted the program budget that they had designed. This budgeting system had the familiar features of the planning-programming-budgeting system that grew out of it: a multiyear expenditure plan, memoranda delineating program choices in certain areas, and analyses underlying the program memoranda.

The Expenditure Plan. The basic program structure of the Defense Department was set forth in the Five Year Force Structure and Financial Program (later renamed the Five Year Defense Program, FYDP). The FYDP established nine major programs, shown in Table 15.1, to summarize all Defense activities. Each program details *total* Defense spending in a mission area, cutting across the Services' appropriation categories. Planned expenditures in each program are shown over a five-year period, a major improvement over the previous system in which all funding had been on a year-to-year basis. Within each program, activities are broken down into subprograms and program elements, as shown for Program I in Table 15.2. Some of the program elements include many expenditure units (such as fighter aircraft wings, infantry divisions); others have few major components (such as the nuclear aircraft carrier Enterprise, which singly constitutes an entire program element).

TABLE 15.1   Defense Department Program Structure

Strategic forces
  Offense (Program I)
  Air and missile defense (Program II)
  Civil defense (Program IX)

Tactical forces
  General purpose (Program III)
  Airlift and sealift (Program IV)
  Reserves and national guard (Program V)
  Military assistance (Program VIII)

Support activities
  General support (Program VII)
  Research and development (Program VI)
  Retired pay[a]

SOURCE: William A. Niskanen, "The Defense Resource Allocation Process," in Stephen Enke (ed.), *Defense Management* (Englewood Cliffs, N.J.: Prentice-Hall, 1967), p. 8.
  [a] Although retired pay is not a program category for purposes of analysis, it is shown separately in the program budget.

TABLE 15.2   Program Elements in Program I: Strategic Retaliatory
              Forces[a]

Aircraft forces
  B/EB-47
  RB-47
  B-52
  AGM-28 A/B
  GAM-87
  B-58
  KC-97
  KC-135
  RC-135

Missile forces, land based
  Atlas
  Titan
  Minuteman

Missile forces, sea based
  Polaris system
  Regulus system

Command control, communications and support
  SAC control
  PACCS (KC-135/B-47)
  UHF emergency rocket communications system
  Advanced flying and missile training
  Base operating support
  Headquarters and command support

SOURCE: David Novick, "The Department of Defense," in Novick (ed.), *Program Budgeting* (Santa Monica, Calif.: Rand, 1965), p. 61.
  [a] As of 1964.

Program Memoranda. Perhaps more in Defense than in other agencies, program memoranda provide the focus for major decisions about force levels. The basic documents are the presidential memoranda sent to the President by the Secretary of Defense detailing force-level decisions in a dozen different categories. The drafts of these documents, as initially prepared by the Office of the Secretary of Defense and circulated to the Services for comments, describe the conclusions that the Secretary has reached about the different Services' alternative proposals in a given program area. Typical draft memoranda present recommended force levels for Program I (Strategic Retaliatory Forces) or Program IV (Airlift and Sealift).

Analytical Studies. Underlying the draft presidential memoranda and usually circulated with them are analyses of alternative force-level proposals. A good analytical study of a Defense program is a cost-effectiveness comparison of different systems in situations ("scenarios") that are thought to be either probable contingencies or cases that will expose the limitations of the system. The initial draft of a presidential memorandum frequently incorporates earlier studies done by the Services, implicitly requesting competing Services to comment on their methodologies and inviting other studies on different aspects of the same issue.

These cost-effectiveness analyses become the basis for the Services' requests that the Secretary modify his initial force-level recommendations, as well as for the draft memoranda themselves. When a Service has what it thinks is a strong case for a change in the original force levels, it submits a program adjustment request (initially a program change proposal). These can be submitted at any phase of the budget cycle but are most likely to arise during consideration of the draft presidential memoranda.

The FYDP, draft presidential memoranda, and program adjustment requests are the basic elements of the Defense program budgeting process, but much of the budgetary cycle proceeds without them. The cycle begins over eighteen months before the President's budget submission to Congress with the Joint Chiefs's preparation of the joint strategic objectives plan, a military evaluation of geopolitical conditions and the U.S. posture required to meet them. This plan is supposed to provide the Secretary with a basis for his initial force-level decisions, but the formal recommendations it contains usually go well beyond the budgetary ceiling under which the Secretary must work. Nonetheless, the military evaluations contained in the plan are preserved in some of the advice of the Joint Chiefs to the Secretary later in the budget cycle.

In addition to the joint strategic objectives plan and the communications between the Secretary and the Joint Chiefs and the Secretary and the Services, a final hearing for the military viewpoint is provided at the end of the Defense budget cycle (just before submission of the President's budget to Congress). At that time, the Joint Chiefs can appeal the Secretary's final decisions directly to the President, just as an agency head may appeal OMB's decisions. Unlike other agencies, however, Defense is rarely restricted severely by OMB budget analysts. Instead, the Secretary himself exercises a restraining influence upon the Services' requests, a role that began with McNamara and has continued, by and large, with his successors.

When the President's budget goes to Congress, the Defense Department receives the same handling as other agencies. New programs must be examined and authorized by the armed services committees, and new obligational authority must be voted by the appropriations committees. The Defense Department usually has had more friends in Congress than other agencies have, however, and its budget requests have received sympathetic treatment. During the 1950's, it was not unusual for Congressmen to obtain testimony from high-ranking officers that budgetary allocations had been cut too much by the Secretary of Defense or the President and for Congress then to vote the additional funds that the Service originally had requested. Some similar instances arose during the 1960's under McNamara, but the availability of cost-effectiveness studies to support the Secretary's decisions generally offset the military testimony. Interestingly, in the two cases where McNamara's force-level decisions have drawn the most after-the-fact criticism, the TFX fighter aircraft (later the F-111) and the C-5A transport aircraft, cost-effectiveness analyses indicated that the systems were only marginally efficient even at the original cost estimates.

Despite instances like these and a persistent tendency to underestimate the costs of major weapons systems, it seems clear that the program budgeting system introduced by McNamara and Hitch and modified under both of McNamara's successors has led to some significant improvements in Defense decision-making. Perhaps the greatest step is the collection of diverse Service programs into the FYDP, permitting cross-Service comparison where none was possible before 1961. The multiyear aspect of the FYDP is also a major improvement, for it forces the Services to display for the Secretary the eventual budgetary consequences of their recommendations. McNamara's reliance on his analytical staff made the role of systems analysis an important one during his tenure as Secretary. His successors have not had as strong a belief in the power of analysis and quantification, but there is some evidence that cost-effectiveness studies continue to be important factors in the Secretary's force-structure decisions. Perhaps more important, McNamara's success in using systems analysis to support his arguments convinced the Services to develop strong analytical staffs of their own. In many cases the results of systems analyses have complemented or even replaced "military judgment" as the basis of Service recommendations.

PROBLEMS WITH DEFENSE PROGRAM BUDGETING

Despite the improvement that program budgeting has brought to resource allocation in the Defense Department, many problems remain in the budgetary process. Many more exist in the analytical process, leading to incorrect choices among systems. These problems may be either economic, such as basing a procurement decision on erroneous cost estimates, or political, such as investing in a weapon system to placate influential Congressmen even though studies have indicated that the system should not be bought. In this section we will discuss some remedies for institutional shortcomings in the budgetary process. In the next section some particular sources of bias in the choice among systems will be examined.

The Role of Military Judgment. Before the installation of program budgeting, there was little civilian control within Defense over major force-level decisions. Instead, the Services tended to pursue their own policies of developing and purchasing new systems, justifying their decisions when necessary on the basis of "sound military judgment" or "protecting the American fighting man." When program budgeting became operational, the pendulum swung rather far in the other direction. Intangible elements in military decisions were downgraded in favor of the quantifiable aspects of system performance that could be included in cost-effectiveness analyses. The joint strategic objectives plan, which formerly had served as a translation of objectives into force-level decisions, was ignored because of its failure to consider budgetary limitations. Analysts on the Secretary's staff treated the Services' proposals and criticisms as self-serving and insufficiently objective.

There is no question that civilians must exercise ultimate control over the Defense budget as well as over the other activities of the Defense Department. But military officers possess certain kinds of training and experience that should not be disregarded in force-level decisions. One way to incorporate professional military judgment into the analytical process (instead of merely reintroducing the political budgeting process of pre-1961 experience) would be to alter the political role of the Joint Chiefs and to upgrade the analytical capability of the Joint Staff (the Service officers assigned to the Joint Chiefs). At present, the Joint Chiefs attempt to resolve differences among the Services in order to present a united front to the Secretary on force-level decisions. In preparing the joint strategic objectives plan, the Joint Staff shies away from ranking alternative systems, reflecting instead the loyalties of individual officers to their Services. Although both the plan and the recommendations of the Joint Chiefs may be influential in force-level decisions, their impact is political and is exerted at cross-purposes from that of analysts in the Services and on the Secretary's staff.

Planning Under a Budget Constraint. In any year, Defense planners, like employees of any other agency, could easily devise productive allocations of funds far beyond those available in the budget. But resources are scarce, and planners must allocate them among Defense projects in an attempt to achieve some objective (such as getting the greatest "bang for the buck" or obtaining the capability to fight two major wars simultaneously). This allocation process has two steps: defining the objective and evaluating different systems' contributions to it. Both of these functions are now performed by the Secretary and his staff, with comments from the Services and broad guidance from the Joint Chiefs.

One problem with this system is that the Secretary gets only the most casual indications of what military priorities are. The joint strategic objectives plan hardly considers the total budget in its force-level recommendations, and there is no attempt to analyze forces at the margin.[1] The Services are in a poor position to give the Secretary an indication of priorities, for they cannot be expected to evaluate each other's systems objectively. Thus, the Secretary must translate the Services' proposals into an allocation of the available funds without any indication of the importance that senior military officers place on different systems.

Such an indication of military priorities could be obtained under a reform in the development of the joint strategic objectives plan. The Secretary could state his and the President's national security objectives and provide the Joint Chiefs with an indication of the funds that he was prepared to commit to attaining them. The Joint Staff could then prepare a joint plan at different funding levels, perhaps 20 percent above or below the Secretary's budget total. From these recommendations, the Secretary could infer that some systems were considered essential by the military, while others were distinctly marginal. His own analysts could then provide indications of the payoff from these marginal systems as a guide toward final budget decisions.

The advantage of this approach is that it would force the military officers to respond to the Secretary's budget constraint. The Secretary always must act within this constraint, but under current procedures neither the Joint Chiefs nor the Services have to make their plans subject to the same limitation. Since the joint strategic objectives plan is the principal military planning document in the Defense Department,

---

[1] Early in the 1960's, an analyst from the Secretary's staff was briefing a group of generals on a cost-effectiveness analysis. When he began to discuss the increment in effectiveness provided by the marginal force unit, one general snapped, "In my command, there are *no* marginal units!" and stalked out.

incorporating the budget constraint into its recommendations would provide considerable integration of civilian and military planning.

Decentralizing Decisions. One of the major problems in Defense allocation before program budgeting was the duplication of effort by the different Services. Army and Air Force produced similar but quite independent missile systems; Air Force and Navy built competing fighter aircraft; Army and Marines developed alternative land combat logistical systems. Thus, each Service developed its own response to the missions with which it was entrusted, often at the cost of inefficient resource use.

This system was changed by Secretary McNamara, who refused to let the Services develop systems without clearance from his office. The result was to eliminate duplication from major systems (such as fighter aircraft) and minor ones (items of personal clothing), but this saving was not achieved without cost. One of the costs was to worsen the consequences of an incorrect decision. The other was to use the Secretary's own resources inefficiently.

Although program budgeting greatly increased both the degree of civilian control of the Defense Department and the incentives for efficient resource allocation, there are in retrospect many examples of poor choices among alternative systems. Some of these choices were made because the Secretary's staff chose among alternative proposals at a very early stage in system development, rather than permitting parallel development to a later stage. Others were made because of imperfect understandings of the missions for which systems were being designed or because of poor estimates of costs and performance. Thus, one of the effects of centralizing the responsibility for decision-making in the Secretary's office was to cut off competition among the Services in designing and developing systems for mutual missions. Once competing systems were ruled out, however, the Secretary had little choice but to follow his chosen systems through to completion, even if the results were much more costly than would have been true if parallel development had been permitted beyond the planning phase.

By centralizing decision-making, moreover, the Secretary's office assumed control over many issues that simply were not important enough to justify its concern. At one point, for example, McNamara himself decreed that the traditional Marine belt buckle would be replaced with a standard Army buckle. Regardless of the merits of his decision (which was supposed to result in large cost savings), it is nearly inconceivable that such an issue could ever have been allowed to reach his desk. By divesting the Services of virtually all their autonomy, however, the Secretary's office created a vacuum in which only his staff could make decisions. In this situation, there was no guidance as to what issues had to be resolved by the Secretary and which ones could be left to the Services to decide among themselves.

These inefficiencies are precisely those that economists predict under any centralized system. The antidote usually prescribed is some form of decentralization, letting lower-level officials make decisions whose ramifications do not reach throughout the organization. In the case of Defense, one way to achieve some decentralization and competition among the Services would be for the Secretary to specify missions and the funds to be allocated to each one. The Services could then propose (perhaps to the Joint Chiefs) alternative allocations of these totals, and the Joint Chiefs could recommend force levels to the Secretary. The difference between this approach and current practice is that competition among the Services would be encouraged and the initial choice among systems would be made by the military, subject to the Secretary's allocation of funds among missions. Such a procedure would be possible now (as it was not in 1961) because of the growth of the Services' analytical capabilities.

Although McNamara's successors have been sensitive to the issue of centralization of authority, they have not adopted a reform of the type described. Instead, there has been some attempt to reduce the Secretary's area of responsibility, returning more decisions to the sphere of "military judgment." As a result of some unfortunate systems development decisions, the Secretary's office now seems more willing to permit parallel development. Neither of these steps, however, guarantees that the inefficiencies caused by excessive centralization will not be matched by those of lower-level decentralized decisions. In other words, we have seen a retreat from centralization but not necessarily an improvement upon it.

BIASES IN DEFENSE ALLOCATION

In this section we consider some causes of bias in the choice of Defense systems resulting from distortions in the prices that the Defense Department pays for its resources. The first example shows the effect of withdrawing resources from the private sector at a price not equal to their opportunity cost. The second case is that of an internal misallocation.

Military Manpower. Since 1942 (with a brief interlude after World War II), the Defense Department has siphoned manpower out of private labor markets through the Selective Service System. While the draft has taken different forms at various times (sometimes including a lottery, occupational or marital-status deferments, and differing definitions of physical and mental eligibility), its basic feature has remained: it requires young men to serve in the armed forces without compensation enough to induce them to volunteer. By providing manpower at less than the market price, the draft leads to many misallocations by both draftees and the Defense Department.

To indicate the cost of these misallocations, we must compare the draft with a nondistorting alternative in which military manpower is obtained at the market price. Such an alternative is the all-volunteer army, which has been discussed and praised by some politicians and many economists (but which is opposed by the military, for reasons that we will examine shortly). If an all-volunteer army were recruited, then the value that the Defense Department places on manpower (and indirectly the value that society places upon it through its decision to allocate funds to Defense) would be equated with labor's opportunity cost, and the economy's allocation of labor between Defense and non-Defense would be efficient (assuming that other resources were priced efficiently). Thus, the all-volunteer army is the analogue of resource allocation in a competitive market.

When the draft withdraws manpower from private sector production, of course, it imposes a cost equal to labor's opportunity cost. If we ignore differences between draftees and prospective volunteers, then the opportunity cost of the draft is the sum it would take to recruit a volunteer army of the same size, since the draft reduces private sector output by the amount of the draftee's productivity (and by assumption the volunteer's). This opportunity cost must be paid by society as a whole, whether the army is raised by conscription or by recruitment. Under recruitment, the cost is paid by taxpayers at large, as a function of the total cost of the volunteer army (that is, the demand for government revenue) and the distribution of the tax burden. But when the draft is used, most of the cost is paid by the draftees in the form of lower income during their period of service.

Some minor refinements are necessary to make this argument correspond to the real world. Draftees may be relatively more productive in civilian occupations than prospective volunteers, so the opportunity cost of the draft may really be larger than the cost of an all-volunteer army. Under the draft, society at large bears some of the cost in the form of resource misallocations, since relative prices must be affected somewhat by the redistribution of income that the draft causes. Finally, the Defense Department might respond to an all-volunteer army by substituting capital for labor. All in all, however, the estimated cost of an all-volunteer army provides a good approximation to the excess cost that the draft imposes upon draftees (for the benefit of other members of society).

Studies of the cost of an all-volunteer army have estimated that it would require additional budgetary outlays of from $3 billion to $24 billion per year, with most estimates near $6 billion.[2] This is a rather large number, representing about 8 percent of the Defense budget and equivalent to an increase of about 7 percent in personal income tax rates. The political implications of such an increase in the Defense budget certainly would be severe, so it is not surprising that both civilian and military officials of the Defense Department have been hostile to the elimination of the draft. Nonetheless, it is important to realize that this additional cost is imposed upon society even if the draft is retained.

Not all the arguments for conscription are self-serving. Under McNamara, the Defense Department began to use the draft to provide occupational training for some unemployable youths, thus increasing the postservice productivity of these draftees and their civilian employment opportunities. More generally, some economists have recognized that military training is not related solely to combat but includes many civilian specialties (from electronics to piloting) that are highly marketable. Both of these effects, however, should merely reduce the dollar cost of an all-volunteer army, since enlistees would recognize that the real value of their military service would exceed their dollar income. Some politicians have worried about the composition of an all-volunteer army, fearing that it might not be racially representative of the population as a whole or that it would be difficult to impose civilian control on a professional military establishment. No economist can judge whether these concerns justify imposing so large a tax on draftees. All that is clear is that the electorate has never been given an opportunity to discuss the issue fully, and the magnitude of the cost imposed upon draftees has never been stated clearly.

Since the draft imposes high costs on draftees, it is not surprising that they should take elaborate measures to avoid it. Educational deferments probably have inflated the demand for college-level education, including graduate training during those periods when such education was grounds for deferment. Occupational deferments probably have increased the supply of technical manpower at the expense of other occupations. In many cases, the period of military service has affected the future careers of those who accept conscription.

[2] An important variable in these analyses is the civilian unemployment rate. The higher this rate is, the lower are the opportunity costs of military service and the lower are the additional budgetary costs of a volunteer army.

Those who do not accept it are even more seriously affected. In all, the draft almost certainly has a major distorting effect on civilian labor markets and resource allocation, as well as on equity.

Allocational costs also are imposed on the Defense Department. Since the draft only reduces the supply price for first-term manpower, it makes this factor of production inexpensive relative to all other factors, including re-enlistees. Thus, the draft encourages the inefficient use of first-term manpower, inflating the amount of manpower demanded. Moreover, the draft makes manpower of different levels of skill equally inexpensive (for the Services can draft a college graduate for the same price as an elementary school dropout) and thereby encourages the Services to demand more highly skilled manpower than they actually need. Both of these factors act to increase the social costs of the draft.

By reducing the overall cost of labor, the draft deters the Defense Department from introducing efficient substitutions of capital for labor. Although military technology has consistently become more capital-intensive, it is likely that in the absence of the draft even higher levels of capital-intensity would be realized. To see this point, it is necessary only to contemplate the effect on the Defense budget of an additional $6 billion outlay for manpower. There is no question that, rather than incur the additional dollar cost, the Services would abolish many inefficient uses of manpower.

The draft also affects the inter-Service allocation of resources, since not all Services accept the same quality of manpower or the same proportion of draftees. Although the existence of the draft certainly increases the willingness of prospective draftees to enlist in all Services, the average Mental Group scores of entering manpower are substantially lower for the Army than for the other Services. Thus, the cost per "skill unit" of manpower is highest in the Army (and lowest in the Air Force), causing further misallocations in the inter-Service determination of force levels.

Other misallocations of manpower arise due to the high proportion of military real wages that accrues as retirement benefits and the fact that the pay system does not adequately reflect differences in skill levels. These distortions may be even more important than those caused by the draft, but their immediate impact upon budgeting is not as great since the Defense Department's long-run pay levels must be roughly competitive with the private sector. The effect of the draft and these other aspects of military pay is to bias the choice of Defense systems toward labor-intensity and to discourage the efficient use of entering manpower.

Nuclear Materials. During the cold war, especially under the doctrine of massive retaliation in the 1950's, the Defense Department built up an enormous inventory of nuclear bombs and, later, missile warheads. While the basic impetus for this stockpiling was political, the details of budgeting procedures played a part in the decision to acquire this inventory. The misallocation arose because no budgetary charges are made for transactions between government agencies.

Nuclear materials are produced and fashioned into nuclear bombs and warheads by the Atomic Energy Commission (AEC). They are then transferred to the control of the Defense Department, which meanwhile has acquired the other elements of delivery systems: bombers, missiles, communications networks, and artillery pieces for "tactical" nuclear weapons. The cost of producing the nuclear parts of the weapons systems is borne by the AEC; the rest of the systems cost appears in the Defense budget.

The result of this splitting of the budgetary costs of nuclear systems is to bias the choice of Defense systems in favor of nuclear weapons. Consider the problem of choosing between a "tactical" nuclear missile and alternative conventional weapons (either bombs or artillery). The fact that the AEC bears the cost of part of the nuclear system means that its cost to Defense is less than its true cost to society. Thus, the choice by Defense is biased away from the conventional system, all of whose costs appear in the Defense budget. Even if all costs were included in the Defense systems analysis, there would be a political advantage to choosing the nuclear system because the costs would not all be charged to the Defense Department's budget.

When we consider strategic weapons that do not have close non-nuclear substitutes, the distortion is the same. The allocation of the Defense budget between, say, strategic and tactical forces reflects some decision-maker's (the Secretary's or perhaps the President's) trade-off between the costs of strategic and tactical systems and their payoffs. Excluding from the costs of strategic systems the cost of the nuclear components must bias the decision-maker's choice in favor of strategic weapons, just as in the preceding example.

As well as a bias among systems, this treatment of the costs of nuclear weapons also imparts an upward bias to the overall Defense budget and to the AEC's budget as well. Since the costs of some Defense systems are understated, both decision-makers in the executive branch and Congressmen are induced to allocate more funds to Defense at the expense of other agencies. Moreover, Defense officials' demands for more nuclear weapons result in budget increases for the AEC. Especially when there is a sympathetic Congress, the outcome of this game is for Defense to demand all the nuclear weapons that the AEC can produce and for the AEC to produce all the nuclear weapons that the Defense Department demands.

To some extent, this inflationary spiral has been curtailed by the unwillingness of OMB examiners to ignore the relationship between the Defense and AEC budgets. But without a mechanism for transferring resources from one agency to another *at an efficient price,* the OMB's ability to counteract the resource misallocation is extremely limited. This problem is quite general and certainly is not confined simply to the example of nuclear materials. It leads to many instances of inefficient resource use by Defense and other agencies, with goods ranging from land to computers and buildings that are transferred between agencies or sold to the private sector.

SUMMARY

There were many sources of inefficiency in pre-1961 budgeting practices in the Defense Department. Competition among the Services led to wasteful duplication of weapons system development. The budgeting system intended for the new department was foreclosed by the diversification of all the Services into new missions, and close liaisons between the Services and Congress led to bypassing the Secretary and funding many duplicate projects.

After many ineffective attempts to impose civilian control on the Services' budgets, Secretary McNamara introduced program budgeting in 1961. He imposed a mission-oriented program structure that cut across Service lines and forced the Services to consider each others' alternative systems by analyzing mission areas in draft presidential memoranda. Cost-effectiveness analyses were relied upon heavily under the new regime.

McNamara's budgeting system tended to downgrade the role of the professional military, partly because they were not trained in systems analysis and partly because their traditional budgeting practices were at odds with program budgeting. The development of systems analysis capability within the Services since 1961 suggests certain reforms, including making the military respond to the Department's overall budget constraint and inducing the Services to assign priorities to different systems. These changes would permit some decentralization of decision-making authority without returning the Defense budget to the political process that influenced its pre-1961 determination.

Major resource misallocations and biases in the choice among systems result from features of the Defense budgeting process. The existence of the draft imposes extensive distributional and allocational

costs on draftees and society at large and also encourages the inefficient use of manpower within Defense. These costs, compared to the
norm of an all-volunteer army, are quite high and can be justified only
if society believes that the non-economic costs of an all-volunteer
army would be equally high. Other misallocations occur because
Defense purchases from (and sales to) other government agencies
are not entered as either budgetary debits or credits, thus creating
biases in the choice among alternative systems.

16 Financing Education

Education is the largest category of expenditures for state and local governments and recently has begun to attract some federal funds as well. Although private education is also a big business, public funding accounts for about 80 percent of all expenditures on education, over $43 billion in 1968. The predominantly public nature of educational expenditures is partly a historical accident, stemming from the communal responsibility that early Americans felt for their children's education. But public funding must also represent a social consensus, for not only the United States but virtually every other developed country treats education as a governmental function.

Our interest is in whether education constitutes an efficient use of public funds. First we must investigate the nature of the benefits of education to determine whether they can be provided efficiently by the private sector or whether some government intervention is required. Then we shall compare the existing pattern of funding with that justified by economic analysis to discover the extent and direction of the implicit transfer payments that now are present in public funding.

THE BENEFITS OF EDUCATION

Before discussing the private and public benefits derived from education, we should distinguish between general and vocational training. General education may be thought of as the process of learning common skills such as reading and acquiring a body of general information unrelated to the student's future occupation or income. The information (such as an understanding of the legislative process) may help the student function as a member of society, or it may be a kind of consumer good (such as a taste for fifteenth-century music and an understanding of Darwin's theory of evolution) of value to the student only in his private activities. Vocational education, in contrast, is defined broadly as any training that increases the student's productivity and marketability as a member of the labor force. Although both types of education yield private and public benefits, the benefits differ in how well we can evaluate them.

Private Benefits. Education traditionally has been thought of as a civilizing, acculturating process whose output is an improvement in the "quality of life." The great English economist Alfred Marshall considered the value of education to be that it "stimulates mental activity," "fosters . . . a habit of wise inquisitiveness," and "raises the tone of . . . life"; "regarded as an end in itself, it is inferior to none of those which the production of material wealth can be made to subserve."[1] This view clearly considered education to be a substitute for other forms of consumption and took as its value the utility that the individual derives from the educational process. Well-educated people were thought to be happier and capable of greater self-fulfillment than those with little education. There is some evidence that these benefits still provide some rationale for people to acquire education (for example, through adult extension courses or college-level and high school–level electives), but most education today appears to be more of a vocational than of a general nature.

Vocational education can be thought of as an item of capital equipment that the student obtains because he expects to receive net benefits whose present value is positive. This criterion applies whether the education yields an elementary or high school diploma that certifies the student as an employable member of the labor force or whether it leads through an intensive course of study and practice to a lucrative career in neurosurgery. Whatever the type of vocational education, the gross benefit it confers is the present value of the increase in future income that can be attributed to the additional education. Its cost is the present value of the resource cost incurred by the student during the educational process plus the opportunity cost of the income that he could have earned instead of staying out of the labor market and receiving vocational education.

[1] Alfred Marshall, *Principles of Economics*, 8th ed. (New York: Macmillan, 1959), pp. 176–77.

These net benefits of vocational education can be summarized in a fairly simple equation. Suppose that an eighteen-year-old must choose between entering college or taking a full-time job. (He will retire at age sixty-five in either case.) As we saw in Chapter 13, the criterion that he should adopt is to invest in the education if its net present value is positive. Let E_i be the income that the student expects to receive in year i if he is educated, and U_i be the income that he will earn otherwise (E_i is zero until year 5 because the student is in school). We assume that the discount rate is 10 percent and that the student's income during the four years of college is zero. Finally, we denote the annual cost of college by C_i. Under these assumptions, the student can calculate the net present value (NPV) of a four-year college education as

$$NPV = \sum_{i=5}^{47} \frac{E_i - U_i}{(1.10)^i} - \sum_{i=1}^{4} \frac{U_i + C_i}{(1.10)^i}.$$

Alternatively, the student can calculate the internal rate of return, the discount rate that makes the net present value zero. If the internal rate of return is higher than the market interest rate, then it must also be true that the net present value at the market rate is positive. Thus, the student can compare the market and internal rates of return and choose the college education if the internal rate is higher than the market rate.

Many problems arise in estimating the internal rate of return from vocational education. One obvious problem is that the income attributable to education will vary according to the student's ability. It may also vary for reasons beyond his control, such as changes in the prices of labor and capital and cyclical recessions that cause unemployment. The return to education also will vary with the student's occupation, sex, race, place of residence (urban or rural), and geographic location. Nonetheless, the internal rate of return is conceptually the correct measure of the productivity of vocational education compared to other investments, and the net present value is the correct measure of the dollar benefits to the student.

Attempts have been made to estimate both rates of return and net present values for broad classes of students and different levels of education. The general conclusion reached is that investment in "human capital" offers rather high rates of return and large net present values at most levels of education. Some of the estimates include a 29 percent rate of return for an elementary diploma, a 15 to 20 percent return for a high school education, and 12 to 15 percent returns for a college degree.[2] The rates of return to graduate-level education are somewhat lower. These results should be interpreted skeptically because of the difficulties already noted, but they indicate that the private benefits from vocational education continue to be substantial up to high levels of educational achievement.

These private benefits are high compared to the returns likely to be available from alternative investments. Nonetheless, there are some reasons to believe that students will not invest in human capital up to the point where the expected return is equal to the market interest rate. For the individual student, self-investment is risky, for he cannot be sure of his own future productivity. The same risk will deter lenders from offering funds to prospective students, even though the average yield may be well above the market interest rate. And students' ignorance of the returns from education may prevent them from investing up to the efficient point. We will examine the appropriate governmental response to these imperfections in the next section of this chapter. For now, it is enough to note that the very high rates of return that have been estimated as the private benefits of vocational education may be consistent with rational investment behavior by both students and lenders.

Public Benefits. General education confers benefits on society at large in a variety of ways. It is generally accepted that minimal levels of education are necessary to permit the functioning of a developed economy and a democratic society. Literacy, familiarity with elementary mathematics, and an acquaintance with cultural and political institutions are essential for minimal participation in economic and political affairs. Although these minimal skills also convey private benefits, society historically has ignored the private benefits in decreeing that these skills should be provided to all its members and that the costs should be financed out of public revenues. We cannot place a value upon these public benefits of general education, but this social policy is a clear assertion that the social value of the benefits is well in excess of the cost of the general education that provides them. Moreover, this public policy removes from the individual's control the decision of whether to acquire general education.

The level of education involved, however, is quite low. The literacy tests that admit an adult to full participation in the political process usually test a reading standard well below the eighth-grade level.

[2] W. Lee Hansen, "Total and Private Rates of Return to Investment in Schooling," *Journal of Political Economy* 71 (April 1963): 128–40; and Gary Becker, *Human Capital* (New York: National Bureau of Economic Research, 1964).

Basic arithmetic, fractions, and decimals all are learned by the time a child enters high school. The process of learning those facts about society that society deems essential may take longer, but the current consensus is that this process does *not* have to extend through high school. (Compulsory attendance usually ends at either fourteen or sixteen years of age.) Thus, the public benefits of general education are limited to primary and some secondary schooling.

Vocational education confers many kinds of public benefits, although perhaps none as socially vital as those of general education. First, let us consider the different kinds of externalities. One externality arises when education increases the productivity and income of a worker who was formerly supported by redistributional transfer payments. In this case, taxpayers at large receive the external benefit in the form of a reduction in their tax liabilities. The amount of the externality, however, is equal to the reduction in transfer payments, which typically is smaller than the full amount of the increase in productivity. Only if we hold the newly educated worker's income constant does the entire benefit of education accrue as an externality. Conversely, if the worker's income rises by the full amount of his productivity increase, then he and not other taxpayers receives all the benefit of vocational education. The public benefit is nil, since other members of society are not affected in any way.

Another externality that may arise because of the high correlation between education and income is a reduction in crime. By increasing labor productivity, education raises the opportunity cost of crime, the losses that the criminal suffers if he is caught and the income that he might have earned as a member of the labor force. Since the criminal imposes substantial costs on the rest of society whether or not he is caught, a reduction in crime must lead to a decrease in these external costs.

An externality frequently mentioned in discussions of education and training programs is the increase in taxes paid by students or trainees as a result of the higher income they earn because of their training. These taxes constitute an external benefit to the rest of society if they lead to a reduction in others' tax burden. In imputing this external benefit to education, however, we are assuming implicitly that the additional education does not lead to a greater demand for government services, so that society's total tax liability remains constant. This is not a good assumption as long as the income-elasticity of demand for public services is greater than zero. Before we accept increased taxes as an external benefit, therefore, we should net out the increase in the size of the budget that constitutes a claim on these additional revenues.

Inter-regional externalities may arise from educational expenditures since local and state governments, not the federal government, are the principal sources of funding. When a student who has been educated at the expense of New York taxpayers moves to California, the social benefits that California derives from his presence are an externality conferred by New York. Out-migration may be a significant deterrent to local expenditures on education, since local residents will be unwilling to subsidize residents of other areas. Although these externalities obviously cancel out for the United States as a whole (neglecting international flows, which on balance have favored the United States), they do not cancel out for each locality or state.

In addition to the externalities that are conferred on specific recipients (such as particular taxpayers or residents of states that attract in-migrants), education offers some benefits that are best thought of as public goods. One public good is the advance of knowledge produced by people who are highly educated. Basic research, for example, may shift the economy's overall production possibility curve outward, making new levels of output attainable without any increase in resource inputs. But the discoveries that lead to this shift are not usually appropriable by the researchers who make them; instead, the value of the discoveries can be thought of as a public good and the researchers' incomes as its cost of supply.

As well as increasing the level of aggregate income, education may contribute to an increase in the growth rate. The overall efficiency of resource use apparently is higher in economies with high general levels of education than in those with lower average educational attainment. Education seems to increase the productivity of factors of production in a multiplicative way, so that the increase in productivity that can be attributed to the training of each worker is amplified by the increased productivity of everyone else.

Another public benefit often claimed for education is that it enables society to provide for its future manpower needs by training students in the specialties and skills that will be essential for tomorrow's or the next decade's economic growth. Usually underlying this argument is the claim that we will experience a shortage of engineers, physicists, doctors, or even economists, unless our government takes action (such as subsidizing certain types of education) to insure that the needed future supply is forthcoming. There are two problems with this argument. One is technical, that we are not able to specify accurately what the occupational distribution of the demand for labor will be ten or twenty years from now. Thus, a policy of publicly providing for future manpower needs is as likely to yield future costs as it is to yield future benefits.

The other problem is that a shortage can exist only if markets are not functioning or if the implicit distribution of income is unacceptable to society. Suppose that we foresee the prospect of a severe shortage of doctors twenty years from now (based on current ratios of doctors to total population). If markets work properly, two things may happen: (1) more students will enter the medical profession in the expectation of higher future incomes that will result from an increase in the demand for medical care relative to its supply; and (2) there may be a substitution of capital-intensive medical techniques for the traditional labor-intensive methods. The "shortage" will only cause an increase in the price of medical services (and even then, perhaps, only for a short time while supply adjusts to the increase in demand).

This market adjustment will not be acceptable if we have some commitment to supply medical care at a fixed price, perhaps in order to make it available to low-income families. But such a policy simply amounts to subsidizing low-income families (or, more generally, consumers of medical care) *inefficiently,* through a transfer payment to future doctors.[3] For society in general, medical care is no more a "free good" than water is and is no more suitable a subject for supply at a price below marginal cost. Since this argument also applies to other kinds of education (in addition to medical training), providing for future manpower "needs" through subsidies to certain types of education does not confer a benefit upon society but only constitutes a redistribution of income in favor of certain groups of consumers.

Summary. The private benefit of general education is the utility that the student derives from developing basic skills and from broadening his horizons in a way not related to his occupation or income. The public benefits of general education are the value to society of the individual's possession of basic skills, cultural values, and information about political and economic institutions. These public benefits are sufficient to justify public insistence upon a minimum level of educational attainment. Compulsory attendance laws, however, suggest that the minimum level is something less than a high school education.

Vocational education yields private benefits in the form of increased future income for the student. In obtaining vocational education, the individual must make an investment decision in which he compares

---

[3] An efficient subsidy would be simply a grant of either income or medical services to give low-income families access to medical care. For some evidence that the market for medical services is inefficient and that direct subsidies are ineffective, see Martin Feldstein, "The Rising Price of Physicians' Services," *Review of Economics and Statistics* 52 (May 1970): 121–33.

the rate of return he can expect from investing in himself with the return he could earn from a non-educational allocation of resources. Despite difficulties in estimating the rates of return from education, many studies have concluded that education is an attractive investment compared to physical assets.

The public benefits of vocational education include reduced levels of crime, lower tax costs of supporting untrained indigents, and perhaps the increased future taxes that trained workers will pay. Other benefits are a more efficient use of resources and the nonappropriable research discoveries made by highly trained personnel. Inter-regional and international externalities may also arise from the migration of productive workers. The provision of skilled manpower to meet future demands is not a benefit of education but constitutes only an inefficient transfer to particular consumer groups.

EFFICIENT SUPPLY OF EDUCATION

The existence of public benefits (public goods and externalities) from education offers a reason for governments to intervene in the private sector's allocation of resources for education. The first question to answer is whether the conditions of production are such that the private sector is unable to supply the efficient amount of education even if there is a public expression of demand. As we saw in Chapter 5, public supply may be justified if a good is produced under conditions of decreasing cost, so that market demand is large enough to support only one producer.

Although indivisibilities characterize the supply of education when the only schooling is provided by the local municipal school district, there is no conclusive evidence that the average (per-pupil) cost of education falls as the size of a school rises. A particular school or district may exhibit decreasing costs temporarily because its physical plant is fixed in supply in the short run, but school facilities are not usually overbuilt to take advantage of decreasing costs. Hirsch has concluded that the average cost of schooling is constant over wide variations in school enrollment.[4] The successful operation of many private and parochial schools of different sizes is a corroborating bit of evidence, attesting to the fact that the basic unit of schooling is the classroom and that factor proportions cannot vary widely within its walls. On economic grounds, public supply of education does not appear to be preferable to private supply.

[4] Werner Z. Hirsch, *The Economics of State and Local Government* (New York: McGraw-Hill, 1970), pp. 176–82 and Table 8–1.

Public demand for education and public supply have not been sep-arated in the past either because of a confusion between general and vocational education or because of a desire to redistribute income through education or to achieve non-economic goals. The most dra-matic example of non-economic objectives is the use of schools to pro-mote social and racial integration, objectives the schools have attained less than perfectly. Nonetheless, the existence of social objectives like these is a constraint on any proposal to separate public supply from public demand for education. Society's demand that particular skills and attitudes be taught in the early years of the educational process also constitutes a restriction on the private supply of education.

An interesting proposal for separating public demand for education from private supply was initially presented by Friedman and has since received some attention within the federal government.[5] Fried-man suggests that virtually all the public benefits from education, whether general or vocational, accrue at the primary and secondary levels of education. For the sake of economic efficiency, accordingly, the public sector should confine its activities to ensuring that all members of society receive these minimum levels of education and to imposing upon the private suppliers of education whatever non-eco-nomic objectives society may specify.[6] Parents and children would then be left to obtain whatever schooling they wanted in excess of the social minimum, subject to these public constraints.

Friedman envisioned his system as working around a government voucher for schooling that would be distributed to parents. The voucher would enable a school to collect from the government an annual sum representing the value that society places on minimal levels of education. In practice, the value of the voucher would have to be roughly equal to the current cost of a year of primary or secon-dary public education, for (1) there is no other way to specify the qual-ity of education that society demands and (2) it can be argued that the cost of public education provides an indication of the value that soci-ety places upon it. Private schools, however, would not be prevented from charging parents more than the value of the voucher, and parents presumably would accept prices in excess of the voucher if the quality of schooling and their demand for it were both sufficiently high.

The chief advantage that Friedman claims for his proposal is that it would permit students and parents to express their demand for differ-

---

[5] Milton Friedman, *Capitalism and Freedom* (Chicago: University of Chi-cago Press, 1962), ch. 6.

[6] Although such objectives can be introduced compatibly with Friedman's proposal, his own preference is for none at all to be imposed.

ent qualities of education. Through such an expression of demand, schools would be forced to compete for students and for good teachers, and the overall quality of education (including that provided by schools that accepted vouchers without any surcharge) would rise. Wealthy parents probably would buy more and better schooling for their children than poor parents, just as they do now. But it would be easier for poor families who place a high value on education to obtain good schooling than is the case under current public school operation.

Friedman's proposal separates not only the supply and demand for education but also efficiency and equity considerations. The social objective of economic integration, equality of opportunity, dictates that all children must have access to equally good schooling. In practice, however, this objective is never attained, even within those school districts that encompass neighborhoods with wide variations in income and racial composition. Public supply of education amounts to a form of transfer to low-income families, but the transfer is never as great in fact as in theory. Thus, even if we agree with the goal of equal educational opportunity, we may agree with Friedman that public supply of education is not a good way to achieve it.

In criticizing Friedman's simple voucher scheme, Levin has claimed that its effects on the poor would be very different from what Friedman predicts.[7] One problem is that private schools might refuse to locate in poor neighborhoods, preferring instead to compete for wealthier students. Thus, economic and social segregation might be increased by the voucher system. Another difficulty is that vouchers would perpetuate inequities in the distribution of income, since wealthy parents would have a stronger incentive to invest in more education and higher future incomes for their children.

Levin accepts Friedman's basic premise, that public supply of education is unsatisfactory and that some way must be found to encourage competition. One way is to combine vouchers with direct income redistribution, either through offering vouchers only to the poor or by making the size of the voucher vary with income. Or local communities might contract out the educational function to private companies. This step has been taken by some school systems for particular activities such as remedial reading. Modifications of this kind in Friedman's voucher proposal may be more acceptable to the electorate than the analytically correct measure, direct income transfers to poor families.

[7] Henry M. Levin, "The Failure of the Public Schools and the Free Market Remedy," *Urban Review* 2 (June 1968): 32–37.

Friedman denies that there is any reason for governments to be concerned with vocational education, for he believes that the full value of vocational training can be captured by the student. In the preceding section, however, we mentioned several sources of external and public-good benefits in vocational education. Adopting Friedman's argument, we may conclude that even if students were to invest in the privately efficient amount of vocational education (that is, the amount that makes the internal rate of return equal to the market interest rate), there would be some basis for public subsidization of vocational training, although not for public provision of it.

Most of the external benefits mentioned are derived from rather low levels of vocational training (primary and secondary schooling). In addition, training programs that supplement formal schooling for dropouts and workers whose skills have become technologically obsolete frequently provide these externalities. Friedman's argument, therefore, justifies some public support for these kinds of vocational education. If efficiency is our objective, the amount of public support should be limited to the value of the externalities that society as a whole derives from the programs (net of the value that the trainee derives). Otherwise, the government voucher would include a transfer element and the efficient amount of vocational education would not be supplied.

This approach suggests that there should be no governmental support of higher education, since the externalities cited earlier are generally received from low levels of education and training. Some of the benefits from higher education may be public goods in the form of new research discoveries and overall productivity increases. The latter, however, cannot be attributed solely or even primarily to higher education, since most members of the labor force are not formally educated beyond high school. (Although on-the-job training is a major source of education, it does not receive much governmental support.) Basic research should be supported directly, rather than implicitly in the form of subsidies to higher education, if our goal is to undertake the efficient amount of research investment. Public support for higher education, therefore, cannot seriously be justified on the grounds that higher education confers extensive public benefits.

Nonetheless, the studies cited earlier indicated that society probably underinvests in education (including higher education) compared to its investment in physical capital goods. The market imperfections that give rise to this underinvestment provide a basis for particular kinds of public support for higher education as well as for vocational training at lower levels. Three of these market imperfections are risk, lack of information, and differences in rates of time-preference.

Risk and Educational Investment. There are several sources of risk in educational investment. A student (borrower) cannot be sure of his own ability to repay a loan. Lenders will view student loans as risky because of variations in students' abilities and motivation. The high levels of investment needed for some kinds of professional education necessitate lengthy repayment periods, in turn increasing lenders' uncertainty about borrowers' abilities to repay. Moreover, students may develop a distaste for the process of education itself, leading them to curtail their self-investment before they had planned to do so.

The proper governmental policy in these cases, as in other instances of capital-market imperfections, is to bring the private (risky) rate of return into equilibrium with the social (risk-free) rate. One way to do this is for the government to insure loans to students as it insures home mortgages, in effect reducing the lender's risk to zero. Students would then be on a par with other borrowers of investible funds and would not invest in higher education unless they believed that the increase in their future incomes warranted such self-investment. Since there is no reason to believe that students' risk aversion is any more intense than that of other borrowers, the bias against educational investment should be eliminated by this policy.

Information About the Returns to Education. There is no question that most students do not have accurate information about the value of different levels of education. In large part, this shortcoming arises because accurate information is scarce and poorly disseminated. As risk averters, accordingly, students will underinvest in education compared to what their level of investment would be if the rate of return were known.

In this case, the appropriate public policy is to provide information about the returns that students can expect from different amounts of education. To offer a complete guide to efficient investment, such information should be very detailed, including breakdowns by age, sex, race, residence, region, occupation, and "ability" (measured, perhaps, by standardized tests). Econometric studies of the value of education have not yet provided such detailed estimates of rates of return. Public policy should be concentrated on improving the quality of information of this type, rather than on offering blanket support for all types of higher education.

Differences in Rates of Time-Preference. Some economists have argued that too little educational investment is undertaken because students' rates of time-preference are higher than those of the population at large. This argument is often applied to poor students and blacks in an attempt to explain high dropout rates. Rather than a high rate of time-preference, however, it seems likely that these groups have low expectations of their future incomes and that in many cases these expectations are well founded in past experience. Active governmental policies designed to increase the equality of opportunity, especially for blacks and residents of depressed regions such as Appalachia, probably would be effective in increasing the demand for higher levels of educational achievement. There is no evidence that rates of time-preference differ systematically among population groups, although they certainly may differ widely among individuals.

Some of the federal government's policies toward higher education are consistent with our conclusion that efficient public policies should be aimed at removing market imperfections. For example, the federal government increases the supply of loans to students directly, through extensions of capital to colleges and universities, and indirectly, by underwriting private loans through the Office of Education. Some studies of the private returns to education are supported by federal funds, although there is no broad program of financing such studies. But the bulk of the public funds used to finance education comes from state and local governments, whose expenditures all too often do not satisfy the criterion of allocational efficiency or of distributional equity.

PATTERNS OF FUNDING EDUCATION

Most expenditures on primary and secondary education are financed by the real property taxes levied by local governments. As we saw in Chapter 10, the incidence of this tax is probably close to proportional with respect to total income. The vocational training component of formal education can be assumed to lead to a proportional increase in all students' incomes, so that the net redistribution of income from the tax and vocational training "package" is nil. (At a more detailed level of analysis, we would have to note the slightly higher returns to low levels of education and the probable slight regressivity of the property tax, leading on balance to the same negligible redistribution of income.) The incidence of taxes used to fund the general education component of primary and secondary schooling can be thought of as representing a social judgment about the equitable means of financing these benefits, which are impossible to evaluate. In sum, there may be no significant redistribution from rich to poor (or vice versa) in the funding of lower-level education.

The principal transfer that arises in funding primary and secondary education is an intergenerational one. Especially with respect to the benefits of vocational education, the beneficiaries of lower-level schooling are primarily the students themselves. The costs of their schooling, however, are financed by taxes on their parents, who may eventually receive secondary benefits in either a monetary or a non-monetary form, and on other members of society who receive at most some benefits from the general education component of schooling. Although the size distribution of income may not be altered by this transfer, the age distribution of income and wealth certainly is affected. The cost of schooling through high school is at least $10,000 per child in most parts of the United States and is frequently considerably more. Since the rate of return to primary and secondary schooling is high, the value of this transfer to the student is well above this amount. Thus, the funding of lower-level education out of tax revenues creates a large transfer of income and wealth from older generations to younger ones.

The same intergenerational transfer applies when we shift our attention to higher education and supplemental training for dropouts and workers whose skills have become technologically obsolete. Public funding of higher education causes a number of transfers and allocational inefficiencies. First, by lowering the price of higher education to the student, public higher education induces overinvestment in education, especially by encouraging college attendance by some students who cannot profit from it. Second, public funding of particular institutions (state universities, colleges, and junior colleges) discriminates against private institutions offering education of equal caliber. Third is the intergenerational transfer that arises because students' vocational education is financed by older taxpayers at large. Fourth, the income size distribution of the beneficiaries of public support of higher education differs substantially from that of taxpayers at large.

This last point is a new one and needs some elaboration. Hansen and Weisbrod examined the subsidies that students in various California state institutions of higher education received in the form of the difference between the resource costs of their education and prices that they actually paid.[8] As we might expect, the subsidy was smallest ($720 per year) for junior college students, larger ($1400) for students in the state college systems, and highest ($1700) for those enrolled in the University of California system. Hansen and Weisbrod found a

---

[8] W. Lee Hansen and Burton A. Weisbrod, "The Search for Equity in the Provision and Finance of Higher Education," in Joint Economic Committee, *The Economics and Financing of Higher Education in the United States* (1969), pp. 107–23.

high correlation between family income and the institution in which a student was enrolled: thus, in 1964 the median family income of junior college students was $8800, that of state college attendees was $10,000, and that of enrollees in the University of California was $12,000. Since the tax structure of California (state and local taxes) was regressive or proportional up to the $25,000 level of family income, the distribution of tax payments was not as progressive as the distribution of subsidies. In particular, the annual net subsidy (the difference between the gross subsidy and average *total* state and local taxes) for families with a child in junior colleges was $40. Families with a child enrolled in state colleges received a $630 annual net subsidy, and those with a University of California student received an annual net subsidy of $790. In contrast, families without children enrolled in the state system of higher education paid a net transfer of $650 per year out of their median income of only $7900.

It is difficult to justify this redistribution of income. It is not efficient, for the external benefits from higher education are unlikely to be very valuable. It cannot be equitable if society's concept of equity is that embodied in either the personal income tax or the (nearly proportional) overall federal, state, and local tax structure. It does not promote equality of educational opportunity, for it does not make higher education *relatively* more available to students from poor families than to those from rich ones. On the basis of this redistribution and the misallocations mentioned earlier, we can only conclude that current methods for funding public higher education in California and probably in other states as well are inferior from the standpoints of equity and efficiency to a system of charging students for the full resource cost of their education, as long as the latter system includes some distributional transfers and public policies to eliminate market imperfections.

Redistributional aspects also dominate the benefits of remedial and retraining programs such as the Job Corps and the Manpower Development and Training Act. These programs are usually defended as efficient investments in human resources, a claim that becomes embarrassing when studies of the increase in labor productivity conclude that the net benefits of the programs are close to zero and in many cases are probably negative. This approach to evaluating such programs ignores their two most important characteristics: (1) they confer sizable externalities in the way that any other program of lower-level vocational education confers external benefits; (2) they are a means for transferring income from rich to poor. Public funding of such programs may be justified, regardless of their net benefits (or benefit-cost ratio), if the combination of the externalities they confer and the amount and direction of redistribution they provide makes them attractive to the electorate.

SUMMARY

Both vocational and general education confer private and public benefits. Lower-level (primary and secondary) education has a strong general component, which perhaps confers more public benefits than private ones. Some secondary and nearly all higher education is vocational, with some public benefits but, especially in the case of higher education, primarily private ones in the form of increased labor productivity.

Because of its public benefits, primary and secondary education should be supported publicly. There is no evidence, however, that the supply conditions of education necessitate public supply. Just such a separation of public demand and private supply is at the heart of Friedman's voucher scheme, which would enable the public sector to express the benefits that it receives from education while letting individual students and parents express the strength of their own demands. Although this approach would justify supporting some (lower-level and remedial) vocational education, it suggests that governments should not support higher education.

Nonetheless, a basis for public action can be found in the existence of market imperfections that make the allocation of resources to higher education inefficient. The presence of risk aversion justifies public insurance programs that would make the private discount rate for "human capital" investments equal to the social rate of return on other investments. Students' lack of information about the returns to education provide an incentive for the public sector to make this information available in a sufficiently detailed manner to be useful inputs to students' investment decisions. These policies should eliminate whatever bias exists in investment markets against making investments in human capital.

Actual patterns of public funding for education are extensively redistributional. Even though state and local funding of primary and secondary education probably is close to neutral with respect to total income, it creates a large intergenerational transfer in favor of the young. When we consider higher education, however, we find that usual methods of funding public institutions lead to a large net subsidy in favor of high-income families at the expense of the poor. This subsidy arises because students do not pay the full resource cost of their education and because enrollees in institutions of higher learning come predominantly from high-income families while taxes fall more heavily on low-income families. Redistributional effects also arise with remedial education and retraining programs, but in these cases the redistribution is in favor of the poor. Even if these programs lead to negative net benefits, they may be justified by the externalities that they confer and the redistribution that they accomplish.

17 Urban Problems

During the decade of the 1960's, the plight of central cities received increasing attention. Changes in the racial composition of urban populations accompanied the deterioration of housing in large urban neighborhoods. The rapid growth of the suburbs led to demands for improved transportation networks and to the construction of many new freeways, often through urban residential areas. Reliance upon the automobile as the principal mode of transportation caused increased pollution and permitted an "urban sprawl" pattern of development.

There is no one central problem of our large cities, for many elements of an urban complex are interrelated. Housing is affected by racial composition, which in turn is influenced by the location of employment, macroeconomic variables, and many different governmental policies. Demands for urban transportation depend on many of the same factors and also affect housing and are affected by it. In this chapter we will concentrate on two urban subproblems: slum and low-income housing, and transportation within a metropolitan area. Not only are these problem areas of great contemporary importance but they illustrate the usefulness of economic analysis and some of its limitations.

HOUSING

Nobody knows quite how to define "slum," but everyone knows what it connotes. The housing that slums contain is usually dilapidated, frequently a fire hazard, rat infested, and dirty often to the point of being dangerous to health. Typically, slum housing is also over-crowded; families of six or more members may live in only one or two rooms. Although slums in many large cities are created in part by racial discrimination that prevents or at least restricts the exodus of slum dwellers to other urban and suburban neighborhoods, one basic cause of slums is that slum families simply are too poor to be able to afford better housing. The spread of slums is also affected by external-ities in the supply of housing and elements of the urban-suburban interaction.

Efficiency in Slum Housing. The outstanding characteristic that poor families have in common is that their incomes are low. The budget constraint that affects all consumers' attempts to maximize utility becomes effective at a lower income level for poor families than for middle-income groups. Without knowing anything else about either the poor or the goods they consume, we might expect low-income families to spend less on housing, food, clothing, transportation, recre-ation, and every other budget category for which the income-elasticity of demand is positive. (As we saw in Chapter 10, the income-elasticity of demand for housing is close to 1.0 for the population as a whole, and there is no reason to expect the preferences of low-income groups to be very different from those of the rest of society.)

One way that poor families could spend less on housing would be to occupy less space. But poor families often are large ones and place a high premium on space. The alternative, to accept housing of lower quality, thus may represent a rational allocation of poor families' housing budgets. As long as there are low-income families, therefore, the existence of slums and poor housing may simply indicate that housing markets are responding efficiently to the rational demands of consumers.

There is probably some validity to this explanation of why slums exist, although it certainly is not the whole story. In rural areas, especially, the most likely cause of dilapidated housing is the low in-come of the residents, and in urban areas, where the poor usually live in rented housing, property owners have no incentive to rehabilitate their property if the residents of a neighborhood are not willing to pay for higher-quality housing. Housing is not a "free good" any more than water and medical care are. The decision to improve the quality of housing, like the quantity (or quality) of water, should rest upon an analysis of the social and private benefits and costs.

If there are no market imperfections, so that slum housing is an efficient allocation of resources caused by low-income families' demand for housing, it is clear that any improvement in the quality of slum housing is primarily a redistribution of income. If there are externalities, they are probably income related (such as crime, as discussed in Chapter 16) or perhaps the psychic cost that higher-income people suffer from contemplating the slum. In any case, a redistribution of income is the appropriate response to the existence of the slum, whether the redistribution is motivated by altruism or by benefit-cost calculations. This approach recognizes that the basic problem is poverty, not imperfections in the allocation of resources. Eradication of poverty will eliminate its manifestation, slum housing.

Many different governmental programs are aimed at reducing the incidence of poverty. Some of these programs include income transfers, grants of education, attempts to eliminate discrimination, and transfers of particular commodities such as food. Many of the transfers of specific goods revolve around housing: rent controls, public housing, rent subsidies. The important point is that, from the point of view of economic welfare, all transfers of specific commodities are inferior to the alternative, transfers of income. If a poor family receives a rent subsidy (by far the best of the housing transfers), it can improve both the quality and quantity of housing it consumes. But if it had received a straight cash grant of an equal amount, the family could have chosen the same improvement in its housing, or else it could have selected some other allocation of its incremental income. The transfer of housing forecloses these other options, even though they might have yielded greater utility to the poor family. Thus, the increase in utility derived from transfers in kind is smaller than from cash transfers of the same cost to society.[1]

As well as being inferior from a welfare viewpoint, grants of housing usually are administratively inefficient. Public housing has been criticized as drab, overly utilitarian, expensive, regimented, and paternalistic. Moreover, there are many inequities in deciding which poor families to admit, since rationing or some other nonmarket criterion for admission must be used. Rent controls are even less efficient, since they lead to the further deterioration of housing and perhaps even to the abandonment of property in the face of rising taxes and maintenance costs and rigidly stable rents. Rent supplements are also paternalistic, but they offer a wider range of flexibility and individual choice than other transfers, and they also encourage the participation

---

[1] This conclusion may be incorrect if there are other imperfections, such as decreasing-cost production of goods that are transferred, or if taxpayers are not indifferent between cash transfers and transfers in kind. In general, however, income transfers are more likely than transfers of goods to be consistent with economic efficiency.

of the private sector in supplying housing. Nonetheless, even an efficient transfer in kind can be preferred to an efficient transfer of income only if the income transfer is politically unacceptable. The movement toward a federal family assistance plan suggests that the political barriers to income transfers may be falling.

Externalities in Slum Housing. Even if we ignore the externalities (crime and psychic costs) mentioned in the preceding section, the existence of slums and "blighted" neighborhoods may be due in part to a market imperfection. The imperfection arises because an individual property owner may not be able to capture all the benefits that his investment confers upon a neighborhood. The residential character of a neighborhood, or its attractiveness as a commercial location, depends on the joint behavior of all its residents, property owners, and businessmen. In these circumstances, the conduct of any one member of the neighborhood confers externalities (either costs or benefits) on all the rest.[2]

To see how this externality can affect the supply of low-income housing, consider the following example. Landlords Green and Gold must make independent decisions about renovating their slum properties. Their buildings are identical and next door to each other. Because the condition of Green's building affects the residential desirability of Gold's and vice versa, the returns that each can expect from investing $100,000 in his property depend on the other's investment decision. The net returns (in thousands of dollars) are shown in Figure 17.1. Green's payoff is shown in the lower half of each cell; Gold's appears in the upper portion. Thus, if both Green and Gold invest, each will receive a net return of $25,000. If Green invests but Gold does not, Gold's rental income will rise by $50,000 (despite his investment of zero), but Green will lose $25,000. If Gold invests but Green does not, Gold will lose $25,000 while Green receives a net return of $50,000. Finally, if neither landlord renovates his property, each will continue to receive his annual profit of $20,000.

Each landlord must make his investment decision independently. Gold considers his two alternatives, recognizing that he has no control over Green's decision. If Gold invests, he will gain $25,000 if Green invests and will lose $25,000 if Green does not. If Gold does not invest, he will gain $50,000 if Green invests and will gain $20,000 if Green does not. Regardless of Green's decision, Gold will profit more from not investing than from investing. Green, of course, faces the

[2] This analysis of externalities is derived from Otto A. Davis and Andrew B. Whinston, "The Economics of Urban Renewal," *Law and Contemporary Problems* 26 (Winter 1961): 105–17.

Green ＼Gold	If Green invests	If Green does not invest
If Gold invests	25 25	−25 50
If Gold does not invest	50 −25	20 20

FIGURE 17.1   Neighborhood Externalities

same decision with the same "payoff matrix," and he will also choose not to invest. Thus, the neighborhood will not be renovated, and both landlords will land in the lower right-hand cell of the matrix in Figure 17.1.

The trouble with this solution is that it is economically inefficient. Both Green and Gold (and society) would be better off if they could move to the upper left-hand cell of the matrix, for they would both receive higher net returns. Society's investible funds would then be allocated efficiently, and the blighted neighborhood would also be improved. But this solution can never be reached as long as the land-lords behave independently, ignoring the fact that each one's action confers an externality on the other.

It is important to note that the foregoing example assumes that renovations would be profitable if externalities were taken into account. That is, there must be prospective tenants for the renovated buildings who would be willing to pay the higher rents necessary to make the renovation profitable. To this extent, we have departed from the conclusion of the preceding section that slum housing represents, in part, an efficient response to poor families' demands for low-income housing. But our analysis suggests that once a neighborhood becomes blighted, it will be virtually impossible for the individual decisions of property owners to change its overall character. This difficulty is heightened by the presence in real-world neighborhoods of dozens of landlords, each making his independent decision about renovation. In such a situation of large-number externalities, some form of collective action is called for.

We can think of many kinds of governmental action that might remove this market imperfection. The government might simply buy up slum properties and develop them in packages, somewhat as New

York City has done in parts of Manhattan. Or the government could acquire the slum properties and then sell them, in packages, to the highest bidders among private developers. The advantage of this approach is that it would encourage land to be developed in its most profitable use. As a third policy, the government could offer inducements to landlords to renovate their properties, in effect altering the payoff matrix for independent decisions. All these policies would affect the price of land by compensating for externalities, but none need entail a direct redistribution of income. The increases in property tax revenues that would result from property improvements would help to defray the costs of these public policies.

The usual public response to slums and blight has been a mixture of the first two policies called urban renewal. Although individual cities had renewal programs earlier, large-scale federal participation in urban renewal dates from the National Housing Act of 1949 (since amended many times). The federal program authorizes the federal government to contribute up to two-thirds of the total cost incurred by a local government agency for a renewal project. The program has been focused primarily on residential construction, but it has also been applied to commercial and even industrial development.

Under the federal urban renewal program, a local government agency develops a renewal plan in conjunction with the federal Department of Housing and Urban Development. After agreement on the plan, the local government acquires all the property lying within the blighted area designated for redevelopment. When all the land has been assembled (either by condemnation or by agreement on "fair market value"), tenants are evicted and presumably relocated, and the site is cleared and prepared for development. The property then may be sold to a private developer or retained for use by the local government. If it is sold, as is usually the case, the developer may choose to erect high-rise apartments, shopping centers, and whatever else he thinks is profitable. If the land is retained for public use, public housing is most frequently constructed.

Several stages in this process have given rise to extensive criticism of the urban renewal program. The relocation of existing tenants of redevelopment areas is often difficult since low-income housing is usually scarce in any city. The local government is required to provide "decent, safe, and sanitary" housing, but an insensitivity to this requirement and to the general issue of slum overcrowding marked the early years of the urban renewal program. This problem has been aggravated by private developers' tendency to erect expensive housing and commercial buildings, thus actually reducing the supply of low-income housing. In this way, one of the principal costs of urban renewal is paid by the very low-income families who were supposed to be helped by it.

Another criticism of urban renewal is that the complete redevelopment process is quite lengthy, with the average project completion time reaching twelve years (as of 1961). This slow process imposes many costs related to idle land and discourages private investment from clustering around the fringes of the redeveloped area. One of the benefits of urban renewal was supposed to be this "pump-priming" effect, but even if we attribute to the program all relocations of investment from the suburbs into downtown areas, urban renewal has been less effective than its proponents hoped.

Most of these criticisms have been incorporated in modifications of the federal urban renewal program. In order to gain federal approval, recent projects have had to make more provision for replacing the low-income housing that originally occupied the redevelopment site. Completion time seems to have fallen somewhat, and there is more concern for relocation (although renewal still results in the breakup of established neighborhoods). Nonetheless, the urban renewal program is something less than an unqualified success. Its impact upon the problem of slum housing has not been dramatic partly because of the scale of the problem and partly because the renewal program has not been focused upon housing the poor.

The difficulties associated with urban renewal strengthen the case for other public policies, such as inducements for slum property owners to rehabilitate their buildings. Under current tax law, landlords have many incentives *not* to rehabilitate. The most important provisions are the short lifetimes and accelerated depreciation allowed on residences, which encourage landlords to sell their property after a short period rather than make long-term investments in rental property. Local building codes also deter rehabilitation in many instances by forcing landlords to "overbuild" if they decide to renovate their property. Some public subsidies for urban rehabilitation (rather than renewal) would be justified to compensate for the disincentives of tax and building codes even if there were no true externalities. Overall, there is a strong case for flexible public policy rather than the "blockbuster" approach of urban renewal.

Slum Housing in a Metropolitan Area. Some of the characteristics of typical urban-suburban metropolitan areas reinforce the tendencies already noted for slums to grow in core cities. Most cities' revenues are limited chiefly to the yield of the property tax, plus transfers from the state or federal government for specific programs (such as "welfare") and whatever local licenses or fees they can assess. Residents of suburban areas are largely beyond the tax base of the core cities. Suburbanites, however, impose costs on the cities through their use of city services: fire and police protection, transportation facilities, communications, and utilities. These costs are imposed as suburbanites work in the city or as they enjoy its recreation and entertainment facilities. No such costs, however, typically are imposed upon the suburbs by city residents.[3]

As a result of these factors, city expenditures per resident are likely to be substantially higher than suburban expenditures for the same services. These higher expenditures necessitate higher taxes, in particular higher property taxes, to finance them. Rising city taxes drive residents to the suburbs, and the threat of this kind of flight squeezes urban expenditures and forces cities to reduce the quantity and quality of their services. The resulting deterioration of schools, parks, and public services stimulates still more flight to the suburbs, further tightening the noose around the central city.

This process creates spiraling property taxes, particularly on residences. City officials may fear that raising taxes on commercial property will encourage businesses to follow their employees to the suburbs, but they know that slum residents are a captive population, prevented from moving outside the city by economic factors (the cost of housing or commuting) and non-economic ones (predominantly racial discrimination). But rising property taxes, in turn, squeeze urban landlords. Their ability to raise rents is limited by tenants' ability to pay, so they cannot shift the higher taxes completely. Instead, there is some reduction in landlords' profits, some increase in rents, and some decline in landlords' willingness to maintain their property. The combination of these factors (the exodus to the suburbs, rising city expenditures and taxes, and declining maintenance of urban residences) leads to an extension and aggravation of slum housing conditions.

This is not a pretty picture, but it is common among American cities. Most large cities have been losing population since 1950, usually because white emigration to the suburbs has been faster than black immigration into the core cities. The changing racial composition has been accompanied by a reduction in the per capita income of urban residents relative to that of residents of metropolitan areas. Rothenberg points out that even though the United States experienced a great housing boom from 1950 well into the 1960's, the annual decline in the number of "substandard" rental housing units tapered off

[3] For some information on these net costs, see William B. Neenan, "Suburban-Central City Exploitation Thesis: One City's Tale," *National Tax Journal* 23 (June 1970): 117–39.

after 1960.[4] Since substandard rental units are located primarily in urban slums, this statistic supports the hypothesis that the problem of urban slums has grown proportionally worse since 1960.

Officials of core cities and the federal government have recognized that this problem cannot be solved by the cities alone. The federal approach is to institute revenue sharing, distributing some of its revenues to states and letting them pass it on to cities. Some cities (notably New York) have imposed local income taxes on noncity residents, with withholding by the employer to ease the problem of compliance. Each of these policies has its advantages and its drawbacks.

Revenue sharing has been heralded as the fiscal element in a new approach to cooperation among the different levels of government. It has strong support from both ends of the political spectrum among both economists and political figures. The heart of all the revenue-sharing plans that have been proposed is a formula for distributing on a nondiscretionary basis a specific amount or portion of annual federal revenues to state and local governments. Different plans specify various formulas and revenue totals, and also differ in their specification of which governments are to receive the revenue.

The advantages of revenue sharing would be felt principally at the state level under the "pass-through" approach, which gives states control over shared revenue. States could plan on additional revenue without worrying about the progress of particular grant-in-aid programs through Congress. State officials could either spend the additional funds or use them to reduce state taxes. One of the major constraints upon states's ability to raise revenues, local taxpayer reaction, would be eliminated.

The chief drawback of revenue sharing as a solution to the problem of cities' fiscal inadequacy is that its impact upon the cities is likely to be very small. Although the details of revenue sharing remain to be worked out by Congress, it seems clear that the magnitude of any revenue-sharing program will be too small to redress the imbalance between cities and suburbs. Most shared revenue probably will be retained by states to fund state programs rather than city ones. Although individual states may elect to fund city programs, there will be no systematic attempt to compensate the cities for the costs that suburbanites impose upon them. Moreover, suburbanites' incentives to leave the cities will not be removed. By the time state funds trickle down to cities and then are split up among the multitude of city programs, the impact of revenue sharing upon slum housing is likely to be negligible.

[4] Jerome Rothenberg, *Economic Evaluation of Urban Renewal* (Washington, D.C.: Brookings Institution, 1967), p. 206.

A nonresident city income tax offers more theoretical advantages than revenue sharing. By taxing suburbanites who work in the city, such a tax reduces their incentives to flee the city. Not only is the city's tax base increased and the city is enabled to reduce its taxes on residents, but some of the fiscal squeeze is transferred to the suburbs. Urban property taxes can be lowered, perhaps leading to some improvement in property maintenance. Overall, such a tax can go far toward redressing the balance between city and suburbs.

The shortcomings of such a tax are both political and economic. As might be expected, suburban residents bitterly oppose city income taxation, for it would increase their tax burden while conferring benefits largely on urban residents. Suburbanites' political power usually is great enough to block such taxation, for cities do not ordinarily have the authority to levy income taxes without state approval. Even if nonresident income taxes are levied, moreover, they may induce businesses to leave the city rather than incur the additional administrative costs and employee resentment that the tax brings. Few cities probably would be badly hurt by such emigration, for studies of business location decisions all suggest that taxes are not an important incentive. But the combination of political and economic factors has deterred most cities from implementing nonresident income taxation.

TRANSPORTATION

As metropolitan areas have grown in both population and geographic area, the problem of intra-urban transportation has become increasingly acute. Cities with highly developed public transportation systems, such as New York, experience congestion on arterial highways as well as on rapid transit at every rush hour. Cities that have virtually no public transportation networks, such as Los Angeles, develop massive traffic jams on commuter roads. Two problems are involved, although they are not completely separable: (1) how to encourage the efficient use of existing transportation facilities and the efficient design of new ones and (2) how to offset the damage to the urban environment inflicted by large amounts of automobile traffic.

Congestion. In our discussion of this topic, we will assume that the capacity of transportation systems—highways, subways, commuter trains—is adequate for all demands except those at the hours of peak use (typically, 7 to 9 on weekday mornings and 4 to 6 on weekday afternoons). Dropping this assumption does not change the analysis very much, but it makes the results more complicated. Moreover, the assumption of excess off-peak capacity is realistic for most transportation systems.

The key step in analyzing the problem is a simple one. The good that is supplied by a transportation system at a peak hour is not the same good that the system supplies off-peak. The goods are not the same because consumers are not indifferent between them. This statement is generally true for most consumer goods; for example, toast and coffee at 7 A.M. does not provide the same utility as toast and coffee at noon. But for commuters who use a transportation system at the peak hours, a trip at noon is not even a fairly close substitute for one at 7 A.M. If peak and off-peak use are not the same good, however, then different prices can be charged for them. Our only problem is to set the prices for both peak and off-peak use that will equate the cost to the user with the marginal cost that he imposes upon society.

The problem is a minor one for off-peak use. Since (by assumption) the transportation system has more than enough capacity to accommodate all off-peak travelers, the marginal cost of an additional user is close to zero. At off-peak hours, transportation systems are decreasing-cost goods and should be priced accordingly. The resulting operating deficit might be recovered from taxes or admission tickets for users, as we saw in Chapter 5.

At peak hours (by assumption and observation), transportation systems are crowded. Cars queue up at intersections and on bridges, and travel times increase. Delays also affect buses, and the conditions of travel are much less comfortable than at off-peak hours. Congestion also characterizes rush-hour subway traffic in every city equipped with a rapid transit system. One way to look at this congestion and delay is as an external cost that each commuter imposes on everyone else. In highway traffic, for example, everyone at the head of the queue imposes delays and costs on all those behind him. In a crowded bus, each rider decreases the space available for everyone else. The marginal cost (in either delay or congestion) is a sharply rising function of the number of travelers, for the greater is the number of commuters, the longer are delays and the tighter is congestion.

This marginal cost arises as an externality because the price that each commuter pays for his travel is its average cost. Consider the example of a line of traffic at a crowded bridge. We can assume that each commuter's place in line is determined at random, perhaps varying from day to day. In deciding whether or not to use the bridge, each commuter weighs the expected travel time against alternatives and ignores the costs that his travel imposes on all other commuters. Adding another car at some random point within the line of traffic does not change the average crossing time very much, but it does make the crossing time longer for half of the cars (on the average). Clearly, this marginal cost is greater the longer the line of traffic is. The average cost the commuter pays in delay time is much less than the marginal cost he imposes externally on other commuters.

Because of the large number of commuters, there is no possibility of bilateral agreements or a market solution to internalize these external costs. Moreover, it might be difficult for commuters to estimate the value they place on their time. Public action is needed to introduce the external costs into commuters' marginal evaluations of different forms of transportation (or the alternative, closer-in residence). For highways, the appropriate action is peak-hour tolls that will bring the price to the individual commuter into line with the marginal costs he imposes on society. Peak-hour prices on mass transit systems also should be increased for the same reason.

A short-run benefit of such a pricing policy would be to encourage efficient use of existing transportation facilities. If commuters were forced to pay a price equal to marginal cost, the probable result would be to reduce delay times and congestion as people responded to the increase in the price of commuting by substituting other goods (either off-peak travel or changes in residence). Commuters who place a high value on their time would be able to equate their marginal rate of substitution between time and other goods with society's marginal rate of transformation. Commuters who do not value their time highly would be discouraged from imposing external costs on others in the form of increased delays.

In the long run, such a pricing policy would provide society with an indication of the efficient level of supply for transportation systems. An efficient pricing policy would tell the government the value that commuters place on additional peak-hour capacity, and this demand could then be compared to the long-run supply cost to decide whether or not capacity should be expanded. "Capacity," of course, should be interpreted broadly as the overall capability of an integrated transportation network, *not* (as was argued in Chapter 9) just the capacity of highways or subways. In other words, the demand for increased capacity should be compared to the efficient method of supplying the additional capacity, even if the efficient method entails a change in transportation mode. This approach to the problem of determining the optimal level of capacity is equivalent to a broad concept of the proper functioning of trust funds (that is, a transportation trust fund instead of the highway trust fund).

Peak-hour pricing is used by some transportation systems, but it is the exception rather than the rule. The best examples of its application are found in airline fares. The New York–Washington air shuttle charges a higher price at the peak weekday travel hours than at other times during weekdays or on weekends. Air fares to overseas destinations vary with the season, rising during peak tourist seasons (winter to the Caribbean, summer to Europe) and falling at other times of the year. Commuter highways, however, typically are toll free. Even worse from the standpoint of efficiency, bottleneck facilities like bridges and commuter railroads frequently offer discounts for peak-hour use through "commuter tickets." Our analysis suggests strongly that these discounts should be eliminated and that governments should move toward a policy of charging commuters for peak-hour travel in order to improve both the long-run and short-run allocation of resources.

Automobiles and the Urban Environment. Automobiles are certainly not the only source of external costs imposed upon urban areas, although they are one of the principal offenders. We have singled out automobile traffic for analysis because it has proved to be a difficult offender tb control. The principles we develop for internalizing the external costs that automobiles impose upon urban environments should apply equally well to other sources of externalities.

There is no doubt that the external costs of automobile traffic are very high. Automobiles are the principal source of air pollutants, which always lead to health problems for people with certain bronchial conditions and which can occasionally cause fatalities. An equally insidious (although less well documented) cost is that of noise. Studies of the effects of noise have concluded that people never lose their sensitivity to it, although they may develop a tolerance that permits them to function at a reduced level of efficiency. Other external costs that have been attributed in whole or in part to the automobile include urban dirt from exhausts and a decline in the "quality of life" as the flight to the suburbs turns cities into night-time ghost towns. In addition, city driving can cause as intense congestion as commuting, with similar external costs imposed on other drivers.

Externalities arising from automobile traffic, like other externalities, probably should not be eliminated completely in the interests of efficiency. That is, the solution to the problem of the external costs imposed by automobiles probably is not to ban cars completely from city streets. Instead, we should design pricing schemes that will force drivers of private cars to take into account the external costs of driving as well as the private costs. One such plan would levy explicit charges for in-town driving. Others involve indirect taxes on auto-related activities.

Vickrey has catalogued a number of technological devices capable of establishing charges for urban street use.[5] One plan would involve equipping cars with electronic identifiers and then having scanning devices register the identities of cars using particularly busy intersections. Billing could be computerized, with owners being charged a fee for each crossing of a "toll" intersection. Another scheme would require the installation of metering devices in cars and electronic cables in roadways. Each time the driver crossed a cable, the signal that it emitted would cause another charge to be rung up by the meter. Other pricing mechanisms could also be devised.

Under plans like these, charges could be displayed to motorists to inform them about the price of driving on different routes and at different hours. The cost of installation and obtaining compliance is not known, but the use of similar systems (say, for electronic scanning of personal checks) suggests that traffic pricing would not be prohibitively expensive. Probably the chief obstacle to introducing such a system would be the hostility of motorists and the extremely vocal opposition of businessmen in auto-related industries. But there is every reason to believe that technology-intensive systems like those Vickrey describes represent feasible techniques for internalizing the external costs of urban driving.

The charges that would be set under such systems are a little more difficult to calculate. Vickrey's concern in presenting the devices was with reducing congestion, an objective that can be realized with a flexible pricing system. Since congestion is directly observable, a government would only have to be willing to raise prices high enough to reduce congestion to acceptable levels. The costs of pollution are more difficult to calculate, for we do not yet know either the impact of different levels of pollution upon health or the relation between different kinds of pollution and property values. In practice, any pricing scheme that attempted to force drivers to pay for these externalities probably would have to establish pollution charges by some sort of trial and error process, observing at each step how pollution and congestion were related to particular sets of prices. The problems posed by such an approach to pricing the use of urban streets are no more difficult than those faced by many industries that produce joint outputs.

Perhaps the simplest indirect tax that a city could impose on automobile use would be a surtax on gasoline. To avoid merely shifting gasoline sales to the suburbs, such a tax would have to be levied on an area-wide basis. By using a gasoline tax, cities would, in effect, be

---

[5] William S. Vickrey, "Pricing in Urban and Suburban Transport," *American Economic Review (Papers and Proceedings)* 53 (May 1963): 452–65.

applying the "user charge" principle that federal and state governments already use to finance highway construction. As was argued in Chapter 9, however, the revenues from such user charges should not be used solely to improve highways or city streets. Instead, the funds should be used to provide alternative transportation modes and to take antipollution measures. The rationale for such a use of funds is that market imperfections (externalities, decreasing costs, public goods) prevent private suppliers from satisfying consumers' demands for either other forms of transportation or antipollution activities.

Other indirect taxes might be more effective weapons against pollution and congestion. Automobile license fees could vary with engine size, or higher taxes might be levied on high-pollutant gasolines. A parking tax might encourage drivers to shift to smaller cars if the tax rate varied with automobile size. In all these case, however, overall demand for automobile use is likely to be quite inelastic. If taxes are to be effective devices for encouraging the reallocation of resources, then tax rates may have to be very high.

Two other points are worth mentioning. The regulatory measures that have been introduced by the federal government and especially the state of California do not affect public budgets, but they are taxes all the same. Drivers who are required to have antismog devices on their cars find either that they must buy the devices separately or pay dealers to install them. In either case, the effect of the regulation is to shift the supply curve upward (a higher price for the same transportation), just as would occur if an excise tax were levied on automobiles.

Second, governments may try to encourage the use of nonautomobile transportation by offering subsidies. In many cases subsidies are efficient because of the decreasing-cost nature of alternative modes of transportation, such as rapid transit. But for subsidies to have the same allocational effect as taxes or prices on driving, the subsidies would have to be financed by charges on automobile owners. Since subsidies usually are financed out of general revenues, they are not, in fact, allocationally equivalent to user charges levied on motorists.

SUMMARY

Our discussion of slum housing included three factors that contribute to the existence of slums. Low-quality housing may represent a rational response by poor families to the tightness of their budget constraint. If this is the cause of slum housing, then the appropriate policy is to transfer income or housing to the low-income families. Income transfers are preferable to transfers of housing, but if transfers in kind are chosen by society, there are many reasons in practice for using flexible transfers such as rent supplements rather than rigid ones like public housing or rent control.

Externalities may lead to the expansion of slums even if it would be economically efficient to renovate or rehabilitate slum property. Unless a government can internalize the external benefits that one landlord receives from another's housing investment, overall investment will be less than socially optimal. The federal urban renewal program represents such an attempt to internalize external effects, but it has not been entirely successful. Other public policies, such as more flexible inducements to property owners, should be tried.

The relation between city and suburbs can also aggravate the problem of slum housing. Suburbanites are encouraged to leave central cities to reduce their tax burden, but their exodus sets in motion a spiraling process of deterioration in urban housing. The remedy for this situation is some device to make suburbanites responsible for the costs that they impose upon cities. Revenue sharing and nonresident income taxes are two approaches, with nonresident income taxation offering somewhat more promise than revenue sharing.

Congestion in transportation facilities is common to all large American cities. The economically correct device for reducing congestion is to levy peak-hour user charges to compensate for the external costs that commuters impose upon each other. While such charges are neither theoretically nor practically difficult to establish, they are the exception rather than the rule in metropolitan transportation facilities.

Automobile-induced urban pollution and congestion could be reduced by some form of user charge. Direct charges are technologically feasible, but it would be difficult to establish the correct level for prices. Indirect taxes on automobile use are simpler to institute, whether they appear in the public budget as taxes and expenditures or affect private resource allocation only through regulation. In either case, market imperfections require that governments subsidize other forms of transportation. Efficiency requires that such subsidies be financed by charges on automobile users.

Index